Chris Crawford on Interactive Storytelling

Chris Crawford

New
Riders

NRG

New Riders Games
New Riders
1249 Eighth Street • Berkeley, CA 94710

Chris Crawford on Interactive Storytelling
Chris Crawford

Copyright © 2005 by Chris Crawford

Published by New Riders. For information on New Riders Games books, contact:

New Riders
1249 Eighth Street
Berkeley, CA 94710
510/524-2178
800/283-9444
510/524-2221 (fax)
Find us on the World Wide Web at: www.peachpit.com
To report errors, please send a note to errata@peachpit.com
New Riders is an imprint of Peachpit, a division of Pearson Education

Acquisitions Editor: Wendy Sharp
Development/Copy Editor: Lisa M. Lord
Production Coordinator: Andrei Pasternak
Technical Reviewers: Mark Barrett, Aria Danika
Compositor: Amy Hassos
Indexer: Lynne M. Grimes/Interactive Composition Corporation
Cover Design: Charlene Charles Will
Cover Illustration: Andrei Pasternak
Interior Design: Mimi Heft

ISBN 0-321-27890-9
9 8 7 6 5 4 3 2 1
Printed and bound in the United States of America

I dedicate this book to my long-suffering wife Kathy, who has supported me emotionally and financially for thirteen years as I have worked on interactive storytelling, patiently enduring my endless promises that "commercialization is just around the corner."

Acknowledgements

My thanks go to Laura Mixon for serving as sounding board, mother confessor, critic, and fellow explorer as I have groped through the complexities of interactive storytelling. Thanks also to Dave Walker for his many contributions to the development of the Erasmatron technology, both technical and artistic.

Lisa Lord, Mark Barrett, and Aria Danika struggled through the morass of my verbosities and helped me clean up the mess, de-polysyllabic-ize my vocabulary, and actually make some sense. Linda Harrison, Stephanie Wall, Wendy Sharp, and Andrei Pasternak provided top cover, bottom cover, and side cover for the project. The gestation period for this book, about 21 months, was the same as an elephant's, and now we all know what an elephant pregnancy feels like.

Contents at a Glance

Table of Contents

About the Author

Chris Crawford was one of the leading lights of the computer games industry. He led the games research group at Atari, where he wrote *The Art of Computer Game Design*, one of the classics in the field. He designed and programmed fourteen published computer games and wrote five books on software design. He founded and led the Computer Game Developers Conference, now known as the Game Developers Conference. Then in 1992 he walked away from computer games to work on interactive storytelling. Over the intervening years, Crawford has created and developed the Erasmatron interactive storytelling technology, portions of which he has patented. Crawford continues to advance the state of the art through his writings, lectures, and Phrontisterion, an annual conference on interactive storytelling. Crawford lives in the mountains of southern Oregon with his wife, Kathy, and with two dogs, eleven cats, three ducks, three burros, and one pig. He also had two goats and two emus, but the mountain lion ate them.

About the Technical Reviewers

Mark Barrett has been a freelance designer and writer in the interactive entertainment industry since 1995. During that time, he has performed a variety of services for his clients, including scriptwriting, game design, design consulting, mission design, and voiceover direction. From 2000 to 2002, Mark was a speaker at the Game Developers Conference, moderating roundtables on emotional involvement in interactive entertainment. He has also written a number of essays and articles on game design theory and practice, which are available at `www.prairiearts.com/design.htm`.

Aria Danika is an independent filmmaker and digital artist based in Brooklyn, New York. She is the co-author of *Flash MX Magic* and *Flash MX 2004 Magic* (New Riders Publishing) and the technical editor of *Object-Oriented Programming with ActionScript 2.0* (New Riders Publishing) and has written numerous online articles, interviews, and reviews. Aria has worked for BBCi (B&P Director) for five years and was part of the team that launched the new media services, including interactive TV and online communities. She has been a Macromedia beta tester since 2000 and has developed and taught courses in Flash Experience Design. In August 2003, she co-founded openedsource.net to focus on interactive design and digital art. Her research interests include intersections of media, particularly film, and the adoption of filmic language in video games and online art. She's currently spending her free time blogging, skateboarding, and exploring interactivity across different platforms, which has resulted in a series of audiovisual experiments, installations, and web toys.

Introduction

Many years ago I was a bigshot in the games industry. I led the games research group at Atari. My face oozed over the covers of magazines; store shelves sagged under the weight of the fourteen games I created. Five books (before this one) bear the scarlet letters of my name as author. I founded and ran the Computer Game Developers Conference in its early years. But in 1991, dissatisfied with the ever narrower stance the computer games industry had taken, I decided to stop working on games and instead focus my energies on interactive storytelling. It was unknown territory to me, but with my generous assessment of my ability to conquer all problems, I pulled out my machete and began hacking my way forward.

At that time, only a few prescient people had recognized the importance of storytelling. Brenda Laurel had done a great deal of impressive work on the relationship between drama and computers, but it was of a character that scientists call *hand-waving*: speculative and lacking in the detail needed to provide a solid foundation for future elaborations. Cognitive scientists were developing ideas about *narrative intelligence*, and these concepts looked promising, but they had not been developed far enough to be useful. A group of graduate students at MIT had formed a reading group on narrative intelligence, attempting to apply some of these newly developing ideas to computer science, but again, they couldn't get far with the still-forming concepts of the time.

Most of my game designer colleagues reacted to my decision with incomprehension; they were sure I had finally floated off to cloud-cuckoo land. Their responses to my excited jabbering could be summarized in a single word: "Stories?!"

Thirteen years later, the world seems to have caught on to the importance of storytelling; now that people are willing to listen, I have a lot to say. Others have made their contributions, and although some are important (and are described in this book), there's a lot of taurine coprotext[1] out there; this stuff incites me to make some of my points more sharply than you might otherwise expect. Every new field attracts its instant experts eager to cash in on the credulity of newcomers. Bah on them!

The Erasmatron

The result of my labors is a technology I call the Erasmatron, the core components of which I have patented. This book is about interactive storytelling, not the Erasmatron. My vision of interactive storytelling is unavoidably colored by my work with the Erasmatron, but over the years I have experimented with or read about a number of other concepts in interactive storytelling, and this book is my attempt to gather all those ideas together under one roof. This topic is a lot bigger than the Erasmatron, and I hope this book reflects that difference.

Lessons and the Alter Ego

I have set off some of my most important conclusions as numbered lessons; you'll find them scattered through the book. They seek to summarize my conclusions in catchy slogans. If I could, I would have added a snappy jingle to accompany each of them. Aren't you glad I couldn't?

This book reeks of the crotchetiness that is my alliterative middle name. It's also highlighted by plenty of Absolute Truths that might strike skeptical readers as less than absolute. Fortunately, I'm blessed with a schizophrenic personality that harbors my Alter Ego, an intellect more nuanced, more even-handed, and more sensitive to the thinking of those unlike myself (normal people). I'd like you to meet him:

Thank you, Chris. I hope to provide useful counterpoints to your elucidations and look forward to our continuing productive relationship.

As you can see, Alter Ego tends to feckless blather.

Just as you tend to wild, inflammatory generalizations!

Sez you!

Let's just get on with it, okay?

Typographic Conventions

The following typographic conventions are used in this book:

▶ A monospace font is used for code terms, such as statements and functions, and to indicate programming variables, such as the verb `RunAway` or the mood `Anger/Fear`.

▶ *Italics* are used to introduce new terms; to denote titles of plays, movies, and books; and to convey emphasis.

---

1. *taurine*: of, or relating to, the bull; *copro-* : a combining form meaning dung, excrement, or feces.

PART I

From Story to Interactive Storytelling

CHAPTER 1
Story

STORYTELLING ISN'T AN IDLE leisure activity that humans developed to while away the hours: It evolved for serious purposes, as a necessary component in the development of human culture. Without storytelling, humans could never have communicated complex information. Storytelling isn't merely characteristic or even definitive of the human condition—it's absolutely necessary to the existence of human culture.

The Development of Storytelling

Storytelling was a natural, almost inevitable consequence of human evolution. The human brain developed in response to the environmental pressures facing early hominids. Each major problem triggered some sort of change in the human body; if a problem could be solved by mental effort, an existing part of the brain took over that problem, often expanding as a consequence. Most of the time, these new mental abilities were cobbled together from a combination of existing parts of the brain, so they weren't often cleanly localized to one region of the brain. As they developed, these "mental modules" were in turn recruited to solve new but related problems.

Because mental modules aren't tightly localized, scientists can't pin them down with anatomical precision; brain function is so complex that one mental module blends into the next. This makes the job of identifying mental modules a subjective task; every scientist slices the pie a little differently. Nevertheless, some slices seem to be more popular than others. Here are four of the most commonly recognized mental modules:

► **Visual-spatial:** Handles visual perception and spatial imagination; based on pattern recognition.

► **Social:** Handles relationships with others; also based on pattern recognition.

► **Natural history:** Storage of facts about the environment and logical analysis of those facts; some sequential processing.

► **Language:** Permits communication and ties together all the other mental modules; sequential processing.

Mental Modules Interact

Once the development of language had pulled the mental modules into communication, all sorts of fascinating interactions began between them. For example, the natural history module and the social relationships module interacted in a surprising fashion. The natural history module impelled humans to inquire into the causes of phenomena they observed in their environment, but all too often a clear cause was wanting. For example, an especially important question for the early farmers was "Why does it rain?" Or, more to the point, "Why does it sometimes fail to rain?"

When language put the natural history module in touch with the social relation-ships module, these two modules interacted to devise an answer that made some sense: Natural phenomena were caused by "powerful people"—gods. Whenever a phenomenon lacked an obvious cause, assigning the phenomenon to a god and then explaining the apparently erratic behavior with the deity's mood swings was a simple matter. Not only did the social relationships module suggest an explana-tion to the problem; it also offered the solution: propitiate the god. A huge array of behaviors became associated with various gods. Some acts were forbidden; others were mandatory. And because the gods seemed so arbitrary, it behooved society to have someone on hand who could communicate with the gods. There was never any shortage of applicants for the position; whoever communicated with the gods was, essentially, in charge of the society. There, now you know where religion came from.

But the natural history module also interacted with the language module, pro-ducing "sequential thinking natural history"—science. Sequential thinking took a long time to develop, but once the idea of syllogisms and chains of deduction took hold, science took off. The conflict between science and religion becomes clearer when viewed in this fashion. Both arose from the natural history module; both attempt to explain the world in which we live. Religion takes the social rela-tionship route, and science takes the sequential logic route. The choice between them might have more to do with relative strengths of these two modules than anything else.

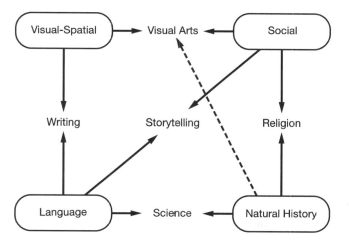

FIGURE 1.1: Interactions between the mental modules.

There are still four more interactions to consider. I lump two of them together: the combination of the visual/spatial module with the natural history and social relationships modules to produce representational art.

When visual/spatial reasoning combined with the language module, we got writing, an impressive result. And when the language module combined with the social relationships module, it produced storytelling.

For those whose spatial reasoning module is stronger than their verbal reasoning module, **Figure 1.1** (on the preceding page) shows a graphical summary of these results.

At Last, Narrative

Why is storytelling such an important component of culture? All cultures have their stories. Why are they universal? The obvious answer, of course, is that stories are the vehicle by which cultural knowledge is communicated from one generation to the next. They're not the only vehicle, of course, but they certainly play an important role in transmitting cultural information. Storytelling is an ancient technique, probably developing hand in hand with language.

But why should information be transmitted by stories? Why couldn't cultures simply compile their knowledge into a simple, compact list of important truths, and then require every young person to memorize them? This approach would probably be quicker and more efficient than the long-winded storytelling system, so why didn't any culture ever adapt such a superior alternative?

The answer has to do with the character of the information being transmitted. Most of the information content of these stories pertains to social reasoning. Some pertains to the natural history module, but the bulk of these stories concern interpersonal behavior: trustworthiness, marriage, perseverance, and so forth. The social relationships mental module relies on pattern recognition, which raises a nasty problem: How do you communicate pattern-type information to a pattern-recognizing mental module using a sequential medium such as language? In computer terms, the data is in the wrong format for the communications link!

What's needed is a reformatter, something that converts one thinking format to the other. Narrative is that reformatter. It's an ad-hoc solution to an ugly interfacing problem that arose early in the development of language.

Consider: A story is definitely a linear sequence of events; its architecture is even referred to as a "plotline." That linearity is the inevitable outcome of using language to relate the story. Yet the story's content can't be understood until the story has been completely received. If I'm downloading my email and the transmission link breaks 90 percent of the way through, I can still read the email and figure out most of its content. But if you're watching a movie in a theater and the projector breaks down 90 percent of the way through the movie, you have every right to demand a 100 percent refund; without that last 10 percent, the story never snaps into place and is a useless communication.

In other words, stories are complete patterns that communicate a special kind of knowledge to our pattern-recognizing mental modules. How does that happen? I'll use a visual metaphor that clearly shows what happens (well, it's clear to visual thinkers…). Imagine your knowledge to consist of a meshwork of connected ideas, something like the diagram in **Figure 1.2**.

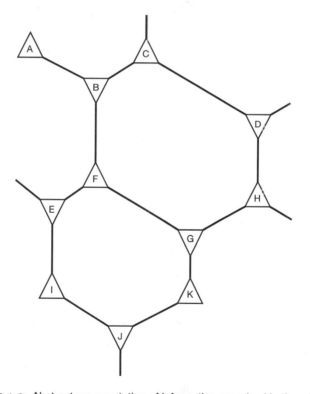

FIGURE 1.2: Abstract representation of information organized in the mind.

The triangles represent ideas or concepts inside your mind. All your ideas and memories exist in some association with other ideas and memories; in other words, you have associative memories. Now Figure 1.2 is misleading in two ways: First, it's a conceptual diagram, not a blueprint. It sketches out some imaginary set of relationships, not a real structure inside your brain. Second, it's vastly over-simplified. Mental associations are far bigger, richer, and denser than this little diagram. I present it only to prepare you for a little exercise in visual reasoning.

I can improve on this diagram by taking into account two facts: first, that some ideas hook up to more than three other ideas, and second, that often the connections between different ideas are strained (see **Figure 1.3**).

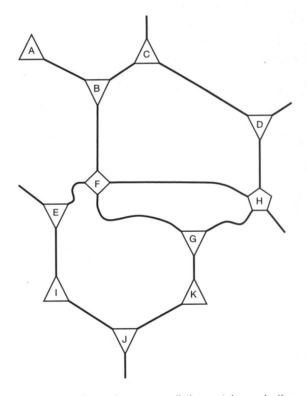

FIGURE 1.3: A messier, more realistic mental organization.

Now consider how learning is represented in this diagram. Sometimes learning is just a matter of adding new ideas, as represented in **Figure 1.4**.

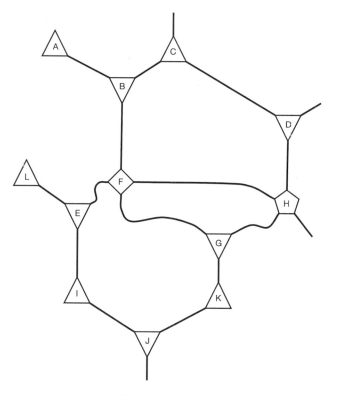

FIGURE 1.4: Simple learning without the "Aha!"

The new triangle on the left, marked as idea L, represents a new idea tacked onto an existing mesh. It doesn't change anything; it's just added on.

The "Aha!" experience comes when a new idea links existing ideas in a new and cleaner arrangement. For example, an exciting moment in learning physics comes with the realization that the sky is blue for exactly the same reason the sunset is red. That realization starts with adding a new link in the mesh, but that addition triggers changes in the mesh to accomodate the new idea, resulting in a cleaner, more tightly woven web. **Figure 1.5** shows how this might happen.

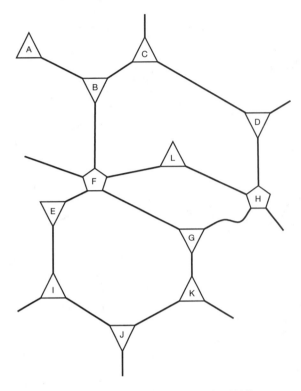

FIGURE 1.5: New idea L triggers "Aha!"

This sudden change of shape in the mesh is the source of the "Aha!" experience, often described as "everything clicking into place." Note also that idea F is now a five-sided hub; learning idea L enriched another idea already in the mesh. As we learn, triangles turn into diamonds, pentagons, and hexagons, and the connections in our mesh grow ever denser.

See Chapter 2, "Interactivity," for more on the "Aha!" experience.

Storytelling's value arises in an attempt to convey a complex mesh containing many linkages. Stories are never told to communicate single, disconnected ideas; you'll never hear a story ending with "And that's why pi is equal to 3.14."

Suppose you want to communicate a set of ideas represented by the mesh in **Figure 1.6**.

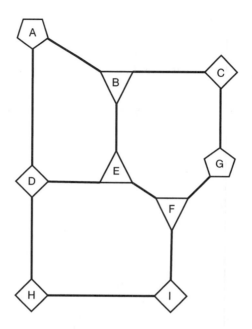

FIGURE 1.6: A wise mesh of ideas.

Suppose further that the person to whom you want to communicate this set of ideas already has a mesh, but her version of the mesh is incomplete (it lacks ideas E and F) and messy (see **Figure 1.7**).

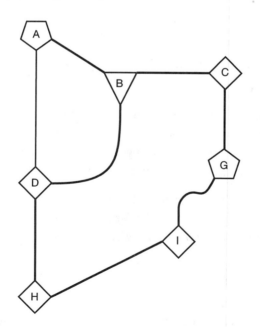

FIGURE 1.7: A student's mesh of ideas.

If you attempt to teach this new mesh in conventional fashion, you must first introduce idea E, forcing the student to make a mess of her mesh (see **Figure 1.8**).

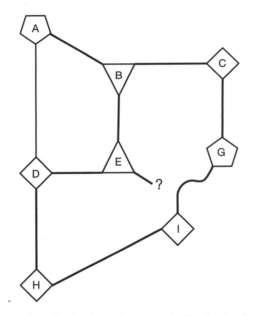

FIGURE 1.8: Student's confused mesh after the first lesson.

The student can clearly see that your ideas make no sense and resists including idea E. Now you must add idea F, but there's still a mess; idea F clashes with idea I, as shown in **Figure 1.9.**

You must explain how idea I is moved and the connections between F, G, H, and I are rearranged. Only then does the student grasp the new mesh. No wonder people have so much trouble learning complexly interconnected ideas—the intermediate steps are discombobulating craziness!

This educational process is made even clumsier by everybody having a slightly different mesh. The adjustments you advise to one student won't work with another; in fact, they could make things worse for the second student!

Stories solve this problem. Remember, a story isn't an isolated fact; it's a connected system of facts. Stories are presented in linear form, but they are understood as a mesh of interrelated ideas, which is why they must be experienced in their entirety to make any sense. If you express Figure 1.6 as a story rather than, say, a lecture or a textbook, the student perceives it as a complete mesh and lays that mesh over her own (see **Figure 1.10**).

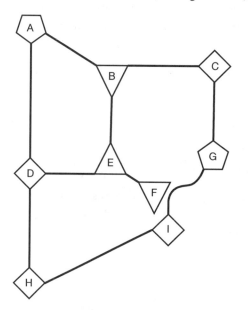

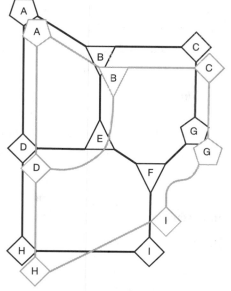

FIGURE 1.9: Student's confused mesh after the second lesson.

FIGURE 1.10: The student overlays the meshes to see the truth in relation to her own mesh.

Because brains are so good at pattern recognition, the student instantly recognizes the changes required to fix the discrepancy. Moreover, the story is more convincing than the expository teaching because the new mesh is obviously cleaner and neater than the student's original mesh. People love to learn, but when it's crammed down their throats in a process that's nonsensical most of the way, they resist. When it's presented to them this cleanly, they embrace it.

That's why storytelling was invented thousands of years ago and why it remains the most powerful medium for communicating complexly interrelated ideas.

The Nature of Stories

So much has been written about the nature of stories that it seems cheeky for me to throw in my own two cents' worth. Nevertheless, there are a few fundamental points I want to emphasize, if only to get you oriented toward the thinking that underlies this book.

Strong Structure

Stories must satisfy tight structural requirements to be acceptable. Many of the definitions I have seen strike me as too academically broad. Yes, any sequence of statements can be construed to be a story, but only in the most academic of senses. I can't specify the structure of stories, but I can point out that even a four-year-old child has a solid grasp of the concept of story. Here are two examples to run by your neighborhood four-year-old:

> *The itsy-bitsy spider crawled up the water spout.*
> *Down came the rain, and washed the spider out.*
> *Out came the sun, and dried up all the rain.*
> *And the itsy-bitsy spider crawled up the spout again.*

Here you have a clear, simple story in four lines. It has a protagonist (spider), conflict (the rain), struggle (being washed out), resolution (crawled back up), and even a moral (the value of perseverence).

Here's another story:

> *Once upon a time, there was a handsome young prince who lived in a shining castle. One day he mounted his beautiful white steed and rode out of the castle into the forest. Inside the forest, his horse fell into a hole and they both died.*

This story has most of the elements of many stories: the classic "Once upon a time" opening, a handsome prince, a beautiful white horse, a castle, and a forest. In these elements, it's quite conventional, but the ending is not at all what's expected. Tell this story to four-year-olds and they'll cry out, "That's not a story!" They'd be right. Whatever structural elements this pseudo-story has, it can't be called a proper story because it violates some fundamental expectations about stories.

Lesson #1
Stories are complex structures that must meet many hard-to-specify requirements.

Games have never paid much attention to the many structural requirements imposed on stories. The story of the prince riding through the forest could easily be an account of a player's experience in a game. Players don't complain when games jerk them through wild dramatic gyrations because they don't expect games to follow the protocols of storytelling.

People

Stories are about people. This is such a simple, basic truth that it's often lost in the high-falutin' analysis of narrative theory. Sometimes the references to people is indirect or symbolic, as in the case of the itsy-bitsy spider, who isn't a person but is understood by the audience to represent a person. An extreme example of this indirection is offered by the movie *Koyaanisqatsi*, which lacks a protagonist or dialogue. The people in this movie are all of us, and we are revealed by our works. The movie presents an artful sequence of images of nature contrasted with the world of civilization. Yet the story is strong and clear, and beautifully summarized in the final long, long shot of a rocket ascending higher and higher into the atmosphere and exploding. The camera centers on the largest fragment and follows it down, down, down. The symbolism is intense and powerful; this movie is about what we have become.

Concomitant with exalting the role of *people* in stories is minimizing the role of *things* in stories. You must concentrate your attention on the people in stories and simultaneously reject any significant role for things.

 But aren't there plenty of stories that revolve around things? What about The Maltese Falcon, Raiders of the Lost Ark, and Lord of the Rings?

No, the objects in the cited stories do not play central roles. *Lord of the Rings*, for example, is not about the ring, but about Frodo's struggle. Replacing the ring with a magic sock or a hat or eyeglasses would not have changed the story much. Replacing Frodo with, say, Han Solo, Don Quixote, or Huck Finn would have changed the story beyond recognition.

This simple truth—that stories about about people, not things—explains the utter failure of games to incorporate storytelling in any but the most mechanical and forced manner. Games concern themselves with things: things you acquire, things you use, things you destroy, and so on. That's why they're so emotionally crippled—when was the last time you gave a damn about a *thing*? Games aren't antisocial; they're a-social. They just don't bother with people other than as walking dolls that perform mechanical functions. The cardboard people in games do for drama what inflatable dolls do for sex.

Lesson #2
Stories are about the most fascinating thing in the universe: people.

Conflict

All stories have some sort of conflict. Sometimes the conflict is direct and violent, as in *Star Wars* or *Lord of the Rings*. The good guys wear white hats and the bad guys wear black hats. The good guys are handsome and noble, and the bad guys are missing some teeth and have bad breath. Youngsters with their simplistic view of the universe favor such stories. But there are also stories in which the conflict is more indirect. Sometimes the conflict is social, sometimes it's symbolic, but there's always conflict of some sort. The second *Jurassic Park* movie illustrates the indirection of conflict. The primary conflict is between the mathematician and the soulless businessman; the conflict is established starkly early in the movie when the mathematician tugs at the businessman's sleeve and the businessman warns "Careful. This suit cost more than your education." As the story progresses, dinosaurs rampage with toothy glee, chomping and stomping people in horrifically entertaining ways, but they aren't the antagonists. Indeed, the dinosaurs are presented as something like "noble savages," devoid of evil intent, merely acting out their reptilian instincts with dinosaur integrity. The central conflict of the movie is indirect: The businessman gives orders to his minions, and the mathematician opposes him with vain pleas and dark warnings. Spielberg could have moved all the dinosaurs offstage, saving millions of dollars, without compromising the integrity of the story—although it wouldn't have been nearly as much fun.

 Well, conflict at least is one place where games shine.

Not exactly. It's true that games have lots of conflict, but it usually takes the simplest and most direct form: violence. Games are deficient in other forms of conflict, such as social conflict. The game designer's spice shelf has lots of sugar and nothing else.

Puzzles

Stories are not puzzles. It's true that puzzles often form a part of the story; indeed, puzzles play a large role in mystery stories. The puzzles in a mystery story are primarily about people, however. The bulk of the story is devoted to detailing the sleuth's machinations in getting people to reveal crucial clues to the mystery.

 But there's also plenty of nonsocial sleuthing going on. Take the television series CSI, *for example. It's about using science to solve crimes, and it has been a big hit.*

True, but the science is not what gives the stories their power. The gee-whiz technology is certainly spectacular, but the strong characters and often poignant storylines are the true strengths of the stories. Without those strong character interactions, *CSI* would be a run-of-the-mill whodunit.

A story always contains some kind of problem or challenge: How is the protagonist to resolve the conflict of the story? If this problem is an intellectual one requiring logical solution, it's called a puzzle, but the exercise of intellectual legerdemain is seldom central to stories. Plenty of great stories do quite well without any puzzle component.

Lesson #3
Puzzles are not a necessary component of stories.

Choices

Ultimately, stories concern the choices that characters make. Indeed, the entire point of many stories is revealed through a key choice the protagonist makes. In *Star Wars*, it's "Trust the force, Luke." In *Macbeth*, it's the decision to murder for ambition. In the third *Matrix* movie, it's Neo's decision to sacrifice himself. In many versions of the Arthurian legends, it's Guinevere's decision to act on her love for Lancelot. In each of these examples, the entire story builds up to or revolves around a key decision.

Spectacle

One of the most direct forms of entertainment is providing novel experiences. Sometimes you try out an exotic food merely for the simple pleasure of tasting something you've never tasted before. A great deal of music, especially popular music, relies on including odd new sounds. Rock music especially reveled in unconventional sounds: The electric guitar, feedback effects, the fuzzbox, and other innovative acoustic effects played a large role in rock music.

The visual form of this "pleasure from novelty" is spectacle: providing exotic imagery as a form of entertainment. Spectacle dominates the movies. The very first movies were spectacles without stories—trains crashing and so forth. *Star Wars* in 1977, *Jurassic Park* in 1991, and *The Matrix* in 1999 exemplify the appeal of spectacle. There's every reason to believe that spectacle will continue to dominate the movies.

Computer games have followed a related course. The earliest computer games offered nothing more than moving squares on a television screen; the evolution of computer games has been dominated by the quest for ever more realistic graphics to provide ever better spectacle. The progress made in the past 25 years is truly astounding. Expect even greater things in the future.

All this fabulous spectacle has engendered in the minds of most younger people an unfortunate confusion between story and spectacle. Many associate spectacle with story so strongly that they believe spectacle is a necessary component of story. But Aristotle, in his classic *Poetics*, ranked spectacle as the least important of the six elements of story. (His priority list was plot, character, thought, diction, song, and spectacle.)

A sad experience of mine forcefully demonstrates the degree to which spectacle has crowded out story in the minds of many. Once upon a time, I acquired a copy of Charlie Chaplin's classic *The Gold Rush*. After watching it, I enthused about the beauty of the story to a young friend, urging him to come watch it with me. With some reluctance, my friend consented. Barely a quarter of the way into the movie, he stood up to leave the room. Chaplin's great work bored him. The scenes were all "plain," the story's pace was torpid, and the movie had literally no color nor sound. How could I expect him to endure such a boring film? In my friend's opinion, a movie without spectacle simply wasn't worth watching.

Lesson #4
Spectacle does not make stories.

The Tyranny of the Visual

Many observers have noted that our culture is increasingly dominated by the image. Indeed, a recent book was titled *The Rise of the Image the Fall of the Word*[1]. No doubt, the image plays a larger role in our culture now than at any time in the past. In many ways, this is good. Glorifying war, for example, is much harder when the news gushes with images of the horrible reality of war. This even applies in fictional representations. Old war movies showed victims clutching their chests and sanitarily falling face down, but a movie like *Saving Private Ryan* shows heads being blown off bodies and people being ripped apart with such graphic realism that a friend of mine, after watching the movie, declared that he could not see how anybody could ever again support a war.

Tremendous effort has gone into improving the quality of images. Computer graphics has absorbed billions of dollars of research and development money and consumed the energies of thousands of our brightest minds. Hundreds of people labor over the computer graphics in a major movie, and their efforts are usually rewarded with bounteous ticket sales. Television is looking forward to the rise of HDTV and the accompanying huge improvement in image quality. Electronic networks are increasing their capacity dramatically, primarily to transmit images. The text you type amounts to a few kilobytes, while images gobble up megabytes.

I won't condemn the rise of the image in our culture, and I will not bemoan the decline of the word. What I want to concentrate on here is the way in which visual thinking has come to dominate our thinking, to the exclusion of everything else.

When I gaze upon a scene, I imagine that I'm perceiving a tiny fragment of reality—perceiving reality through the narrow window of the visual. I look at a tree and perceive so much more than the visual image. I imagine the fluids slowly creeping through its cambium, the photosynthesis taking place in its leaves, the absorption of nutrients from the soil—all these invisible processes that are central to the life of a tree. My eyes tell me only so much about the tree; there's much more going on out of my view.

Note that my perception of the tree is informed, indeed driven, by my education. Because I have read about biology and trees and physics, I bring to bear an understanding that allows me to see deeper inside the tree. My perception of the universe is an integration of my knowledge and my senses.

Here's an analogy: Suppose that you are watching a black-and-white movie. You see an apple presented in shades of gray, but you know that the apple must be red. Your real eyes see a gray apple, but your mind's eye fills in the color. Now extend that analogy. What if you also perceived the smooth texture of the apple's skin, the slow oxidation of the apple's flesh—everything going on in that apple. By living only in the world of the visual, are you "seeing" less of the world than you could?

The Wachowski brothers created a stunning visual analogy to this process in the first *Matrix* movie. At the climax, Neo has returned from the dead and can now see the Matrix for what it is. He looks down the corridor at the three agents and sees not the corridor, but the code behind it. This image communicates the idea of seeing the processes behind reality rather than just the visual skin of reality. Ironic, isn't it: a visual representation of an idea that attempts to get around visual thinking?

Lesson #5
Visual thinking should not dominate storytelling.

Spatial Thinking

Closely related to visual thinking is spatial thinking. Spatial reasoning is one of the brain's greatest achievements. When you reach around behind the refrigerator to retrieve the fallen spoon, you're using spatial reasoning. People often apply spatial reasoning to nonspatial problems, as evidenced by such statements as "Joe and I aren't very *close* friends" or "Your statement is *wide of the mark*." Spatial reasoning used metaphorically, as in these examples, works well. The problem comes when people apply it too literally to storytelling. Spatial reasoning is out of place in the universe of drama because drama is about people, not things.

In my designs for interactive storytelling, I have always used a simple arrangement: Space is composed of individual stages with no spatial relationships whatever between stages. In my definition, a *stage* is simply a location containing actors and props. Actors simply disappear from one stage and reappear on another. Inside a stage, all actors are able to interact with each other without any spatial considerations. It's a simple, robust model and it closely approximates the way in which space operates in most stories. This broader definition of "stage" can be applied in any storytelling medium: theater, cinema, literature, or interactive storytelling.

Most people react to my claim that stories don't rely on spatial considerations with incredulity, but consider the interactions between actors on a stage. How many times do the spatial relationships affect those interactions? Don't think in terms of movies because their visual element automatically includes spatial factors, thereby biasing the analysis. Consider a medium in which spatial factors are not automatically included: literature.

For example, the *Odyssey* is at heart a story of a journey around the Mediterranean. Isn't that fundamentally spatial? Indeed, the journey motif shows up repeatedly in literature, from the *Odyssey* to *Huckleberry Finn* to *Star Wars*. But are the spatial motions central to the story? Are they not merely transitions from one stage to another, without any genuine spatial content? The best evidence for the chimerical nature of spatial factors in stories is the fact that the actual spatial relationships are never specified. Odysseus traveled for many days and came to the Land of the Lotus Eaters—where is that? How far away is it from Scylla and Charybdis? Is it closer to Troy or to Ithaca? These relationships aren't specified in the *Odyssey*—because they're not important.

The same thing goes for other journey stories. *Huckleberry Finn* takes place on a specified river, with specified places that could, I suppose, be established on a map. Yet many of the details just aren't there. Where was it that Huck saw the body of his father? And how far away was that from the town where they tarred and feathered Huck's shyster buddies? Or the place where the feud led to the murders of his hosts? The reader doesn't know because those spatial relationships are irrelevant to the dramatic matters addressed in the story.

Even within a stage, spatial relationships are unimportant. Some people have contested this claim, observing that Cary Grant has to get really close to the actress if he's going to kiss her. But in literature, authors never write "Overpowered with passion, he walked over to her, seized her in his arms, and kissed her frantically." No, the sentence is more like "Overpowered with passion, he seized her in his arms and kissed her frantically." Look at it from the other extreme: "Overpowered with passion, he walked over to her, seized her in his arms, moved his head directly in front of hers, rotated his head slightly to avoid a collision of noses, then closed the gap between her lips and his and kissed her frantically." Pretty silly, eh? Spatial factors just aren't important in drama. If an actor needs to alter a spatial relationship to get something done, he simply does it, and you don't need to worry about the mechanical details of how that's carried out. Stories are about the exercise of emotion, not musculature.

Consider the *Star Trek* universe, developed over the course of more than three decades by hundreds of people. Fat encyclopedias define and list all manner of details of the *Star Trek* universe. You can read technical specifications for all kinds of starships and wondrous devices. There are detailed histories of dozens of different species and their homeworlds. Yet this stupefying mountain of data lacks one of the simplest of all documents: a map. Nobody can tell you whether the planet Vulcan is closer to the Klingon homeworld or to Earth. Where is the planet Andorrea? How do you get to Raisa or Cardassia? There are literally hundreds of stories from the *Star Trek* universe, but a map has never been necessary to understand the stories.

Lesson #6
Stories take place on stages, not maps.

Temporal Discontinuity

Just as stories break up space into discrete chunks called stages, they play havoc with time—breaking it up, jumping backward and forward, and skipping it altogether. Actors are shown embarking on a journey and arriving at their destination; the time the journey itself consumes is simply skipped over. Years are disposed of with the note "Many years later…." Simultaneity is presented sequentially with the simple phrase "Meanwhile, back at the ranch…." Flashbacks jerk you backward in time, and then return you to the present without so much as a by-your-leave. Dramatic time just doesn't behave like physical time; it follows whatever course the story requires.

Fortunately, temporal reasoning facilities aren't as unconsciously pervasive as spatial reasoning facilities, so people seldom have difficulty appreciating the liberties storytellers take with time. Nevertheless, computer game designers contemplating the problems of interactive storytelling should disencumber themselves of the old notions of physical time that so dominate games.

Wrapping Up

This chapter reveals no grand theory of narrative. Instead, it offers a number of separate points about story that are important in considerations of interactive storytelling. Storytelling is so deeply entwined in human nature and cultures that I doubt whether the true essence of stories can ever be nailed down. If you mean to build interactive storytelling systems, however, these few points at least should be clear in your mind before turning to the matter of interactivity.

---

1. Mitchell Stephens, *The Rise of the Image the Fall of the Word* (Oxford University Press, 1998; ISBN 0195098293).

CHAPTER 2
Interactivity

INTERACTIVITY IS WITHOUT DOUBT the most grossly misunderstood and callously misused term associated with computers. Everybody has been using the term for so long that people are quite sure of their appreciation of interactivity. The problem is that everybody seems to have a different conception of interactivity, and most descriptions are fuzzy and accompanied with lots of arm-waving.

Here's a prime example taken from a recent book, *Pause and Effect: The Art of Interactive Narrative*[1]:

> *Interaction can be described as many things. Catchwords abound: "engaging," "immersive," "participatory," "responsive," and "reactive."*
>
> *Interactivity is a continuing increase in participation. It's a bidirectional communication conduit. It's a response to a response. It's "full-duplex." Interaction is a relationship. It's good sex. It's bad conversation. It's indeterminate behavior, and it's redundant result. It's many things, none of which can be done alone. Interaction is a process that dictates communications. It can also be a communication that dictates process. It provides options, necessitates a change in pace, and changes you as you change it.*

Readers who are revolted by this description's semantic smarminess may skip to the next section. If, however, you did not feel your gorge rising while reading the above, read on!

How Wrong Art Thou? Let Me Count the Ways

Engaging: It's true that interactivity is engaging, but then, so is a good movie. Movies aren't interactive, however. (I'll demonstrate this point a few pages further.) There's no value in characterizing interactivity by a trait (engagingness) widely shared by other media.

Immersive: This attribute confuses sensory completeness with interactivity. Immersiveness is an attribute of 3D graphics environments, which immerse the user in a visually complete and consistent space. But 3D graphics are neither necessary nor sufficient for interactivity; indeed, the two have little to do with each other. You can have highly interactive situations with pure text, and you can have truly crappy interactivity with a 3D engine.

Participatory: This attribute involves a common misunderstanding. A participant plays a part in some event. Being a part of the event does not imply any interaction: You can participate in the music by dancing along with it, but dancing to music is not an interaction. You can participate in pushing a car, but there's no significant interaction in pushing something. Interaction entails a lot more than simply being a part of something.

Responsive: This attribute hits on a fragment of the truth, but remains too vague to illuminate the nature of interactivity. Yes, interactivity requires responsiveness, but it's the character of that responsiveness that conveys the value of interactivity.

Reactive: Again, this attribute is partially correct—but don't make the mistake of confusing reaction with interaction. Reaction is a one-way process; interaction is a two-way process. Two people interacting are engaging in a series of reactions to each other. Reaction alone is only a subset of interaction, however. And intense reaction is not the same as interaction; you can't turn reaction into interaction merely by turning up the volume. Reaction is to interaction as moving your left foot is to dancing.

The second paragraph of the opening quotation includes these bloopers:

Interactivity is a continuing increase in participation. This statement is flat-out nonsense. Is a "continuing increase in participation" like dancing faster and faster? Or better and better? Or singing louder and louder? If you figure out what it means, please tell me.

It's a bidirectional communication conduit. As written, this sentence is silly; a length of copper wire in your telephone wiring is a bidirectional communication conduit. If you indulge the sloppy English, however, you can glean some indication that interactivity involves bidirectional communication, and this is indeed correct.

It's a response to a response. Not quite. The response itself is not the interaction; the interaction comprises the entire chain of responses and counter-responses.

It's "full-duplex." This statement is misleading; the correct term would be "duplex." Any duplex communication is bidirectional and so meets the intent of the metaphor. Full-duplex communication permits simultaneous transmission in both directions, rather like two people talking at the same time. Half-duplex communication requires one side to shut up while the other side talks. Hence, half-duplex communication is just as sufficient for interactivity as full-duplex.

Interaction is a relationship. This statement is so stark, so lacking in further explanation or specification of the nature of the relationship, that it can be accepted only as a poetic expression; it certainly conveys nothing of any utility.

It's good sex. It's bad conversation. It's true that both sex and conversation are interactions, but assigning values of good and bad to them confuses the matter with irrelevant distinctions.

It's indeterminate behavior, and it's redundant result. This is drivel. It says nothing—but it sure sounds erudite, doesn't it?

It's many things, none of which can be done alone. The first clause might be improved with a tad more specificity, but the second clause does have some value. It says that interaction requires two agents, and that requirement shows up in my own definition.

Interaction is a process that dictates communications. It can also be a communication that dictates process. As a writer, I am offended by the sacrifice of clarity to cuteness. The use of the verb "dictates" is particularly unfortunate, as it's unclear whether the subject provides the content of the direct object or merely militates the action the direct object specifies. Why is the first sentence absolute and the second sentence tentative? And what relationship between process and communication do these sentences imply? I sure can't tell.

It provides options, necessitates a change in pace, and changes you as you change it. It's true that options are a factor in one step of the process of interaction, but the first clause gives no idea of how those options fit into the bigger picture. This first clause sounds to me rather like the statement "A computer has wires." Yeah, right—so what? The second clause falls outside the pale of relevant comment. What pace is the author talking about here? Why is the pace changed? Does it increase or decrease? Just what does this clause say? The third clause is equally pointless. Interactivity changes you, but every experience changes you. Staring at the wall changes you. Falling on your face changes you. Reading dreck changes you.

I have taken up your time trashing this piece because it represents a school of thought that I regard with alarm and disdain. This school approaches interactive storytelling in much the same manner that a married man regards his mistress: as a plaything, a toy not to be taken seriously. The hallmark of this school is long-winded phrasing and polysyllabic terminology that pretends to erudition through obscurity. Sloppy reasoning, slovenly wording, and the subordination of logic to cleverness are intellectual crimes.

My Definition of Interactivity

So, with the hope of appearing dreckless, I offer this definition of interactivity:

> *A cyclic process between two or more active agents in which each agent alternately listens, thinks, and speaks.*

In this definition, the terms "listen," "think," and "speak" must be taken metaphorically. A computer doesn't listen in the strict sense of the term, but it does listen to its mouse and keyboard, metaphorically speaking. It may not speak, but it does something operationally similar when it displays output on its screen. And, of course, a computer never thinks in the true sense of the word, but it does process data, or calculate. I suppose I could have used the terms "accepts input," "processes input," and "outputs results," but those terms are just as narrow-mindedly computerish as the earlier description's terms are narrow-mindedly humanistic. With this proviso for the broader sense of the terms "listen," "think," and "speak," the definition is a clear statement of exactly what constitutes interactivity.

The value of this definition lies in its reference to conversation, a well-known form of interaction. Our experiences with conversation offer useful guidance in software design. Obviously, the overall quality of a conversation depends on the particular quality with which each step (listening, thinking, and speaking) is carried out. Even more important is the way those three qualities combine. Many people assume that maximizing the quality of each step is all that's required to achieve the maximum quality of interactivity, but the truth is a bit more subtle.

Consider: The overall quality of a conversation doesn't depend on the isolated qualities of each step—each step must be executed well if the conversation is to succeed. Can you recall conversations in which your interlocutors weren't listening to your words? In such cases, no matter how refined their thinking or eloquent their speaking, the conversations were an utter loss because without good listening, the interaction is ruined. In the same fashion, I'm sure you can recall conversations with people who were just too stupid to understand your point— and these conversations were just as frustrating and pointless as the previous type. Last, you can also recall conversations with a tongue-tied, inarticulate clod who simply couldn't rub two words together to save his life. Again, the conversations were failures because without quality in that third step—speaking—the quality of the first two steps didn't matter.

Therefore, Lesson #7 presents a fundamental and rarely appreciated rule of good interactivity.

Lesson #7
The overall quality of interactivity (human-with-human or human-with-computer) depends on the product, not the sum of the individual qualities of the three steps. You must have good listening and *good thinking* and *good speaking to have good interaction.*

My definition rejects a number of phenomena mistakenly held to be interactive. For example, reaction, no matter how intense, is not the same as interaction. If you're watching a great movie, and your heart is pounding with excitement and your fingers trembling with emotion, you're still not interacting with the movie because it's not listening to what you are saying, nor is it thinking about anything. It is only speaking. It speaks well and powerfully—that's good! But it is not interacting.

 Not so! The viewer engages in active interpretation of the movie and, therefore, is not in a passive role.

This argument confuses the active/passive dichotomy with the interactive/reactive dichotomy. Reaction still has action inside it, but that doesn't make it interaction. The audience can actively think, but that doesn't change the fact that the movie *isn't* thinking. The relationship between the movie and the audience is fundamentally one-sided: The movie does all the speaking, and the audience does all the listening and thinking. The audience does not *act on* the movie; it merely *reacts to* the movie.

"Interaction" requires that the "action" be "inter" (between or among) the agents. If the action all goes in one direction, it's not "inter"; it's "re."

I belabor this point because so many people balk at it. Perhaps they are influenced by the current status of "interactivity" as the latest buzzword and the implication that interactivity is somehow "New! Better! Hot! Cool!" My declaration that movies are not interactive becomes, by implication, an assertion that they are "Old! Worse! Tepid!"—a suggestion that any knowledgeable person would reject. Hence, people reject the notion that movies aren't interaction.

Let me set this matter straight: I am not denigrating movies. I like movies. Some of my best friends are movies. I take a movie out to lunch every year on D.W. Griffith's birthday. Cinema is a highly developed medium that does its job very well. But we must render unto Caesar; every medium has its strengths and weaknesses. Movies aren't interactive, and interactive storytelling will never have the highly polished internal structure that movies have. They are two different media.

Second-Person Insight

All great artists have some special insight that gives their work profundity. A brilliant composer has an inner ear that can judge the feel of music. A painter has an eye for form, shape, and color. A deep insight into the language gives a top-notch writer the ability to come up with the perfect phrase. In the same way, the interactive artist needs a special kind of insight, an artistic acuity few others share. I call that acuity *second-person insight*. It's the ability to think primarily in terms of how an expression will be perceived by the audience.

 But every artist worries about how an expression will be perceived by the audience!

True, but this isn't an artist's primary concern. An expository artist's main task is to get the expression right in the first place. A writer prepares a first draft and then attempts to reread it from the reader's point of view. In other words, the primary emphasis is on the expression itself, and only secondary emphasis is on the audience's perception. An artist whose work isn't understood by the masses doesn't seek the nearest tree with noose in hand. Whether it's a play, a painting, a movie, a novel, or a poem, if people don't understand it, that's their problem, not the artist's.

This is true for fine artists, but entertainers cater to the tastes of their audiences. What difference is there between the second-person insight you talk about and the sensitivity to the audience intrinsic to any good entertainer?

Entertainers need insight into how the audience will react to their creations; designers of interactive storytelling need to go even further and anticipate their players' imaginings and whims.

Therefore, second-person insight requires a fundamental and profound shift in attitude. You must go beyond the normal consideration of your audience's perceptions and make those perceptions the entire thrust of your efforts. You must develop the mental discipline to get out of your own mind and get into your audience's mind.

There are two facets to second-person insight. The first is empathy, but it goes much further than an emotional appreciation of the audience's state. It's not just the ability to empathize with their likely emotions, but the ability to empathize with emotions you wouldn't feel. You might design a corner of your storyworld with pathos in mind, but your player might react to that situation with anger. You must not reject or suppress that emotional response; you must anticipate and respect it. The second facet operates on an intellectual plane; you must be able to visualize the confusion audience members bring to the experience. What questions will be going through their heads? What assumptions will they be making? How will their minds mesh with the thinking in your work, and where will their thinking clash with yours? How can you minimize the likely clashes between your product and their thinking?

We spend so much time inside our own heads (24/7 for sane people) that seeing the world through another's eyes is immensely difficult. Indeed, few people appreciate just how differently other people think. Teachers do; it's quite a jolt teaching your first class. You stand up in front of your students, reveal the truth to them in a few clean, simple sentences, and note with shock the utter incomprehension in their faces. So you repeat yourself with more elaboration, and behold the same blank stares. The act of teaching is mostly a matter of finding an infinite number of ways to communicate an idea. All good teachers have strong second-person insight, at least in the intellectual dimension.

A Model for Human Understanding

A detailed appreciation of the nature of human understanding will clarify the role of second-person insight and reveal the importance of interactivity. The starting point is the notion of *associative memory*. Information in the human mind is not stacked neatly in files and folders the way it's organized inside a computer. No, the ideas are organized by association. For example, credit cards and bank accounts are perceptually different from money, yet most people associate credit cards and bank accounts with coins and bills, even though credit cards and bank accounts don't contain actual coins and bills. You might imagine coins and bills moving into or out of your bank account, even though nothing is moving; it's just numbers being added or subtracted. The mental associations spread out from there: Money flowing into accounts from your paychecks, flowing out to pay rent, gaining interest, being transferred to savings or invested in stocks—all an imaginary process carried out in your mind by associations between these concepts.

Many of these associations are natural and logical, but people put different weights on them. Perhaps your view of these associations puts your checking account at the center of a web of connections. Another person might use the credit card as the focal point. A third person, blessed with lots of financial savvy, might well refuse to think in terms of a financial center of gravity and instead connect all these ideas in a more egalitarian style, concentrating on the balance of the overall distribution of assets among stocks, bonds, T-bills, cash accounts, gold, and so forth.

Even more important for interactivity considerations is the idiosyncratic nature of many of these associations. Some people have completely different connections; some people have connections in common but put different weights on those connections. Someone who invested heavily in Enron will have strong emotional associations with stocks; another person who held lots of dotcom stocks will have different emotional associations. A person who recalls grandfather's old safe with its pile of grand stock certificates will always associate stock with certificates; the absence of those certificates from modern stock trading might induce a certain nervousness not shared by others. And what if grandfather had often intoned in his deep, resonant voice "Stocks, my child—you can't go wrong with a solid portfolio!" How would that fond memory distort the web of associations in a person's mind? And what if grandfather had died penniless?

It is this webwork of associations that constitutes human memory and human understanding. We each build our own webwork, node by node, connection by connection, as we learn and grow. Because we all live in the same universe, our webworks often share gross similarities, but the differences in our experiences ensure that each webwork's particular structure is unique to its builder. This explains why we so often misunderstand each other. You and I might have a roughly similar overall understanding of the stock market, but your associations are so different from mine that we can come to stunningly different conclusions. You can explain your reasoning with determination and patience, but if my webwork doesn't coincide closely with yours, I just won't get your point.

These discrepancies of experience and understanding are just part of the human condition; we accept them, shrugging our shoulders and mumbling "*De gustibus non est disputandem.*" ("There's no arguing about taste.") If the audience rejects an artist's work, the artist can dismiss them as obtuse cretins who simply cannot perceive his vision (webwork). Too bad for them.

The revolutionary value of interactivity lies in its ability to get past this limitation. Imagine the teaching process not as expository lecture, but as interactive conversation. The teacher probes the student's webwork, noting carefully the deeper significance of the questions the student asks. The teacher uses that information to infer the structure of that webwork. Here is where the teacher's second-person insight comes into play; a good teacher can quickly reconstruct the student's webwork and identify the misplaced node or incorrectly weighted association. With the problem identified, the teacher can set to work shifting the student's webwork. Initially, the student will resist, attempting to fit the teacher's observations into the webwork in a manner that doesn't stress or distort it. But the teacher presses, and suddenly the student's webwork snaps into place. "Aha!" says the student.

This is the power of interactivity: Interaction reveals the discrepancy between the artist's and the audience's webworks and makes it possible for the artist to address that discrepancy. The result is an ability to reach people with tremendous impact. That's what makes interactivity so powerful and what justifies interactive storytelling's loss in narrative finesse.

To use interactivity effectively, you must deeply understand the human truth that people see and hear what they want to see and hear, and then you must come to understand those desires. Being right is not good enough; you must somehow see your truth through other people's eyes.

Second-person insight, like so many artistic gifts, involves a certain degree of mental aberration. To be of any value, the artistic expression must be unconventional, or at least non-obvious; at the same time, you must see your truth from many points of view. You must be able to see how your truth fits into many different webworks of knowledge. It's a weird way to think, perhaps within the reach of only a gifted/cursed few.

Discipline

Another requirement for the interactive artist is an iron determination to subordinate your own desires and interests to those of your audience. You must push down the artistic egotism that glories in self-expression, replacing it with other-person perception.

 So you want me to abandon my own artistic drive and instead just "give 'em what they want." Sounds more like Barnum and Bailey than Michelangelo.

Absolutely not. I'm not suggesting that you should abandon your own artistic interests; after all, that's what you have to offer your audience. Yes, you want to speak your truth, but that's the easy part; the hard part is making them hear it. Ergo, you must silence the shouts of your ego so that you can hear the whispers of your audience's needs.

Perhaps a metaphor will help. Imagine the king of a medieval country deciding how much of the country's wealth should be dedicated to his own comfort and pleasure. "As the king, I'm the most important decision-maker in this country, so it's vital that I be cushioned against the distracting vexations and tribulations of life. It's my job to concentrate on the highest-level decisions. It is better for all if I wear the finest clothes, eat the best foods, live in the most luxurious palace in the country. Some of the peasants might starve, but it's all for the greater good."

You can instantly see through the selfishness of this argument, but how does it differ from this one: "As the artist, my ideas are the most important in the world, so it's vital that I be cushioned against the distracting desires and interests of my audience. It's my job to concentrate on the grandest artistic ideals. It is better for all if I heed my own voice, aspire to my own goals, and pursue my own interests. Some of the audience might not understand my work, but it's all for the greater good."

 Wouldn't this argument apply to every artist in history? If so, the success of the great artists of history would seem to rebut this argument.

No, this argument doesn't apply to all art—just to interactive art. Artists in other fields are perfectly justified in neglecting the needs and desires of their audiences because their audiences are so large that those needs and desires average out to meaningless gray murk. The great Greek sculptor Polyclitus once proved this point with a simple exercise. He showed a work in progress to a series of critics, asking each what could be done to improve the work. Then he carried out all their suggestions. The result was an ugly monstrosity. A work of expository art must have a single unifying vision; all those audience ideas and variations only muddy the waters.

Interactive art is profoundly different because it's experienced individually by millions of people. Millions of people have seen reproductions of Michelangelo's *The Creation of Adam* on the ceiling of the Sistine Chapel, and every single one of them has seen exactly the same thing because there's just one image. But millions of people can play an interactive storyworld, and each one can experience something that nobody else has ever experienced. That's the whole idea of interactivity: It responds to each person individually. Accordingly, you cannot hide your ego behind the argument that the audience's needs and wishes are all averaged together. You must face each player individually.

Degrees of Interactivity

Interactivity is not a binary quantity like mortality (either you have it or you don't); it's an arithmetic quantity like weight (you can have more or less of it). My favorite example of a low-interactivity phenomenon is the refrigerator light. You open the door and the refrigerator light turns on; you close the door and it turns off. That's interactivity! (The refrigerator light "listens" to the door switch being opened, "thinks" with the simple-minded logic of "Switch open, turn on light!" and "speaks" by turning on the light.) But it's dumb interactivity, hardly worth the candle. It might entertain a three-year-old for a little while, but even a three-year-old quickly outgrows the insipid interactivity of the refrigerator light.

At the other end of the scale, I can offer sex as an example of the most intense interactivity. Powerful lovemaking is the deepest interaction two people can have; is it any wonder that society wraps it in such grand robes? This provides a useful rule of thumb in Lesson #8.

Lesson #8
Your designs should aspire to the ideal of metaphorically having sex with your users.

Three factors determine the degree of interactivity: speed, depth, and choice.

Speed

Speed is the simplest of the three factors to understand. At the bottom end of the scale, slow applications destroy interactivity. Three examples demonstrate this point.

The first example is the spreadsheet. VisiCalc was the first spreadsheet for personal computers, and computer historians agree that this program did more to launch the PC revolution than any other. But VisiCalc wasn't the first spreadsheet—not by a long shot. There were plenty of spreadsheet programs for big mainframe computers, but they were batch-processing programs. You punched your data onto punch cards, submitted your job to the computer center, and then picked up your output the next day. You studied the printouts, made a few changes in your data, punched up the cards, and resubmitted the job. If you were lucky, or you stayed at the computer center until 3 a.m. when nobody else was submitting jobs, you could get your turnaround time down to a few hours, in which case you could run through half a dozen scenarios in one night.

VisiCalc wasn't as powerful as mainframe spreadsheets; after all, it had to run on a tiny microcomputer. Moreover, a PC's small screen showed only a fraction of a typical spreadsheet; the "real" spreadsheets at computer centers could print out their results on big sheets of paper so that you could see everything at once. VisiCalc had just one advantage over conventional mainframe spreadsheets: If you changed a number, it processed the change immediately and presented the results in a flash. In terms of features, display, and overall computational power, VisiCalc was a loser. Its interactivity was thousands of times faster than mainframe spreadsheets, however, and that made all the difference in the world.

The second example is the BASIC programming language, developed at Dartmouth in the late 1960s. A number of languages that emphasized simplicity had been designed for students, but something quite unexpected made BASIC stand out: its interactivity. BASIC was an interpreted language, not a compiled language. Computer languages in those days, and most computer languages today, are compiled. You type up your program, submit it to the compiler (a program that translates your program into machine language), and then run your program to see how it works. The compilation step could take several minutes in the old days, so after submitting your program to the compiler, you would take a coffee break before returning to see how it came out. It probably had a few bugs, so you would fix one or two bugs, submit it again, and go have another cup of coffee. Repeat this process all day long and your eyes were bulging out of their sockets from the caffeine, and you had made only minor progress on your program.

But BASIC is interpreted: It's designed to be run immediately, without compiling. You type up your program and run it; the results appear immediately. If there are bugs (usually the case in a first-cut program), you make a change right then, and run the program again. This process is so quick and easy that you *never* quit for a cup of coffee; you just sit in front of the computer, lost in intense interaction with it.

As a result, BASIC took the programming world by storm. Within just a few years, everybody was using it to teach students. It's actually a crummy language, with all sorts of problems, and it teaches bad habits. The single factor of rapid interactivity, however, put it way ahead of everything else.

On a more modern note, the third example is the "World Wide Wait." Remember how frustrating it was to wait for web pages to download? If you have a broadband connection, do you remember the sense of exhilaration the first time you sat down and worked with fast reaction times? That reduction in turnaround time made a big difference, didn't it?

Lesson #9
Fast turnaround is always better than slow turnaround.

So far I have demonstrated only that moderately fast reaction times are better than very slow reaction times. What about the top end, where you're comparing fast reaction times with moderate reaction times?

Take a simple example: your word processor. When you type, the letters appear on the screen. How much delay is there between striking keys and seeing the letters on the screen? Most of the time, there isn't much delay, but my copy of Microsoft Word, running on a fairly fast Mac, does bog down when vertical scrolling is required. If my text runs over the line and spills underneath the bottom of the window, requiring vertical scrolling, there's a slight delay—perhaps half a second—while the screen scrolls. That slight delay is enough to throw off the stride of my typing; I often make typos during that period.

Or how about the task of scrolling from the top of the document to the bottom? If it's a lengthy document, you can wait a long time while the damn thing slogs through all the pages. My copy of Microsoft Word scrolls through about four pages per second. That's fast, but it's not fast enough. I wish it were faster. Don't you?

Depth

Some of the activities performed on computers are mindless: Searching through a few dozen websites to find a bit of information doesn't take a lot of concentration. A videogame might move at a frantic level, but it doesn't reach deep into the most important areas of your mentality. Other activities require more mental exertion and hence provide deeper interaction. A game of chess, for example, moves slowly but provides a deeper interaction than a game of tic-tac-toe.

By "deeper," I mean "penetrating closer to what makes you human." Computers can easily beat you at tic-tac-toe, but that wouldn't bother you because tic-tac-toe isn't that important. But what if your girlfriend ran away with a computer? "I'm sorry, Mortimer," she says, "but you're just not as exciting, not as sensitive, not as satisfying as R26a here. Sure, he's dull gray, but in every way that counts, he's a real man." Now *that* would strike you in the gut! This is an extreme case, but it serves to illustrate what I mean by penetrating closer to what makes you human.

Many dimensions of depth are available to the artist. Games confine themselves to a few of the simplest modalities of human cognition: hand-eye coordination, puzzle-solving, spatial reasoning, and so forth. For interactive storytelling, however, the foremost cognitive modality at play is social reasoning. The infinite complexity of the dynamics of human social relationships gives the interactive storyteller a bottomless well of material; the problem lies in getting some sort of algorithmic grasp of the problem. Reducing social machinations to mathematical form without compromising their richness, however, requires deftly combining artistic insight and mathematical fluency. This topic is addressed in the discussion on personality modeling in Chapter 11, "Personality Models."

Lesson #10
The overall quality of an interaction depends on its depth as well as its speed.

Choice

Carl Von Clausevitz, in his monumental work *On War*, noted that battle is to war as cash payment is to business. A businessperson can make deals, write contracts, design and build products, obtain loans, and arrange foreign exchange, but in the end, cash payment is the decisive point; everything else is merely a preliminary to that moment. A general can obtain weapons, train troops, and maneuver around with clever strategy, but in the end, battle is the deciding moment. The same idea applies to the process of thinking: Choice is to thinking as battle is to war. You can philosophize and deliberate all day long, but the end result of all your mental gymnastics has to be a choice of some sort. Your choice might not seem like much of a choice (Do I eat lumpy oatmeal or pickled prunes for breakfast?), but it's still a choice, and all your mental processes are geared toward making a choice, even in the absence of clear information (When I hear footsteps behind me in the dark alley, do I run or ignore them?)

The quality of any interaction depends on the richness of choices available to the user. "Richness" breaks down into two factors:

▶ The functional significance of each choice

▶ Perceived completeness: the number of choices in relation to the number of possibilities the user can imagine

"Functional significance" means the degree to which a choice satisfies users' desires, needs, and interests. For example, a word processor could offer a feature that randomly changes fonts and font sizes while typing, but this choice would be useless, so providing it doesn't improve the interaction at all. A better example comes from those games that offer the player the opportunity to wander all over a huge region—but nothing interesting happens in the huge region. The poor player wastes hours of time exploring a dead space that offers no further opportunities for interaction. Sure, the game offers zillions of choices in terms of where the player might go, but none of those choices is functionally significant.

"Feature bloat" is an example of the reverse of this issue. Consider, for example, the Microsoft Word feature that allows you to add borders and shading to a document. I have *never* used this feature, nor do I expect to ever use it. It therefore represents a choice that has no functional significance to me. From my point of view, this choice is a liability in the program. Every time I consult the Format menu, my eye must glance at this option, and I must make a decision to ignore it. Of course, other users might love the feature, throwing in borders and shading all over the document. For them, this feature doesn't constitute a liability—it offers an additional choice that they find functionally significant.

For the second factor, the absolute number of choices isn't important; it's the number of choices offered, compared to the number of possibilities the user can imagine. If the user has reached the climax of the story and must choose between leaving his girlfriend for the war or shirking his duty, having only two choices doesn't detract from the power of the interaction; it's difficult to imagine any other reasonable possibilities.

This brings me to the most important lesson in this book:

Interactivity depends on the choices available to the user.

It is my sincere hope that the font size successfully conveys the importance of this point. In case its significance remains in doubt, I offer a few variations:

▶ The choices available to the user determine the quality of the interactivity.

▶ If the user doesn't have good choices, the interactivity stinks.

▶ Giving the user all the right choices makes perfect software.

▶ If the software is bad, it's probably because it doesn't let you make the choices you want.

▶ Denying choice to the user is the surest way to ruin the interaction.

So What?

All my ranting and raving about interactivity fails to address an important question raised by my Alter Ego:

 Who gives a damn about interactivity? Why bother with it?

I can offer three reasons for getting on the interactivity bandwagon: It's the medium's basis of competitive advantage, it's revolutionary, and it's powerful.

Incentive #1: Basis of Competitive Advantage

One of the great rules of competitive behavior is to set the competition in the context most advantageous to you. In military science, this rule is expressed as the aphorism "Fight on the ground of your own choosing," which means that a general should choose a battlefield best suited to the advantages and disadvantages of his own army. Political pundits always advise their candidates to "fight the campaign on your own issues, not your opponent's." Every MBA quickly learns to identify and exploit a company's "basis of competitive advantage." It's the product or service that the company can supply better than anybody else. Concentrating your efforts on that basis of competitive advantage is the only way to profit.

The computer is a medium of expression, and the artist using this medium must understand its fundamental basis of competitive advantage: interactivity. Computers can do a lot of things well: graphics, animation, music, sound effects, and even text. Plenty of media can do these things better than computers, however. Sure, a computer can present beautiful images, but a printing press can still deliver better images for less money. A $10 calendar or a $20 poster delivers better imagery than a $1000 computer. If you want animation, you can rent a DVD for a few bucks, and it doesn't take a computer to play that DVD—just a DVD player costing perhaps a tenth as much as the computer. You want sound or music? You can buy a CD player for even less than a DVD player. And let's not even talk about the cost and quality of the text in a paperback book compared with what you get on a computer. In all these areas, the computer is second best, an also-ran. The computer might be a great development system for creating your masterpiece, but it's never the delivery system of choice—not if you want to get the best possible presentation of your work.

Interactivity is another matter entirely. No other medium can deliver true red-blooded interactivity—not movies, not audio CDs, not DVDs, and certainly not books. When it comes to interactivity, computers are the only game in town. So if you truly want to get down and dirty with the computer, interactivity is what you want to concentrate on; that's the basis of competitive advantage of this medium.

Incentive #2: Revolutionary

Hey, who wants to work in a tired old field like cinema, music, or literature? Interactive storytelling is so new that nobody has any idea of what it is or how it works. If you're the adventurous type, it's the field for you. Besides, opportunities to get in on the ground floor of a new medium don't come along often. Literature was a hot new field about 3,000 years ago, and the printing press opened up a lot of opportunities 500 years ago. Movies were young and wild a century ago, radio was young in the 1930s, and television had its heyday in the 1950s. I was in on the ground floor of computer games in the early 1980s, and that was fun, but nowadays it's just another case of Big Media, where the accountants have more sway than the designers. If you've got the creative itchies, interactive storytelling is the place to be.

Incentive #3: Power

Perhaps you're the kind of artist who lusts for the power to influence people. You have something you want to say to the world, and you don't want to whisper; you want to shout. You want your message to hit people in the gut, to knock their socks off, to take their breath away. Hearken back to the earlier section in this chapter, "A Model for Human Understanding." Remember how I talked about the "Aha!" experience that people get when their webwork suddenly snaps into a new position? That's what any great work of art does. With expository art, you get one chance to make something so powerful that in one swipe it forces the "Aha!" onto its audience. But with interactivity, you have a better chance of making that "Aha!" experience happen to your audience because they can test their webwork of ideas against yours. Isn't that what you want?

 Why not simply use the computer to enhance conventional storytelling?

The computer has been used to enhance storytelling for a long time; *Jurassic Park*, for example, couldn't have been made without computers. Indeed, there's an entire field of effort known as "digital storytelling" that attends to the problem of using computers to present conventional stories. Sure, the computer makes it possible to do the same old stuff faster and cheaper, and that's great for accountants and creative fuddie-duddies. So if you want to use the computer as a tool rather than a medium, be my guest—and don't forget your Metamucil.

Wrapping Up

Now that I've pumped you up with revolutionary fervor, I shall cut you off at the knees with the warning that this revolutionary stuff is tough, sweaty, bloody business. The road ahead is no cakewalk; those who attempt to travel it will face innumerable difficulties. This book doesn't walk you down that road; it can give you only general guidelines for staying alive as you stumble forward. Remember, it's the choices you offer your player that determine the quality of the interactivity. If those choices permit players to fully engage their personal webwork of ideas with your own, then you can bestow an "Aha!" experience on them.

---

1. Mark S. Meadows, *Pause & Effect: The Art of Interactive Narrative* (New Riders, 2002; ISBN 0735711712).

CHAPTER 3
Interactive Storytelling

HAVING ESTABLISHED SOME BASIC concepts of stories and interactivity, the task now is to combine the two and ask "What is interactive storytelling? What lies at the conjunction of interactivity and stories?"

The plethora of terms used in discussing interactive storytelling indicates the confusion that surrounds the subject. Over the years, people have used "interactive story," "interactive storytelling," "interactive drama," "interactive narrative," "interactive fiction," and "interactive movies" to describe this field. I use "interactive storytelling" because it seems to be the most commonly used term.

Extrapolation from Games

When people are at a loss to understand a new phenomenon, they fall back on what they already know and describe the mysterious phenomenon in familiar terms. Therefore, the American Indians of the nineteenth century saw the railroad as an "iron horse." Americans of the mid-twentieth century perceived the computer as a "giant mechanical brain." In much the same way, people trying to grasp interactive storytelling fall back on games as the closest experience they can imagine. After all, interactive storytelling, like games, is played on a computer, is interactive, and is entertaining. So shouldn't interactive storytelling be some sort of extrapolation of games?

I define a game as "a goal-oriented form of interactive entertainment in which one or more active opponents attempt to hinder the player's attainment of his goal." This definition could apply just as well to almost any interactive story-world. The game's opponent is the same as the story's antagonist. The player in the game is the protagonist in the story. The player has goals, and the opponent acts to hinder those goals. Clearly, in this definition, there's no difference between a game and an interactive storytelling system.

The real world is a messy, complicated place, and all too often definitions run afoul of ugly reality. It's easy to accept a mouse, a deer, or a lion as a mammal, but what about platypuses or whales? They're mammals, too, but they certainly stretch the common notion of mammal. If you define food as a form of nutrition, does a diet soda with no nutrients constitute food? Most definitions of life have the very devil of a time dealing with fire, viruses, and prions.

So too with games. The broad definition I offered is academically correct, but the products that people actually play can be defined in much narrower terms. Here's a definition for videogames as they are actually played:

> *A form of interactive entertainment involving simple and/or violent themes, relying heavily on cosmetic factors, in which players must exercise precise hand-eye coordination, puzzle solution, and resource management skills.*

Although this definition doesn't cover all games, it does a good job of covering most videogames. Perhaps it would be more accurately termed a characterization than a definition.

Now compare the reality of games with stories, piece by piece:

simple and/or violent themes

This piece shows a huge chasm between games and stories. Stories for young children are certainly simple, but the full range of stories is characterized by complexity of themes and story structure. Even the simplest movies, such as *The Terminator* or *Godzilla*, have more plot twists and turns than the most intricate computer game. The level of character development and plot intricacy demanded of stories goes far beyond what games can offer.

relying heavily on cosmetic factors

Cosmetic factors certainly play a role in movies—lately computer graphics advances have made wondrous imagery possible. Yet movies that *rely* on cosmetic factors always fail at the box office. There were some fantastic dinosaur movies in the 1990s, but can you recall any of them other than the *Jurassic Park* series? The movie *Final Fantasy* explicitly relied on cosmetic factors; ads for the movie boasted that it sported the finest computer graphics ever built. It bombed. Movies will take advantage of cosmetic factors wherever possible, but they don't rely on cosmetics to sell the product. Cosmetics are a supporting element; the story comes first.

precise hand-eye coordination

It's true that hand-eye coordination plays a role for some characters in movies; the swordfights of the Jedi knights or the feats of any action hero come to mind. Physical prowess, however, never plays a major role in any genre but action movies, and even those movies often portray physical prowess falling prey to cleverness. The delicate damsel in *The Terminator* eventually crushes the robot in a machine, after spending the entire movie running and hiding from the monster. Luke Skywalker might have used physical prowess to destroy the Death Star in *Star Wars: A New Hope*, but his ultimate triumph came by begging his father, Darth Vader, to help him when the Emperor was torturing him to death. As far as stories are concerned, hand-eye coordination is for the kids.

puzzle solution

Plenty of stories focus on puzzles. All mystery stories are elaborate puzzles, and puzzles often play a role in action movies. Again, however, their role is always subsidiary to the story, but most games include puzzles, and some games revolve around their puzzles. If you were to forbid game designers to include puzzles in games, the games industry would be crippled; if you were to forbid Hollywood from including puzzles in movies, it would lose a genre (mysteries), but little more.

resource management skills

Stories have always played fast and loose with resource management issues. Six-shooters always have more than six shots. In *The Lord of the Rings*, Aragorn, Legolas, and Gimli run all day long for days on end without food or water. And people *never* have to stop and go to the bathroom in movies! Yet games impose all manner of resource management problems on players. Stories don't worry themselves with accounting problems (except as a secondary factor accentuating the stress on the protagonist), but game players revel in maintaining exactly the right amount of ammunition, food, and so forth as they play.

These observations point to the conclusion that stories and games, as they actually exist, are distant cousins at best. Visualizing interactive storytelling in terms of games is rather like describing a whale by using a camel as a reference. Sure, they're both mammals, but they are so different that the effort is a waste of time and ultimately misleading.

I have more to say on this matter in Chapter 7, "Simple Strategies That Don't Work."

Lesson #11
Interactive storytelling systems are not "games with stories."

Interactivized Movies

Some have pursued the notion that interactive storytelling is just like the movies, only the player gets to make all the dramatically interesting decisions. Wouldn't it be wonderful to find yourself playing the role of Luke Skywalker in *Star Wars*, facing evil, becoming a Jedi knight, and swashbuckling across the galaxy?

This possibility has inspired a generation of would-be moviemakers shut out of Hollywood, desperate to prove their talents. The powerful tools the computer makes available to low-budget operations encourage them to experiment, and while they're at it, they figure they might as well toss in some interactivity. The inevitable result is what I call an *interactivized movie*: a product that is for all intents and purposes a movie, but has some interactivity tacked on.

To illustrate the core problem with interactivized movies, I've applied the concept schematically to *Star Wars: A New Hope*. Here is the sequence of key decisions that Luke makes during the course of the movie:

1. Agree to take Obi-Wan partway to Mos Eisley Spaceport?

2. Race home to discover the bodies of uncle and aunt?

3. Decide to accompany Obi-Wan to Alderaan?

4. Rescue Princess Leia?

5. Run away from Darth Vader?

6. Trust the force to blow up the Death Star?

Now I ask you: If you were playing Luke Skywalker and the key decisions were up to you, would you answer any of these questions in the negative? Of course not! So what decisions are available to a person playing a game based on the movie? None!

I have more to say on decisions in Chapter 7.

Plot Versus Interactivity

Comparing plot with interactivity leads many to conclude that there's a fundamental conflict between the two. Academics prefer to use the term *agency* to refer to what most people call "interactivity" and *narrativity* to refer to what most people would call "storiness" (or "plot"). Here are some relevant quotations from various authorities:

> *I will argue that there is a central contradiction within the idea of interactive narrative—that narrative form is fundamentally linear and non-interactive. The interactive story implies a form which is not that of narrative...*[1]

In a narrative, this notion of significance seems inversely defined, since the ability to alter events in the plot actually works to diffuse the significance of the story. If viewers can change characters' actions with the wave of their hands, why should they care about the story? What indeed then is the story?[2]

Some assert that the intersection of interactivity and story is empty:

The popularity of the concept of "interactive fiction" for computer-based stories and games is surprising. Is there anything compelling in our cultural history that suggests people want to participate in received stories? Are there stunning examples of successful interactive fictive experiences that have turned doubting Thomases into true believers? No.
It's the Myth of Interactivity again—recall that this myth tells us: Interactivity makes games better, and a game designer should try to make the experience as richly interactive as possible. And what goes for regular games goes for story games. This belief in the universal power of interactivity is what leads people to try to marry interaction and storytelling.[3]

Dr. Glassner is correct in observing that interactive storytelling has never been done before, but then, lots of things had never been done before, such as interactive word processing, interactive database management, interactive spreadsheets, and, of course, the interactive Internet. Until the advent of the computer, rich interactivity could be accomplished only by committing a human being to the process, and most of the time the human was too slow or too expensive to make the interaction worthwhile. To dismiss interactive storytelling on the grounds that it hasn't been done before is to reject the entire basis of the human intellectual adventure.

The difficulty in building interactive storytelling technology doesn't mean that interactive storytelling is impossible. There are theoretically sound reasons for the apparent conflict between interactivity and plot. The problems are best seen from the plot faction's point of view. Plot creation is an enormously difficult task, demanding talent and creative energy. Permitting the grubby-fingered audience to interact with the carefully crafted plot will surely ruin its delicate balance. Knowing how difficult it is to get a plot to work well, writers insist that any audience intrusion into the process yields only garbage. If interactivity requires the audience to involve itself in the direction of the plot, clearly interactivity and plot are incompatible.

Adding to this apparent incompatibility is the attitude of the other side. The protagonists of interactivity tend to take a dim view of plot. The strongest example of this attitude is the possibly apocryphal story about id Software and the creation of Doom. There was, so the tale goes, some dispute within the organization about the proper role of the story in the game. One faction argued that there should be some story element to tie everything together. The other faction argued that Doom was to be an action game, pure and simple, and that they "didn't need no steenking story." Eventually, the anti-story faction won out, and the losers left the company. So the tale goes. Doom went on to become one of the most successful games in history, which confirmed (in the eyes of the gamers) the uselessness of storytelling.

So you have an apparent incompatibility between plot and interactivity. It would seem, from both theoretical considerations and the experiences of many failed attempts, that plot and interaction cannot be reconciled. This in turn implies that the dream of interactive storytelling is a chimera.

The central issue here isn't new. In slightly different terms, some of the brightest minds in human history have struggled with this problem, often with illuminating results. Now, you might wonder how the problem of interactivity versus plot could have attracted the attentions of august thinkers in times past, but they were working with a bigger problem: the classic theological problem of free will versus determinism.

I'll explain the connection using the terminology of Christian theologians who wrestled with the problem for centuries: God is omniscient and omnipotent. Every event that takes place in the universe happens according to His benevolent design. There are apparent evils in the universe, but they are all part of God's greater intentions. But these God-willed events include the actions of people as well as natural phenomena. Thus, a terrible disaster is an "act of God," but so is a murder. So how can human beings have any free will? They are pawns in the hands of an omnipotent God. If humans did have free will, God would be neither omnipotent nor omniscient, for then He wouldn't control or know what we would do. But if He is neither omnipotent nor omniscient, how can He fit any definition of God? Therefore, free will clashes with determinism.

The connection with interactive storytelling should be obvious. Determinism in theology is analogous to plot in storytelling. The plot is the storyteller's predestined plan for the story's outcome. Free will is analogous to interaction, for how else can players interact without exercising their free will? To make the theological analogy more explicit, view the storybuilder as the creator of a miniature universe. The storybuilder, for example, creates an imaginary universe populated by characters. Like some omnipotent god, the storybuilder decides their actions and predestines their fates. Conversely, the history of the universe is nothing more than a huge story written by God that we act out.

But wait! The game designer is also a god of sorts. He too creates a tiny universe and exercises godlike control over that universe. Yet free will seems to exist in the game universe. What's the difference?

The difference lies in the intended experience. The game designer doesn't specify what path the player takes to get to the victory condition, only the rules by which the player can attempt to do so. The gameworld is an orderly place with free will for the player. That's because the designer's control is exercised through the *rules* of the gameworld rather than the *events* of the gameworld. Therein lies the resolution of the dilemma of plot versus interactivity. A plot specifies events, not rules.

Therefore, the pessimists are correct: Plot and interactivity are incompatible. However, there's something higher, more abstract than plot. Call it "metaplot," if you like. It's something like a plot, only it's specified by rules, not events. And there's no clash between interactivity and this kind of metaplot.

I'll be expanding on these concepts in Chapter 5, "Abstraction," after I have explained some points about abstraction.

It's Different

The conclusion you must draw from these considerations is that interactive storytelling is a whole 'nuther ball game, a horse of a different color, a rare bird, a queer duck. You cannot apply tried and true expertise (from games or from stories) to this unprecedented medium. You're navigating through uncharted waters, and the rules of thumb that work so well in familiar waters simply don't work here.

So it's back to basics—all the way back to the absolute fundamentals and working your way forward from there. The most fundamental rule is Crawford's First

Rule of Software Design: Ask "What does the user DO?" So ask yourself "What should the user of an interactive storyworld be able to do?"

When you frame the question in that way, the answer is obvious: The user should be able to make lots of dramatically interesting decisions. Conversely, the user should not have to make boring decisions, such as when to go to the bathroom.

Three problems arise automatically from this answer:

▶ How do you generate enough interesting decisions?

▶ How do you pare away the boring decisions?

▶ How do you keep the storyworld interesting?

How Do You Generate Enough Interesting Decisions?

Consider the earlier example with Luke Skywalker: He made a total of only six dramatically significant decisions in the movie, and none is a particularly interesting decision because it's implausible that Luke would have made any other choices.

This is a gigantic problem because stories as we know them are designed this way. At each step in the storyline, the character's decisions must be so natural, so obvious, that the audience believes them. If a character violates the audience's expectations, the story loses credibility. For this reason, storytellers bend over backward to create circumstances that make a character's decisions believable.

For example, in *Star Wars: The Phantom Menace*, Queen Amidala violates Qui-Gon Jin's instructions not to contact Naboo because she's concerned about the fate of her people, but, more important, the storyteller has contrived a series of disagreements between her and Qui-Gon Jin that serve to undermine her willingness to obey his orders. In doing so, she gives away their location to the Sith Lord, who sends Darth Maul to capture her. This otherwise idiotic decision on her part had to be justified, so the storyteller contrived not one but three cases in which, with increasing rancor, she disagreed with Qui-Gon's decisions.

Even if you could design algorithms that successfully create plot elements to justify otherwise unbelievable character decisions, you would be ill-advised to use this method, for it would rob the player of any sense of free will. Would you really enjoy playing the role of Luke Skywalker when all your major decisions are forced on you by circumstances?

This discussion leads to one of the most important design factors in interactive storytelling. This lesson is difficult to accept because it contradicts one of the fundamental rules of conventional storytelling. The interactive storyworld must present the player with decisions that hang on a razor's edge, decisions that could readily go either way; the conventional story must give its characters decisions that can be made in only one way.

Lesson #12
A storyworld is composed of closely balanced decisions that can reasonably go either way.

You will immediately recognize Lesson #12 if you're familiar with information theory. This lesson amounts to nothing more than a dictum that the user be able to communicate significant information content to the software. If all decisions are heavily slanted in one direction, users don't get the opportunity to communicate much information reflecting their wishes. "You can have any color you want so long as it's black" is just another way of saying you have no choice, and "You may choose to fail to shoot down the enemy tie fighters" is a choice that isn't plausible because taking this choice ends the story right then and there.

Lesson #12 presents one of the most important conceptual shifts the storybuilder must make in moving from conventional stories to interactive storyworlds. A storyteller creates a conventional story by striving hard to create a sequence of entirely reasonable decisions that lead to an interesting and perhaps unexpected conclusion. The storybuilder, however, must banish such thinking and instead concentrate on decisions that could plausibly go either way. This concept is totally new in storytelling, so alien that it could excite suspicion or rejection. If you review the logic of the preceding paragraphs, however, you'll find that it's an inevitable conclusion.

Oftentimes the focal point of a story is a fundamental decision or change that a character must make. Darth Vader looks back and forth between the Emperor and Luke, trying to decide whether loyalty to the Emperor outweighs love for his son. The entire story builds up to that one decision. A storyworld must be equipped with dozens or even hundreds of such decisions. Many of these razor's-edge choices will have less dramatic import than Vader's decision, but they must still carry some dramatic import if they are to be interesting to the player.

Clearly, the task of creating so many decisions is a gigantic one; stitching them together into a coherent whole is an even bigger task. Because these tasks are clearly the most difficult ones a storybuilder must face, they become the focus of the creative efforts in building a storyworld.

Lesson #13
The storybuilder's most important task is creating and harmonizing a large set of dramatically significant, closely balanced choices for the player.

How Do You Pare Away the Boring Decisions?

The negative side of this effort is eliminating dramatically uninteresting decisions. Actually, this task is easy to implement: You simply bundle them together as inevitable outcomes. Suppose, for example, that the villain gets the drop on the protagonist and cries "Drop your gun!" The protagonist can choose between dropping his gun or offering some kind of resistance. If the protagonist chooses to drop his gun, you don't need to follow that decision with verbs for the villain to command "Turn around and march to the dungeon!" and the protagonist to decide whether to comply. Having made the decision to surrender to the villain, these subsequent events are essentially moot. The storyworld need merely announce something like "The villain marches you to the dungeon, where he has imprisoned his other captives. You see this and that. Then the villain says some villainous words, and you decide to choose [Door A], [Door B], or [Door C].

In other words, you simply bundle together all the consequent events as part of the reaction to the protagonist's decision, jumping the story ahead to the next interesting decision. You do *not* saddle the player with endless trivial decisions about where his feet should be or whether he'll have one lump of sugar with his tea or two. There's no reason that an interactive storyworld can't have long chunks of noninteractive exposition—so long as those chunks are necessary to set up the context for the next stage of interaction.

Indeed, if the story is well designed, those long chunks of noninteractive exposition shouldn't be necessary. In a well-written story, the gap between the protagonist dropping his gun and finding himself in the dungeon should be minimized (unless, of course, the storyteller wants to introduce some interesting tidbit of information during the trip to the dungeon).

How Do You Keep the Storyworld Interesting?

Here lies the real meat of the storybuilder's task in interactive storytelling, and the essential task is to envision a dramatic *storyworld*, not a *storyline*. If you perceive your creation as a storyline, you are doomed to failure. If you have a story to tell, you should tell it by traditional means: cinema, literature, or theater. If you want to build an interactive storyworld, you must banish all notions of plot and storyline from your head and instead think in terms of a storyworld: a universe of dramatic possibilities, revolving around a central theme and exploring all the variations on that theme.

This topic cries out for an example. Consider, in the broadest terms, a storyworld about the Arthurian legends. It's a promising foundation to work on because a large and varied collection of stories already exists within this body of literature. If you start off thinking in terms of a single story, such as *Romeo and Juliet* or *For Whom the Bell Tolls*, your efforts are doomed because a single storyline dominates your thoughts. But the Arthurian legends offer all manner of different stories; it's impossible to think of these legends in terms of a single storyline. Yes, some dominant threads should show up in any interactive Arthurian storyworld: the love triangle involving Arthur, Guinevere, and Lancelot; the search for the Grail; the conflict with Mordred. But none of these primary themes must come out in any predetermined fashion, and the stories have other subthemes as well. It's still possible to have a worthy Arthurian storyworld without any love triangle or one in which Mordred reconciles with Arthur. This is the key to creating interactive storyworlds: multiple but connected themes. An interactive storyworld must present the possibility of romance, betrayal, battle, spiritual growth, and many other possibilities. Only in this way can the player explore a dramatically interesting universe. If the storyworld is confined to a single theme, such as a love triangle, it can develop and conclude in only a few ways.

So a simple version of the Arthurian storyworld includes the love triangle, the search for the Grail, and the final battle with Mordred. At the outset of the storyworld, young Mordred is seeking to unseat Arthur as king; Lancelot has just arrived at Camelot; Guinevere has been Arthur's queen for some years; and the Saxons are continually raiding the lands of Arthur's people, killing peasants and stealing cattle. Arthur must organize war parties, lead counterattacks against the Saxons, fight battles against them, and drive them back. He must fairly distribute the spoils of war among his subordinates, rewarding those who fight well without antagonizing others. Mordred attempts to foment trouble by playing on the rivalries and resentments of those who believe Arthur hasn't properly recognized them. Arthur must also adjudicate disputes among his people, which sometimes requires more diplomacy than justice. Meanwhile, Guinevere, as queen, is responsible for running Camelot, and her activities generate new difficulties demanding Arthur's interventions. If Guinevere feels unsupported by Arthur, her resentment might flower into a relationship with Lancelot—assuming that he too is somewhat disenchanted with Arthur. Or perhaps it won't. Either way, Mordred spreads tales besmirching Arthur's reputation and Guinevere's purity. The situation comes to a head when Mordred declares a rebellion against Arthur. The nobles choose sides, based largely on their respect and affection for Arthur. In a final battle, numbers will likely determine the outcome. Of course, if Arthur has maintained peace and prosperity for all, Mordred will never get his chance and Arthur will die in his bed, beloved of all.

This example shows only one way to build a storyworld. There are many other possibilities. The key realization is that a storyworld is a much larger creation than a story. This makes perfect sense when you realize a simple theorem about storyworlds: A single playing of any storyworld generates a single story. In other words, when a player goes through a storyworld, he produces a story. The player's path is a linear sequence of events—a *storyline*. He could relate his experiences to another person, and the listener would perceive the player's experience as a story. Different playings of the storyworld can yield many different stories, however. Hence, a storyworld contains zillions of incipient stories. Clearly, this creation is much larger than any single story. Building storyworlds is necessarily a huge task.

Atoms of Interactive Storytelling

No matter what technology is used for interactive storytelling, it must somehow assemble pieces into a complete story. There's one exception to this simple statement, however. It's possible to think of a computer story technology in which players make all their decisions at the outset of the story. Perhaps a player specifies some character traits for the protagonist; perhaps she answers a questionnaire. Whatever method is used, the player's contribution is complete before the story begins. The software then creates a story using these specified parameters. This technology would certainly be interesting, but I wouldn't accept it as interactive storytelling because it's not interactive. The player speaks just once to the computer, and then the computer thinks it over and speaks back to the player with a long story. Interaction requires an alternating cycle of speaking, listening, and thinking. One step doesn't cut the mustard.

For true interactive storytelling, however, you can be sure that the computer assembles the complete story out of little story fragments. This process is fundamental to computing. A computer sees an image as a big collection of little image fragments called *pixels* and manipulates the image by changing the individual pixels. A word processor sees a document as a collection of text characters mixed with a set of formatting commands. Deep inside the heart of every computer program is at least one central quantity or concept broken up into lots of tiny fragments, and the computer executes processes on this set of fragments to generate its output. This concept is absolutely fundamental to all computing; it applies to interactive storytelling just as well. The question, then, is "What are those little story fragments that the computer plays with?" In other words, what are the atoms of storytelling?

I use the term *substory* to describe the atoms of storytelling, but giving these atoms a name doesn't answer the question. What are substories?

A substory is a single dramatic step; it's an event or a change. It can be described in a sentence that specifies an event: "Jan realized the significance of the white dog" or "Andre lived happily in his new life." This event can be tiny ("James sidestepped the descending sword and swung to his right") or big ("James killed Thomas in a swordfight").

Note that substories aren't measured with a clock. That is, a substory cannot be a chunk of time. Stories don't move forward in synch with the clock; they crawl through moments of intense emotion, and then leap forward hours, days, even years. Some substories can take place in a flash ("In an instant, Jan realized the significance of the white dog"); others can span years ("and so Andre lived happily in his new life, until one day…").

These examples show that the data structure defining a substory is the same as that for a sentence. There must be a subject, a verb, and, most likely, a direct object. A substory probably also includes additional information in the form of prepositional phrases, adverbial phrases, and so forth. Its basic form, however, must be functionally similar to a sentence.

What about exposition? Every story has to provide context and background through straightforward exposition, and exposition doesn't necessarily involve events. For example, "The cavern was astounding; on the walls, fist-sized jewels glistered in the light of their torches, while the path on which they walked was paved with golden bricks."

This substory doesn't fit the standard sentence template you described. It doesn't represent any event or change. It's a state. Doesn't this invalidate your description of a substory?

I don't think so. While working on the Erasmatron, I did encounter some problems with exposition because exposition must never be repeated. So I designed a special object called an *exposition* to describe some stage, actor, or prop when first encountered. But expositions never interfere with the flow of the story; the story development is independent of expositions. An exposition is, in effect, an unrepeatable substory.

The Ideal Scale of Dramatic Resolution

How big should substories be? At what level of dramatic resolution should players experience the storyworld? At one extreme, you could offer players the opportunity to make only the key decisions in the storyworld, such as the six decisions that Luke Skywalker made. This method would keep the storyworld small, but would be unsatisfying to players, as the storyworld wouldn't offer many variations on the basic storyline. In the Luke Skywalker example, all six decisions are simple binary decisions; therefore, the story has (theoretically speaking) only 64 possible outcomes, and in practice players would experience far fewer. After all, should a player decide not to take Obi-Wan partway to Mos Eisely, he returns home and is killed along with Uncle Owen and Aunt Berue. End of story. In truth, the original story has only eight variations, one of which matches the original movie. The other seven all end abruptly with the player being killed or living out the remainder of his life in obscurity. Therefore, restricting a storyworld to only gigantic decisions keeps things too simple to be interesting. Perhaps a simple system would be useful for children first experiencing interactive storytelling, but adults would find it dull.

At the other extreme is something like a stream of consciousness. Every experience, thought, and perception is treated as a substory and presented to the player. As with conventional stories using stream of consciousness, the result can be overwhelming, impossible to follow, and tedious.

My belief is that the size of substories is one of the fundamental artistic decisions every storybuilder must make. Dramatic emphasis is achieved by using small substories; tedious material can be compressed into a single larger substory. The storybuilder's ambition and effort determine the total number of substories in any storyworld. Tolstoy could have written *War and Peace* as a short story or regular-size novel, but he chose to write a behemoth. To each his own.

You could refer to traditional story forms to determine the ideal scale of dramatic resolution. In literature, you can choose between a sentence and a paragraph as your atoms. A typical novel has so many sentences, however, that using paragraphs is preferable; the number of paragraphs in a novel seems a manageable and appropriate number of decisions for the player to make. Again, you see that the length of a substory is variable; some paragraphs in a novel are short and some are long. Comics provide a particularly useful angle on the problem of determining the ideal scale. You can view a single frame of a comic as a substory; no other medium has such a cleanly quantifiable structure.

The conclusion is that the ideal resolution for interactive storytelling is somewhere between literature's sentence and paragraph. However, it's too early to close this topic; I suspect that creative artists will expand the boundaries of this concept.

What Can't Be Part of Interactive Storytelling

Some elements of traditional storytelling cannot be used in interactive storytelling. For example, you can't have what I call the "Third Option": the protagonist's stroke of genius that gives him a third option for escaping the sharp horns of a dilemma.

Here's a somewhat obscure example requiring some explanation. In the movie *Bless the Child*, a devil-worshiping cultist accosts a God-fearing little girl on the roof of a high building. He taunts her faith in God and forces a test upon her. Placing her on the ledge of the roof, he demands that she prove her faith. She must leap off the roof and trust God to save her, or she must reject God and declare her faith in the Devil by taking the hand of the cultist. A dark shroud of menace hangs over the scene; neither the audience nor the little girl can guess whether the cultist will throw her off the roof if she refuses to make the impossible choice he is forcing upon her. After a nerve-wracking pause, the little girl turns to the cultist, smiles, and says invitingly "After you!"

This scene actually contains two important lessons about interactive storytelling. First, consider the long logical train her response triggers. She is suggesting that the cultist should prove his own faith in his own god (the Devil) by making exactly the same leap he's trying to force on her. If the cultist is unwilling to leap off the building, how can he ask the girl to do so? He is revealed as a hypocrite, and his either-or choice is ruined. It's a complex logical twist that comes as a complete surprise to the audience. Although it's impressive work, I think you can discount the possibility of a computer coming up with a similar option. It's simply too hairy and requires too deep an understanding of human nature. Perhaps next century.

Second, even if an interactive storytelling system could concoct such a stroke of genius, it couldn't offer it to the player. If the system were to present the girl's choices in that form, the list would read:

▶ Leap off the building to your death.

▶ Reject God and embrace the Devil.

▶ Say "After you!"

This list doesn't present a true choice; only the third option is viable. This scene had great dramatic power in the movie, but it would fall flat on its face in an interactive storyworld. The trick lies in the fact that the audience couldn't have anticipated the third option. It was so clever that it took the audience by surprise. Suppose you restaged the scene, replacing the vulnerable little girl with, say, Arnold Schwarzenegger. Sure, the cultist might give Arnold only the two choices, but any audience could anticipate that Arnold would simply shout "Hasta la vista!" and mow down the cultist. No surprise there, and no drama to the scene.

A variation on the Third Option is the "Creative Option." One early tester of my Erasmatron technology complained that it didn't offer "creative options." When I asked what that meant, she could say only that she wanted to be able to do things I might not have thought of. The problem is, how can I provide software to handle situations I haven't thought of? There's something of a Catch-22 here.

Another element that simply can't be included in interactive storytelling is real-time play. This rule is a natural result of Lesson #12, which posits that a storyworld is composed of closely balanced decisions that could reasonably go either way. These decisions require thought from players; they cannot be made in a split second. If the story just keeps moving along in real time, however, players might have lost the opportunity to choose by the time they make up their minds. Therefore, the storyworld must come to a halt whenever it presents a decision to the player.

There have been some attempts at using unbroken time flow in interactive storytelling. The first was Mixed Emotions, by Rosa Freitag, produced in 1995. This product uses continuous video to tell the story of a woman facing problems in her marriage. During the course of the story, she occasionally pauses to think, at which time two icons appear over her head, one blue and the other red. The blue icon always indicates a morally conservative course of action; the red icon represents an adventurous or risky course of action. The player can click on one of these icons to guide the protagonist through the story. If the player doesn't select an icon within a few seconds, the story proceeds using the blue icon as the default choice. The system did succeed in presenting real-time interactive storytelling, but only because the choices were so simple.

Andrew Stern and Michael Mateas have produced an interactive storytelling system (Fac[cd]ade) that operates in real time, but it too has restrictions. More on their technology in Chapter 19, "Story Generators."

Wrapping Up

▶ Interactive storytelling systems are *not* "games with stories."

▶ There's a fundamental conflict between plot and interactivity, but not between metaplot and interactivity.

▶ A storyworld is composed of closely balanced decisions that can reasonably go either way.

▶ The storybuilder's most important task is creating and harmonizing a large set of dramatically significant, closely balanced choices for the player.

▶ The fundamental atom of interactive storytelling is the substory, which is best imagined as a sentence.

---

1. Andy Cameron, www.hrc.wmin.ac.uk/hrc/theory/dissimulations/t.3.html.

2. Michael Murtaugh, http://ic.media.mit.edu/Publications/Thesis/murtaughMS/HTML/InteractiveNarrative/InteractiveNarrative.html.

3. Andrew Glassner, www.glassner.com.

PART II

Styles of Thinking

CHAPTER 4
Two Cultures, No Hits, No Runs

IT'S BEEN NEARLY 50 YEARS since C.P. Snow[1] warned of the emerging problem of "the two cultures." The scientific community and the arts/humanities community were drawing apart in mutual incomprehension and antagonism. Snow believed strongly in the necessity for the two cultures to work together in solving the problems that bedevil Western civilization.

Although his thesis caused a sensation and triggered much subsequent discussion, the problem has grown worse. Scientists, engineers, and mathematicians are not just unschooled in the humanities; they actively dismiss the arts and humanities as soft-headed wastes of time. The arts and humanities people have gone just as far in the other direction: They simply refuse to have anything to do with the sciences and disparage science as "linear thinking."

A variety of causes have been offered for this yawning divergence. The iron rule of academia, "publish or perish," rewards specialists and punishes generalists, driving academics ever further into their narrow rabbitholes. The fundamental difference in style between the rigorous sequential thinking of the sciences and the pattern-recognizing thinking of the arts and humanities divides the two camps even more. There's even a bit of gender factor here, with the sciences attracting more than its share of men and the arts and humanities grabbing up more of the women. Whatever the cause, the basic trend is undeniable: The two sides are drawing further apart.

We're paying the price for this pigheadedness in the field of interactive storytelling. A physicist doesn't really need to know the Louvre from the loo, and an artist can get along quite well without knowing the difference between energy and entropy. Interactive storytelling, however, requires creative people who straddle the divide. The verb thinking I discuss in Chapter 6 is really a generalization of the algorithmic thinking that scientists routinely engage in, and who can deny that a solid appreciation of the nature of storytelling is necessary to success in interactive storytelling?

All of Me (1984), a delightful comedy starring Steve Martin and Lily Tomlin, told the story of Edwina Cutwaters (Lily Tomlin's character) getting stuck inside the brain of Roger Cobb (Steve Martin's character). Edwina gets control of Roger's left side, while Roger retains control of his right side. The consequences are demonstrated in a hilarious scene in which Roger attempts to walk down the sidewalk. Edwina, wanting to go one way, uses her left leg and hand to march one way, while Roger, using the other side, desperately tries to do the opposite. Steve Martin's physical comedy is magnificent; you can see the battle between the two sides of his body as they struggle against each other. Of course, they get nowhere.

That's pretty much the situation with interactive storytelling. The programmers and games people on one side struggle against the new media people on the other, and with all the spastic staggering, nobody gets anywhere. In the movie, the two antagonists eventually learn to work together and fall in love in the end. Would that interactive storytelling has such a happy ending.

Techies: Programmers and Games People

Now take a look at how this polarization has played out in the computer games industry. The programmers and games people, educated in the technical tradition, are comfortably ensconced in their world, making really "cool" action games with plenty of graphics, animation, and throbbing music. They're successful and making lots of money—and that's the first major obstacle to interactive storytelling: Comfortable people never change. The games people are too comfortable to seriously consider the major effort required to realize interactive storytelling.

Instead, they seek a quick, easy way to "story-ize" their games. Games people see stories as a desirable feature to add to their games, not the defining aspect of games. They design the game first, and then add a story the same way they add animation, sound effects, and music. It's just another tacked-on feature. At conferences, they eagerly discuss the many tricks they can use to "fake" a story, although they don't see it as faking.

Their fundamental mistake is applying science's standard analysis-and-synthesis approach to storytelling. They believe that a story can be taken apart into components just like any machine, and then they merely need to reassemble those components and voilá—a story! So they apply whatever random bits of information they've picked up about storytelling and assemble their parts list:

▶ Characters, preferably with good backstories

▶ A beginning, a middle, and an end

▶ Plot twists

▶ A romantic interest for the male protagonist

▶ Obstacles to overcome

Then they tack these components onto their game design as best they can. The result is a game containing some of the elements of storytelling. "Huzzah!" they exult. "We're already halfway there!"

A classic example of this add-on approach is the game Half-Life (1998), which won awards and critical acclaim as a breakthrough product. The game itself was nothing more than a standard 3D shoot-'em-up embellished with a sequence of cut-scenes smoothly integrated into the 3D display engine. These cut-scenes were just like all previous cut-scenes, but because they were presented using the same graphics engine that handled the game, they were less obtrusive. What set the techies' hearts racing was a genuine, honest-to-gum plot twist. After blasting uncounted monsters, the player hears the sounds of approaching soldiers. Thinking himself saved, he rushes in that direction. Before he reaches the soldiers, he sees another person also running toward the soldiers. The soldiers shoot the fellow, and the player hears a voice shout that no witnesses to the monsters must be allowed to live. So now the player finds himself in a shoot-'em-up against soldiers. What gut-wrenching drama! What a breakthrough!

What a laugh.

In the years since Half-Life, games people have scrambled to expand on the concept, and we have seen all the obvious extensions: multiple plot twists, more characters, cut-scenes for victory or defeat, and dozens of random ideas. Nobody has come close to achieving anything like interactive storytelling, however. Despite repeated failures, the games people just don't get it; they keep trying the same basic analysis-and-synthesis approach.

Admittedly, the analysis-and-synthesis approach can be made to yield fruit; if it couldn't, interactive storytelling with computers would be an impossibility. The trick is, it must be applied with considerably more knowledge of drama than techies are willing to bring. Dr. Frankenstein provides the perfect analogy. He figured he could just stitch body parts together, zap them with enough electricity, and voilá—life! In the most basic terms, he was correct in believing that assembling the right parts, in the correct manner, could yield life, but he vastly underestimated the complexity of the task or the amount of biological knowledge necessary for success. In the same way, techies stitch together bits and pieces of a story, zapping them with ever-snazzier algorithms, and expecting a story to emerge—but they fail to appreciate the complexity of the task and the amount of storytelling knowledge necessary for success. They disdain the vast store of storytelling knowledge that people on the "wrong" side of the tracks have accumulated.

Indeed, many techies are infused with a deep-seated contempt for people from the arts and humanities. For several years, I have hosted a conference on interactive storytelling for a small group of people. Time and again, the techies grow bored with the contributions of the storytelling people, dismissing them as a bunch of meaningless hot air.

Yes, techies appreciate the work of the artists, so long as artists keep their place. In techie eyes, the proper role for artists of all kinds is providing artistic flesh for the techie bones. Techies design a game's basic skeleton, and artists fill in the snazzy graphics, animation, sound, and music that make their techie game design come alive. Artists don't design games, however; that task is reserved for techies.

Walk into a typical techie's home, and you'll find the bookshelves stocked with technical manuals, a few science books, and some science fiction novels. That's the extent of their taste in literature. Their video library consists of action and science films—no Jane Austen adaptations for these guys. Once I overheard a techie dismissing *A Beautiful Mind* as a total bore, saying that all the characters did was sit around and talk. How dull!

Their thinking also includes a brutal materialism that views selling products as the true measure of accomplishment. They reject suggestions that might improve a game's artistic qualities with the observation that they're not in business to make a statement, but to sell games. Entertainment, they declare, has nothing to do with art, and making money is the sole metric of success. Their idol is John Carmack, creator of the 3D algorithms that made possible a generation of blood-soaked shoot-'em-ups. Carmack recently retired young and rich to spend his days playing with big rockets, the ultimate high-tech toys. Game design techies the world over swoon over his example.

 You grossly exaggerate the nature of the problem. There are techies who don't fit these generalizations.

Well, *of course* there are exceptions; every generalization about human beings has exceptions. The larger the group, the more exceptions. I trust my readers know this and can accept my claims for what they are: generalizations that apply to a *typical* techie, not *every* techie.

Artsies: The New Media People

My ferocious assaults on techies don't indicate any preference for the other side, whom I call the "artsies." Having smeared one group, I shall now level my trusty mudslinger at the other.

Techies created the computer games revolution, and artsies took a while to get on the bandwagon. Once they got going, they refused to have anything to do with techies. Perhaps the most revealing tidbit is their refusal to learn programming. It's not universal; there are a few notable exceptions. But the majority of artsies who have jumped on the games bandwagon have never written a program.

I've tried several times to teach artsies to program, and I have found that their mental orientation does them in, not any lack of intelligence. They simply refuse to knuckle down and think in terms of deductive logic. In artistic communities, a linear style of thinking has been so denigrated that artsies simply can't bring themselves to embrace it. It's rather like my attitude toward eating fish. I never ate it as a child and now, as an adult, I simply can't bring myself to enjoy it. Knowing that it's good for me, I occasionally make the attempt, but try as I may, I simply can't get it down my gullet. Artsies seem to have the same hangup with programming.

I don't mean to suggest that expertise with programming is essential to understanding interactive storytelling. It's possible, I suppose, for somebody to make useful contributions in the field without any technical background. After all, you don't need to understand internal combustion engines to drive a car. However, you *do* need to understand such engines to design a car, and you really should understand computer technology if you hope to design computer applications, including interactive storytelling. Leonardo da Vinci spent plenty of time watching dissections of human bodies so that he could understand human anatomy better. Artists don't need to dissect human bodies to draw the human body, but knowing something about human anatomy certainly helps. Sculptors need to understand the properties of the materials they work with; painters must understand the dynamics of light and color; musicians must understand something of acoustics. All artists need to understand the warp and woof of the medium they work with.

Despite the example of great artists such as Leonardo, most artsies just won't roll up their sleeves and learn programming. Instead, they insist on regarding interactive storytelling as an extension of conventional storytelling—in exactly the same way that techies insist on regarding interactive storytelling as an extension of game design.

Bubble Intellectualism

"Bubble intellectualism, arises when a group has become so ingrown that it loses all contact with the rest of the intellectual universe and drifts off into its own self-reinforcing universe. I must confess that I don't understand any of the artsies' discussions on interactive storytelling or, for that matter, games. Despite my substantial credentials as a designer and theoretician, I can't understand what these people are talking about. It's not just one of them that bewilders me—it's the whole kit 'n caboodle. The works of the media theorists impress me with their erudition and cleverness, but they never leave me with anything to grab hold of.

 This demonstrates your own ignorance, not their impenetrability. You're on the science side of the Two Cultures divide, and you just don't get the top thinkers on the other side of the chasm.

Yes, there's plenty of truth in that assertion. Whenever artsies start talking about semiotics, I feel like they must feel when confronting a mathematical formula. Yet there's a difference, I think, between their grand theory and the grand theories of science. Even the most abstruse, exotic scientific theories ultimately relate back to the real world in some useful way. To put it in cruel terms, the physicist's motto might well be "Give me a new theory, and I'll make a weapon out of it!" We're surrounded by a myriad of actual, working technological devices derived from abstruse scientific principles that the average person couldn't comprehend—but that average person can still use the devices.

The geniuses of the artsy side of interactive storytelling don't seem to have produced anything that could be boiled down to practice, however. I struggle through their works, trying to glean some useful bit of information that I can apply to my own work, and everything I read is obvious or irrelevant—or so it seems to me.

Aren't you expecting too much? After all, Einstein never bothered to build a nuclear reactor, and Maxwell didn't build any radios. Why should the top people on the artsy side have to worry about products?

Einstein and Maxwell never worried about practicalities, but others used their theories to build products. The metaphorical pair of pyramids in **Figure 4.1** explains my idea.

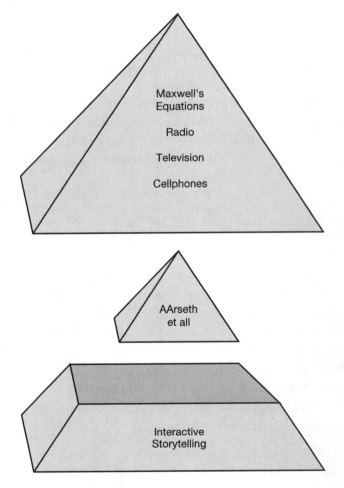

FIGURE 4.1: Electromagnetic theory and interactive storytelling theory.

The physics pyramid has a base: all the ideas and products that flowed from Maxwell's theories. The theorists of interactive storytelling, however, seem to be disconnected from the base of their pyramid. Nothing connects their work with the actual creating of interactive storytelling.

 That's not fair. The theory these people are working on is still in its early stages. More than a century separates Maxwell from cellphones. These people have had less than a decade. Give them some time!

No, there's still a difference. Maxwell's theory wasn't immediately *applied*, but it was immediately *applicable*. That is, any physicist of the time could see how to take existing technology and extend and improve it by using Maxwell's theory. The time delay in applying Maxwell's theory had more to do with the pace of technological development in the nineteenth century than the utility of the theory. The theory's full ramifications weren't immediately obvious, of course. That took further effort, but there was no question the theory fit into the rest of the sciences and would lead to new ideas and new technologies. Such is not the case with the artsies' theories about interactive storytelling. I'm a practitioner *and* a theorist, and I can't see how their work could be applied to anything other than more theory. This is what I mean by "bubble intellectualism." It's a complete, consistent, and impressive body of thought that has no connection with the rest of the intellectual universe.

Cross-disciplinary Futility

I have to give artsies credit for trying to bridge the gap, at least socially. They have organized conferences on interactive entertainment and games, to which they always invite some representatives of the techie/games community. (It's revealing that techies have never reciprocated, but merely acquiesced to an artsie initiative.) These conferences always start off with an earnest declaration of the need for academia and industry to work hand in hand. Then a techie gets up and talks about what he wants from academia: students trained in 3D artwork, programming, and animation. An artsie gets up and lectures about the semiotics of Mario Brothers. A techie follows with a lecture on production techniques in the games industry. Another artsie analyses the modalities of mimetics in text adventures. And so it goes, both sides happily talking right past each other, and neither side having the slightest interest in or comprehension of the other side's work.

As always, you're exaggerating the problem and neglecting the important exceptions. Carnegie-Mellon, MIT, and other universities have good cross-disciplinary programs, and the Europeans are taking the lead in educating artist-programmers.

Yes, there are some good cross-disciplinary programs, but most are recognizable as either an arts program spiffed up with some programming and interactivity, or a computer science program spiffed up with some coursework on media. The projects students build always fall into one of two categories: a highly creative use of computer imagery and sound with nothing in the way of substantial programming, or a clever new algorithmic technique to do the same old stuff faster and with more colors or fewer polygons than anything done before. I have yet to see a single project at any of these schools that married creative use of imagery or sound with creative use of algorithms.

However, I'll concede the point about Europe. The Two Cultures divide has never seriously affected continental Europeans; this problem seems to be a particularly American one. Perhaps European techies are inoculated against the Two Cultures virus by the experience of living in cities bursting with art. I suspect Europeans will eventually take the lead in interactive storytelling technology; perhaps then Americans will realize the seriousness of the problem and make serious efforts to catch up.

Neurophysiological Basis

To some degree, the Two Cultures problem can be traced to events during the evolution of the human brain. As humans faced new challenges, various mental modules (refer back to Chapter 1, "Story") developed to address those challenges. Two broad classes of mental modules developed: pattern-recognizing and sequential. The pattern-recognizing modules were finely tuned to process complex patterns, such as visual processing and social reasoning. Sequential thinking is used for auditory and language processing; it's also important for the natural history module.

These two basic styles of thinking (pattern recognition and sequential) exist in every brain, but some minor genetic predispositions affect them. Gender specialization in hunter-gatherers (men did more of the hunting, women did more of the gathering) endowed men with slightly stronger skills in sequential thinking, and the richer social environment of the base camp gave women a slight advantage in pattern-recognition. The cultural milieu in which children are raised magnify these small tendencies. The net effect is that men have traditionally dominated the sequential-thinking social functions, and women have played a larger role in the pattern-recognition social functions.

Guess what? There's a bit of correlation between logic-versus-pattern and science-versus-art. It's not an iron law, just a vague correlation. People who are stronger in sequential thinking gravitate toward the science and engineering side of the Two Cultures polarity. People who are stronger in the pattern-recognizing side are more comfortable in the arts and humanities end of the polarity. Therefore, the Two Cultures war is to some extent based on styles of thinking that stretch back millions of years.

Exhortations and Prognostications

What can you do to combat this sad state of affairs? First, fight intolerance. The next time somebody asks you how many artists it takes to screw in a light bulb, don't go along with the joke; answer by calling the joker a pointy-headed nerd. That ought to put the joke in the proper light. If somebody makes a derisive comment about linear thinkers, tell 'em you prefer linear thinking to intolerant thinking. Don't let people get away with the crude behaviors that divide us from each other.

Second, take the time to really listen to people from the other side. It's frustrating, I know, but it can be life-changing.

Let me tell you a story about a friend who changed my life. Veronique is all intuition and no logic. Because I worship at the altar of Reason, you might think that Vero and I were fated for mutual disdain, but when we first met, some sort of emotional connection transcended our differences. Perhaps it was the attraction of yin for yang; perhaps it was platonic romance. I don't know. It certainly wasn't a sexual attraction—I'm older and not up to the standards of this hot-blooded Frenchwoman. Whatever the attraction, we always enjoy our time together, talking endlessly about all manner of things.

One day we got into a discussion of reincarnation. Being a rationalist, I reject this notion as idle superstition. Vero thinks differently. So I decided to walk her down the primrose path of logic, right into a trap. Step by step I led her toward my inexorable conclusion, making each step absolutely bulletproof. However, one step in my logical sequence was unavoidably soft. It wasn't wrong, of course—I would never engage in deliberate mendacity. Although every other logical step was adamantine, however, this one wasn't quite ironclad. I rushed through it and moved onto the next step. Vero listened politely as I went a couple of steps further, and then pounced on the vulnerable spot. With unerring accuracy, she stripped bare the flaw in my logic and demolished my argument. I was flabbergasted. How could she have seen the flaw? I interrogated her, trying to determine what logic had led to her discovery. There wasn't any; she just knew.

From that day forward, I have held Vero and other intuitive thinkers in much higher regard. I don't understand how they do it, and it bothers me that they can't justify their conclusions, but unquestionably they are capable of intellectual feats that defy my comprehension. I have started cultivating my own intuitive faculties. Maybe I can learn how to do it, too! So far, though, I feel like a clumsy child learning to ride a bicycle.

Third, take the time to cultivate the other style of thinking. If you're an intuitive, pattern-recognizing artist, put your nose to the grindstone and tackle some icy cold logic. Remember, it doesn't come easily to anybody—we all have to learn it. If you're a sequential-thinking person, take some time to enjoy art. Don't force yourself to endure art that you don't appreciate; just delve deeper into something that does appeal to you. Something important is going on there, some strand of human genius you need to respect and appreciate.

Generally, scientists admit that the most powerful force for change in science isn't rational analysis but the mortality of older scientists. A similar pessimism permeates my appreciation of the current Two Cultures problem. The prejudices that underlie this problem are immune to reason, and this chapter won't rehabilitate any combatants in the Two Cultures wars. Ultimately, however, you can't beat Mother Nature; those who continue to man the barricades will surely fail one day. With the passage of time, we'll see individual acts of treason, brave souls who dare to cross no man's land and consort with the enemy. Those few brave souls will enjoy some measure of success, and that success will encourage more to follow. Eventually, the Two Cultures divide will be bridged, at least in the field of interactive storytelling, but I fear that such a deep cultural shift won't be completed in my lifetime.

Wrapping Up

▶ The Two Cultures war is deeply rooted in our psyches and our culture.

▶ Techies concentrate on linear thinking; artsies focus on pattern thinking.

▶ Linear thinking is required to understand the computer; pattern thinking is needed to understand storytelling.

▶ Therefore, interactive storytelling requires creative people who can straddle the Two Cultures divide.

---

1. C. P. Snow, *The Two Cultures* (Cambridge University Press, 1993; ISBN 0521457300).

CHAPTER 5
Abstraction

THE PROBLEM OF PLOT VERSUS interactivity discussed in Chapter 3, "Interactive Storytelling," sometimes takes another form: control versus interactivity. In its simplest form, the problem is phrased as follows:

If the story is to be truly interactive, the player must be able to change the story, but if the player changes the story, the artist cannot control its development, and the player will likely ruin the story.

The solution to the problem is, in a word, abstraction, and I ask you to stay with me as I demonstrate the truth of this point. As soon as you're absolutely, completely, totally, and utterly convinced that abstraction is, in fact, the solution to the problem of control versus interactivity, you may move on to the next chapter.

Justice

The problem of exercising control over a complex system is an old one, and in every case, the solution has always been a resort to higher levels of abstraction. For example, consider the problem of providing justice to society. In small societies, justice can be provided by a single chief. Disputants present their case to the chief, who hears each side out and then pronounces judgment. All very simple. As societies grow, however, the number of cases grows and the chief—now known as "king"—finds himself overwhelmed with an impossible caseload. The solution is to delegate his powers of adjudication, but this creates a new problem: How is the king to maintain control over the judges so as to ensure fair justice?

The solution is law. The king declares the rules under which judges will operate, and those rules are then applied to all concerned. The solution isn't perfect; judges can still apply the laws unevenly if they are biased, or they can misinterpret the laws or even apply the wrong law to a situation. Disputants who feel they have been short-changed, however, can appeal to the king in hope of a correct application of the law.

In this manner, the king can continue to exercise control over the society. That control is not direct; it's indirect. The king's power is exerted through the laws the judges apply. Ultimate power still resides with the king, whose laws control every aspect of daily life. The king might not be looking over the shoulder of each of his subjects, but he still retains control.

The killer problem with the use of law isn't so much applying law as formulating law. The king must bring great insight and care to bear in creating his laws.

Here's an example from the first recorded set of laws. Nearly 4,000 years ago, Hammurabi of Babylonia promulgated a set of 281 laws. Among the laws were these two:

If any one steal the property of a temple or of the court, he shall be put to death, and also the one who receives the thing from him shall be put to death.

If any one steal cattle or sheep, or ass, or pig, or goat, if it belong to a god or to the court, the thief shall pay thirtyfold for it; if they belonged to a freed man, he shall pay tenfold; if the thief has nothing with which to pay, he shall be put to death.

These two laws contradict each other. One says that the punishment is death; the other that it is 30 times the value of the stolen item. In the babble of 281 laws, Hammurabi overlooked this little detail.

This problem of abstracting reality to terms that can be addressed in a law haunts all lawmaking processes. Courts sometimes annul poorly worded laws that permit entirely unintended results. It's a tough problem.

Science

Now turn to the biggest, most complex system of all: reality. The efforts to understand reality have yielded an increasingly complex intellectual system: science. At first, science was a huge mass of disconnected tidbits of information, random fragments of data that people had noticed over the generations. The big step forward was the realization that different tidbits of information could be connected to form a more coherent, albeit more abstract, whole. For example, people had long been aware that there were stars in the sky, which moved in relation to each other. Some moved faster and some moved slower, and they all seemed to move along the same path. Ptolemy assembled these disparate facts into a coherent whole, suggesting that all the planets (previously called "stars") circled around the earth. This theory was an abstraction; nobody could actually see the planets from a distant viewpoint that directly demonstrated their motion around the earth. It was all based on indirect evidence, but this more abstract view of the solar system tied together many observations and, therefore, supplied a better explanation.

That trick—finding an abstraction that ties together simpler truths—has been the basic strategy of all science ever since. Chemistry stumbled forward, building up a mass of knowledge about how chemicals reacted with each other, until the idea of atoms forming molecules took hold and explained these reactions in a more powerful, unifying, and abstract fashion. With the development of the theory of quantum mechanics, scientists were able to explain the mechanics of chemical reactions, thereby creating a more broadly encompassing view of chemistry—at the cost of using abstractions that are more difficult for mere humans to understand. The development of biochemistry merged chemistry and biology at a fundamental level that offered insights into the genetic processes that govern all living systems—but again, the price was more abstraction.

Meanwhile, physicists continued their search for the fundamental laws of the universe. James Clerk Maxwell unified electric theory with magnetic theory and light to demonstrate that all light is an electromagnetic wave. Einstein unified electricity with magnetism by showing that magnetism is a relativistic effect of electricity. Chemistry was further unified when physicists showed that all atoms are combinations of electrons, protons, and neutrons. In probing the nature of these three particles, physicists discovered a whole zoo of new particles—and then reduced them further by showing them to be composed of yet more fundamental (and even weirder, more abstract) particles called "quarks." Meanwhile, theoreticians struggled to reduce the universe to its most fundamental constants and equations, making slow and jerky progress. The end result of all these labors is a highly abstract system of ideas that explain the most profound workings of the universe—and are beyond the reach of all but a few people.

Mathematics followed a similar course. Starting with simple counting combined with simple addition and subtraction, people developed the ideas of multiplication and division, and arithmetic was born. Algebra, a more abstract approach to mathematics, came next. In the seventeenth century, mathematics exploded with analytic geometry, calculus, probability, and so forth. Nowadays, of course, mathematics has reached levels of abstraction utterly beyond everybody but specialists.

Pulling It Together

Over and over, we see the same idea: To grow intellectually, to understand and cope with ever larger problems, we always move to higher levels of abstraction. This idea can be summarized in a simple lesson.

Lesson #14
When you can't bash through a problem, go over its head.

Lesson #14 resolves the apparent dilemma of control versus interactivity. The solution is to exert control at a higher level of abstraction. As with all the examples, that abstraction is more difficult to understand, but it certainly extends our intellectual reach. Many storytellers, frozen in the traditions of storytelling, are unable (and somewhat unwilling) to grasp the novel abstractions and reject the whole concept. No matter; there's always plenty of room in this world for traditional stories, but interactive storytelling demands more.

To understand the abstractions I'm presenting in this book, you must first let go of the notion of plot. A plot is a fixed sequence of events that communicates some larger message about the human condition. In interactive storytelling, plot is replaced with a web of possibilities that communicate the same message. Because this concept confuses most people, I'll provide a number of examples at various levels.

As a starting point, I use the classic movie *Star Wars: A New Hope*. Here's the direct representation of the story:

> *Luke Skywalker leaves home, meets Obi-Wan, travels with him to Mos Eisley spaceport, and flies away in a spaceship. The ship is captured by the bad guys; they fool the bad guys, rescue Princess Leia, and escape from the Death Star. The bad guys attack the last bastion of the rebels, and Luke helps attack the Death Star. Luke destroys the Death Star and gets rewarded by the Princess.*

Now look at the same story in a more abstract fashion:

> *A young man ventures out into the world, makes new friends, and experiences many adventures. He learns much and triumphs over adversity, winning the respect of a pretty girl.*

Now make it even more abstract:

> *A boy confronts the challenge of growing up to become a man. He faces many difficulties, but ultimately triumphs over adversity and establishes his manhood.*

Storyworlds are designed at these higher levels of abstraction, not assembled event by event. Instead, a high-level design requires you to consider storytelling in a more abstract fashion. It's difficult to think of many variations of "rescue Princess Leia," but there are plenty of ways to present "faces many difficulties." Put another way, there's only one version of the first story, but there are thousands of versions of the second story and millions of versions of the third story.

Here's another, less directly pertinent example. Suppose you wanted to build an "addition machine" that must be able to carry out additions, such as 2+2=4 and 3+4=7. If you think of addition as a set of all those little formulas, you have an impossibly difficult task. How could you ever program your addition machine to remember that 3+5=8 and 9+2=11 and 18+27=45? There are just too many possible variations—it could never be done!

Indeed, if you insist on thinking of addition as a collection of numerical formulas, you're correct in concluding that an addition machine is a physical impossibility. But if you think of addition as a process rather than a set of formulas, and you mentally replace actual numbers with variables, suddenly the problem becomes much simpler. You merely program your addition machine with the laws of addition, and it will work with any set of numbers.

Playing God

Resorting to a higher level of abstraction also offers a partial solution to the knotty problem of free will versus determinism discussed in Chapter 3. This solution embraces physics and rationalizes faith. It says that God is omnipotent with respect to process, not data. That is, God controls the universe through His laws, but not through the details. God does not dictate the position and velocity of every electron and proton in the universe; instead, He merely declares "Let there be physics," and then allows the clockwork of the universe to run according to His laws. In an indirect way, you could say that He does control everything that happens in the universe, but it's abstract control. God determines the principles under which the universe operates, but grants us free will to choose as we wish within that universe. He even works a little randomness into the system to ensure that we aren't automatons responding robotlike to our environments. The important point is this: God is an abstract designer!

The same resolution works with the apparent conflict between plot and interactivity. If you are a data-intensive designer, you are necessarily a deterministic one. Like some Bible-thumping fundamentalist, you insist that your story's characters must obey literally every single word you write. The fundamentalist focuses all his beliefs in the explicit data of the Bible rather than the abstract processes behind it.

If you're a process-intensive designer like God, however, the characters in your universe can have free will within the confines of your laws of physics. To accomplish this, however, you must abandon the self-indulgence of direct control and instead rely on indirect, abstract control. That is, instead of specifying the data of the plotline, you must specify the processes of the dramatic conflict. Instead of defining who does what to whom, you must define how people can do various things to each other.

 This is too esoteric, too indirect to allow the richness of tone that a good story requires.

Consider what a story really communicates. A story is an instance that communicates a principle. *Moby Dick* is not about a whale; it's about obsession. Luke Skywalker never really existed, but the movie's truths about growing up and facing the challenges of manhood are its real message. Stories are literally false, but they embody higher truths. The instances they relate didn't actually happen, but the principles they embody are the truth that readers appreciate. They are false in their data but true in their process.

Given that stories communicate principles, consider the nature of the communication between storyteller and audience. The storyteller seeks to communicate some truth, some principle of the human condition. Rather than communicate the truth itself, he creates a set of circumstances that instantiate the truth he seeks to communicate. This instantiation is what he communicates to his audience. The audience then interprets the story; it induces the higher principles from the story's details. Note, however, the circumlocution of this process. The storyteller seeks to communicate some truth of the human condition; the audience seeks to learn the same. Instead of just telling the principle, the storyteller translates the principle into an instantiation, then communicates the instantiation, and then the audience translates the instantiation back into a principle.

This is truly a roundabout way to get the job done—but it's what works best with people.

Interactive storytelling differs from this process in two fundamental ways. First, the process of translating principle into instance is delegated to the computer. The storybuilder retains indirect artistic control, but must now exercise that control at a more abstract level. The basic process of translating principle into instance is retained, but is now performed by the computer. This of course entails considerable effort in algorithm creation. The second fundamental difference is that because the story is generated in real time in direct response to the player's actions, the resulting story is customized to the audience's needs and interests, and thereby more than makes up for any loss in polish with its deeper emotional involvement.

 This is great theory, but in practice, the act of reducing storytelling to grand principles is beyond human intellectual ability. Nobody could ever handle so deeply intellectual a process.

This process-intensive style of storytelling is done all the time, and by amateurs, no less. Here's Grandpa taking little Annie up to bed:

"Tell me a story, Grandpa?" she asks.

"Okay," he replies. "Once upon a time there was a pretty little girl who had a pony…"

"Was it a white pony?" Annie interrupts.

"Oh, my, yes, it was as white as snow. It was so white that the sunlight reflected off its coat dazzled the eye. And the little girl and the pony would go riding along the beach…"

"Did they go riding in the mountains too?"

"Why yes, as a matter of fact, they did. After riding along the beach, they would ride up the green canyons, jumping over the brush and ducking under tree branches, until they came to the very top of the mountains. And there they would play at jumping over boulders…"

"I don't like to jump."

"Well then, instead of jumping, she would let her pony graze in the rich deep grass on the mountain's summit while she sat in the sun…"

And so the story goes on. Note that Grandpa doesn't respond to Annie's interruptions with "Shuddup, kid, you're messing up my carefully prepared plot!" He wants those interruptions; his storytelling thrives on them. Grandpa doesn't enter the room with a carefully planned and polished plot, all set to dazzle Annie. He comes in with basic principles of storytelling, and then he makes up the story as he goes along—in response to Annie's needs and interests. The story he creates is his special story, just for Annie and himself, and no other story will ever be the same. Because it's their special story, it means more and has more emotional power than any high-tech Hollywood extravaganza. Yes, it lacks the careful plotting, the intricate development, and the glorious special effects of the Hollywood product. Its roughness is more than compensated for by its customization, however. Sure, Annie likes *The Lion King*—but she treasures *Annie and the White Pony*.

Now, if an amateur storytelling grandpa can pull that off, why can't big-shot professionals do the same? Sure, genuine interactive storytelling presents a bigger challenge than Grandpa faces. Granddaughters are forgiving audiences, and they don't pay for the service. On the other hand, Grandpa doesn't have to suffer through wretched books like this one to make up his stories.

Wrapping Up

▶ To understand and cope with ever-larger problems, we always move to higher levels of abstraction.

▶ Storyworlds are designed at higher levels of abstraction than stories.

▶ In interactive storytelling, plot is replaced with a web of possibilities that communicate the same message.

CHAPTER 6
Verb Thinking

THE GREATEST OBSTACLE TO THE advancement of interactive storytelling is the difficulty of *verb thinking*. This is an unconventional and almost unnatural style of thinking that is nevertheless central to understanding interactivity.

Verb thinking can be appreciated only in the context of its yin-yang relationship with *noun thinking*.

Verb Thinking Versus Noun Thinking

What is the universe? Most people answer this question by describing a collection of objects existing in a space. The universe is so many stars, galaxies, planets, and so forth. Our corner of the universe is composed of so many rocks, trees, animals, plants, houses, cars, and so on. To completely describe the universe, you need to list all the objects within it. Practically, it's an impossibly huge task, but conceptually, it's simple enough.

But there's another way to think of the universe: You can think of it in terms of the processes that shape it, the dynamic forces at work. Instead of thinking in terms of objects embedded in space, you could just as well think in terms of events embedded in time.

These two ways of looking at the universe compose the yin and yang of reality. They show up in every field of thought. In linguistics, you can see this yin and yang in the two most fundamental components of all languages: nouns and verbs. Nouns specify things, and verbs describe events. Nouns are about existence; verbs about action. Together they make it possible to talk about anything under the sun.

In other fields, the yin/yang shows up in economics as goods and services. Goods are objects, things that exist. Services are actions, desirable processes. Goods are (mostly) permanent, and services are transitory. In physics, you talk about particles and waves. Particles are things; waves are transitory processes.

Military theorists worry about assets and operations. Assets are the troops, weapons, and ammunition that can be used in a war; operations are the military actions carried out with these assets. Together, assets and operations define military science.

Programmers see the dichotomy even more clearly: They have memory for storing data, and the CPU for processing data. *Data* is the "noun" of computers: It's what is chewed up, sorted out, and worked over. *Processing* is the "verb" of computers, what does the chewing, sorting, and working over.

Even a factory manager unconsciously thinks in these terms. The factory starts with parts, the nouns of the operation, and applies labor, the verb of the operation, to build its products.

A simple table of terms that touch on this dichotomy demonstrates just how fundamental it is:

Noun	Verb
goods	services
particle	wave
assets	operations
data	processing
number	algorithm
fact	idea
truth	logic
knowledge	understanding
parts	labor
character	plot

Because these two approaches of noun thinking and verb thinking constitute a dichotomy, we often think in terms of one side versus the other (nouns versus verbs, goods versus services, and so forth), but in fact the dichotomy is illusory; it's really a polarity. A big gray zone where the two sides blend together shows up in every one of the human activities listed previously:

▶ **Language:** Nouns can be verbified ("*Trash* that memo!"), and verbs can be nounified ("That was a good *play*."). In the process, the word's definition can blur. Is "trash" intrinsically a noun or a verb? How about "play"?

▶ **Economics:** You purchase a hamburger at a fast-food restaurant. Are you purchasing goods (the burger itself) or services (the preparation of the burger)? When you hire a tax preparer, are you purchasing a good (the completed tax return) or a service (the efforts of the tax preparer)?

▶ **Physics:** The wave-particle duality drives everybody nuts. If you shoot electrons through a double slit, they'll diffract, just like a wave. Yet you can detect each electron individually, just like a particle. So are electrons waves or particles? It depends. Massive objects behave more like particles. Tiny objects behave more like waves—but you can never isolate a single aspect of the behavior. You can only make one aspect, particleness or waveness, very small compared to the other aspect.

▶ **Military science**: A small number of fast ships aggressively patrolling a sea zone can accomplish just as much as a large number of sluggish ships hanging around port. And obviously, a large army with plenty of assets can still accomplish a great deal if handled properly.

▶ **Computers**: From the earliest days of computers, programmers have realized that any computation can be carried out with almost any combination of data and process. If you can throw more memory at the problem, you require less processing and the program runs faster. If you're short on memory, you can always rewrite the program to use more processing and less memory.

▶ **Factory**: The tradeoff between raw materials and labor consumption is well known. You can work "up the supply chain" by taking in more of the job yourself. Instead of purchasing finished printed circuit boards for your computer, you can purchase the parts and add employees to make the printed circuit boards. More labor means less parts.

Thus, the yin of nouns and the yang of verbs complement each other neatly; you can twist the dial one way to apply a "verbier" approach or the other way to get a "nounier" approach. Plenty of special circumstances, of course, cause you to lean more toward one side or the other. It's a lot easier to think of Jupiter as a particle than to think of it as a wave with a very tiny wavelength. In your factory, if labor is cheap, you want to use fewer finished parts and more labor, but if labor is expensive, you want to use more finished parts.

However, another factor at work heavily biases the noun/verb balance in everything we do: the natural bent of our minds. For some reason, it's easier to think in terms of nouns rather than verbs. This bias shows up in each of the aforementioned fields:

▶ **Language**: I leafed through my dictionary, picking pages at random and counting the number of nouns and verbs on each page. I counted a total of 101 nouns and 26 verbs, a four-to-one ratio. I repeated the experiment with a Latin dictionary and counted 57 nouns to 20 verbs, a mere three-to-one ratio. The English language seems to have a strong preference for nouns.

Contrast that with Hopi, for example, which is famous for its preference for verbs.

▶ **Economics**: Adam Smith's book *The Wealth of Nations* laid the foundations of modern economics, establishing all the basic principles: the relationship between price, demand, and supply; the utility of division of labor; the advantages of free trade; and so forth. Yet the concept of services as a economic entity was poorly developed in Smith's work. He was well aware of the role of labor in economic production, but only as a means of creating goods. Therefore, the father of modern economics never saw the yin/yang of goods and services; he thought almost exclusively in terms of goods. Indeed, the notion of services as an economic output didn't establish itself firmly in economic thought until the early twentieth century. The "goods" side of the dichotomy was figured out quickly; the "services" side took another century.

▶ **Physics**: Isaac Newton laid down the physics of particle motion in 1664; it took another 200 years before scientists worked out the physics of wave behavior in as much detail. Even for the brilliant people who created the science of physics, particles were much easier to understand than waves.

▶ **Military science**: From the beginning of military history, the concept of "assets" was recognized. The actions of generals in ancient times clearly demonstrate that they were quite cognizant of the importance of how many soldiers and weapons they had. Early generals, however, only dimly grasped the notion that the way those assets were applied was just as important as the assets themselves. Alexander the Great seemed to appreciate the idea, but his use of it seems spotty. Napoleon was the first general to demonstrate a consistent application of the idea that armies are only as useful as the extent to which they are maneuvered. It was the military theorists between the two World Wars (Liddell-Hart and Guderian) who first put down on paper the ideas behind the operational approach to military strategy, and it took the Blitzkrieg to wake up the rest of the world to the value of these ideas. Therefore, military thinkers took more than two millennia to recognize the importance of the yang of operations.

▶ **Factory**: The management of raw materials and parts is an advanced field now. Using computers and close communications with suppliers, factory managers can ensure that parts and raw materials arrive at the factory just before they are used, thereby dramatically improving the system's efficiency.

Labor management enjoys no corresponding system, however, so it remains a messy, uncomputerized task. Perhaps it's because labor is done by human beings, who are not so easily pushed around to fit the algorithms. But then, why couldn't algorithms be designed to take into account individual differences in human beings? The fact is, our understanding of the labor flow in a factory is far behind our understanding of the parts flow.

▶ **Computers:** From the start, the relative importance of memory and processing were recognized, largely because memory was in such short supply that computer scientists were desperate to find any way to get the work done. Indeed, the history of the relationship of memory to processing has been almost the reverse of every other field: Hardware limitations forced early programmers to put more emphasis on processing, but as computer memories became larger, programmers put less emphasis on the processing side and more on the data side of the dichotomy. A second factor contributing to this process was the explosion of demand for programmers. In the '50s, '60s, and '70s, there wasn't much demand, so only the best and brightest became programmers. When the demand for programmers exploded in the '80s, however, we could no longer afford to limit the ranks of programmers to the cream of the crop; large numbers of un-brilliant programmers flooded the field, and these people weren't as comfortable working with algorithms as they were slinging bytes around.

The programming microcosm of games clearly shows this shift toward noun thinking. One of the early videogame systems, the Atari 2600, was equipped with a powerful processor: an 8-bit 6502 running at just under 1MHz. However, it initially allowed only 2KB of ROM and just 128 bytes of RAM. Games designed for this system were heavy on processing and light on data. Over the years, games have grown vastly in size. A typical game these days requires a CD-ROM with 650MB of storage. You can see the nature of the change most clearly by comparing the shift in hardware capabilities in videogame machines:

Machine	Atari 2600	Microsoft Xbox	Ratio: Xbox to Atari
RAM	128 bytes	64MB	512,000
ROM	2KB	8GB	4 million
Clock speed	1MHz	733MHz	733
Bus width	8 bits	64 bits	8

Note how data capacity has increased far more than processing capacity. The Xbox is millions of times better than the 2600 when it comes to data, but only hundreds of times better when it comes to processing. Games programming has shifted away from processing and toward data. Now, much of this change is caused by technological limitations; it's easier to improve storage than processing. Nevertheless, this change also represents (to a lesser extent) what people seem to demand in their games as well as programmers' proclivities. And a major question remains: If game machines are millions of times better, why aren't the games themselves millions of times better?

These examples demonstrate just how frozen our minds are into noun thinking. We just can't seem to "get" verb thinking, and when we do, it's always late and second best.

In Chapter 3, "Interactivity," one important point is that the degree or quality of the interactivity increases with the quantity and quality of the choices available to the user. To pursue that idea a little further, you can say that choice takes action as its direct object. You don't choose between an éclair and cotton candy; you choose between *eating* an éclair and *eating* cotton candy. You choose between bowing your head and saying "Yes, sir" to your boss and pulling out a machine gun and blasting him to oblivion. You choose between verbs. Verbs lie at the heart of choice, and choice lies at the heart of interactivity. To put it bluntly:

Lesson #15
Interactivity requires verb thinking.

Lesson #15 is the core reason that software sucks. Good interactivity design requires clear verb thinking, yet most people just don't "get" verb thinking. So we struggle forward with noun thinking, building software that's noun-heavy and verb-light.

Case in Point: Multimedia

Does anybody remember the multimedia craze of the early 1990s? It all started when CD-ROM drives became standard equipment on personal computers, and software developers could take advantage of the storage capacity of these babies.

It might be hard to believe, but the average personal computer back then had only about 4MB of RAM and 100MB of hard disk storage. The floppy disk was the standard means of distributing software, and its capacity was only 1.4MB. By contrast, a CD-ROM boasted 650MB of storage. The transition from floppy disk to CD-ROM increased delivery capacity by a factor of more than 400! To make a similar-sized jump from CD-ROM to something bigger, that bigger medium would need to hold about 260GB—bigger than most hard disks these days.

Freed from the constraints of floppy disks, software developers began stuffing huge quantities of data onto CD-ROMs. That data took the form of graphics. Because most personal computers in those days had 640×480 8-bit displays, requiring only 307KB of data per screen, developers could stuff about 2,000 screen images onto a single CD-ROM. Overnight, the demand for artists to prepare all this artwork exploded.

Joy reigned throughout Software Development Land. The old constraints had been lifted; the sky was the limit. Artists who had previously been discouraged by computers because they required so much programming could now create lots of dumb software with great graphics, and that's exactly what they did. The floodgates opened and out gushed a tidal wave of software called "multimedia." In design terms, all multimedia software was pretty much the same: a big pile of images and sounds presided over by a tiny little program that did little more than shuffle bytes from the CD-ROM to the screen and speakers.

Amid the cheering masses at the grand parade stood one scowling curmudgeon: me. I rained all over their parade, dismissing CD-ROMs and multimedia as a waste of time. After all, I pointed out, the CD-ROM is a data technology, not a processing technology. It gives a huge boost to the noun side of the interactivity, but that's useless: What matters is the verb side. Therefore, CD-ROMs and multimedia weren't going to do much to advance the software revolution.

Nobody believed me; they thought I was crazy. And certainly the sales figures made me look like an idiot. People made millions and millions of dollars creating multimedia. The proof of the pudding is in the eating, and multimedia people were eating quite well.

I had seen it all before. Around 1983, a similar fad swept the world of arcade games: Dragon's Lair. It was the first arcade game to use an optical disk, a precursor to the CD-ROM that was bigger, clumsier, and more expensive. The makers of this game stuffed actual animated video (from Don Bluth, no less!) onto the optical disk with a simple branching system that permitted the internal computer to shunt different video snippets to the screen. The structure of the game was simple (**see Figure 6.1**).

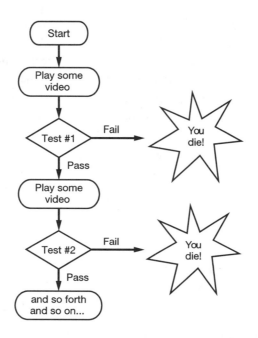

FIGURE 6.1: Game structure of Dragon's Lair.

The game was a huge hit because nobody had ever seen such glorious graphics in an arcade game. Naturally, every other arcade game maker rushed to deliver its own optical disk game. Within a year, arcades were full of optical disk games, which promptly flopped. Optical disk games were a fad, a flash in the pan, because they really weren't fun to play. Sure, they looked great, but they didn't *do* anything interesting. And play, as well as any form of interactivity, succeeds or fails on what the user *does*.

Lesson #16
Crawford's First Rule of Software Design: Ask "What does the user DO?"

Getting back to the 1990s and multimedia, I saw that the whole thing was a fad, just like Dragon's Lair. The multimedia craze would climb a little higher and last a bit longer, but it had no staying power. And that's exactly what happened. The craze lasted three, maybe five years, depending on how you measure it. By the late 1990s, multimedia was dead. The CD-ROM lived on. After all, it was a better distribution medium than the floppy disk. But people stopped selling software on the size of its multimedia content.

It is instructive that, in the games industry, multimedia was killed by 3D graphics. The distinction is lost on most observers, who figure that one graphics medium is pretty much the same as any other. In fact, there's a huge difference between CD-ROM-based multimedia and software-based 3D graphics rendering: The former is data intensive, and the latter is process intensive. Multimedia merely shovels bytes from the CD-ROM onto the screen; multimedia designers sweat data capacity. But 3D graphics software calculates its imagery using the CPU; its designers sweat machine cycles. Because 3D graphics software is processed rather than shoveled, it's far more responsive to the user. The interaction is tighter and more intimate because it's process intensive. Remember, data intensity is noun based; process intensity is verb based.

Getting Started with Verb Thinking

Okay, so I've convinced you. You have seen the light, and you're a True Believer in the gospel of verb thinking. Now how can you learn verb thinking?

First, you lay the foundations by shifting your outlook on the world. Here's that list of dichotomous words again:

Noun	Verb
goods	services
particle	wave
assets	operations
data	processing
number	algorithm
fact	idea
truth	logic
knowledge	understanding

parts	labor
character	plot
story	drama

Every time you think about any of these topics, contrast the left-side word with the right-side word. Are you worrying about the facts of an issue when you could be thinking about the ideas behind it? Go down the street looking at shops and stores. Are they selling goods or services? Can you imagine their output solely in terms of the services that went into the merchandise?

Above all, try to think about things in terms of what things *do*, not what they *are*. A window is not glass; it's something that blocks air movement while permitting light to pass freely. A car is not an engine, a body, seats, and so forth. It's something that moves; everything else is subsidiary. A computer is not a box with a whirring fan; it's a processing machine. A pill is not a bundle of exotic chemicals; it's something that alters the biochemistry of your living processes.

Recall my reference in Chapter 1, "Story," to the image taken from the end of the movie *The Matrix*; I'm going to use it again. The protagonist, Neo, finally realizes his potential to see behind the artificial world of the matrix, to see that it's really just numbers and algorithms. The walls dissolve into numbers, and his antagonists are stacks of numbers; everything is just numbers that he can control at will. This imagery provides the metaphor for how you must see the world. Those aren't walls in the hallway; they're zillions of atoms held together with atomic forces, transmitting weight from roof to floor, interacting with photons of light to bounce those photons in different directions. Things don't just sit there—they happen, and if you can come to understand how and why they happen, you can understand the universe at a deeper level, like Neo. And like Neo, you can freeze bullets in mid-air. That's the power of this kind of thinking.

Everything is connected in intricate webworks of cause and effect, and your goal in life is to understand as much of that webwork as you can. To do so, you must concentrate on causal relationships, on the precise nature of causality. You need a language that allows you to express with clarity and precision the exact nature of each causal relationship you discover. I have good news and bad news for you. The good news is that this language has already been developed; the bad news is that it's mathematics.

I can hear the hissing sound of your deflating balloon. The very thought of using mathematics probably repels and terrifies you, but in my experience, a willingness to embrace mathematics is the single most significant factor in success or failure in software design. Many people refuse to tackle mathematics, like debutantes unwilling to seize a greased pig, and this aversion is natural. Our brains are wired to think in associations and patterns, and mathematical thinking is sequential, step-by-step in style. It requires you to twist your mind around in knots to make it operate in a style it just isn't built for. You have every right to balk at my suggestion that you subject yourself to this kind of mental torture.

But what, I ask you, is wrong with the idea that you have to work to accomplish wonderful things? Great artists have never shied away from unpleasant tasks in pursuit of their artistic goals. The brutal truth is that you must embrace the slobbering monster of mathematics if you are to succeed in interactive storytelling. Here's the true test of your passion: Will you get in bed with this creature to pursue your vision?

And don't kid yourself with the comforting self-deception that there's just got to be another way to do interactive storytelling without mathematics. There's no getting around this one. Lord knows, I've tried. In designing the Erasmatron, I have struggled to cushion the spikiness of mathematics in layers of soft verbal down. I have tried to concoct other forms of expression that skirt mathematics completely. Despite all my creative powers, I have failed to concoct any non-mathematical scheme that adequately empowers storybuilders.

So gather your courage and face the monster; I'll keep him on a chain.

Causal Relationships

We normally think of causality in merely binary terms: Socrates is either mortal or not mortal. If X, then Y, and X is either true or false, as is Y. It's more useful to think of causality in mathematical terms, however: Apples cost $0.60 per pound, so if I buy 2 pounds of apples, I pay $1.20, and if I buy 4 pounds of apples, I pay $2.40. There's a direct mathematical relationship between the cause and the effect, expressed in a simple mathematical formula:

```
Price = $0.60 × Weight of apples
```

Take this idea a half-step further: Suppose somebody discovers that a man's weight in pounds is equal to four times his waist measurement in inches. This isn't actually true, but for purposes of argument, suppose that it is true. Then you could make the following mathematical statement:

```
All men's weight is equal to four times their waist measurement.
```

You can set this up as a kind of syllogism:

All men are mortal.	All men's weight is equal to four times their waist measurement."
Socrates is a man.	Socrates has a 48-inch waist.
Therefore, Socrates is mortal.	Therefore, Socrates weighs 192 pounds.

The difference between the two syllogisms is that the left-side syllogism gives mere binary results (yes or no to the question "Is Socrates mortal?"), but the right-side syllogism can have all sorts of different results, depending on the man's waist size. The left side divides Truth into black and white, yes or no, but the right side permits shades of gray. The left side can address only the most simple-minded questions, but the right side can address far more: anything that can be quantified.

Having established the basic principle that mathematical formulas are simply a kind of syllogism, you can then make those formulas more complex. For example, a more accurate formula for a man's weight might be something like this:

```
All men's weight is equal to 3 times their waist measurement plus their
height.
```

Or to put it in the spare terminology of mathematics:

```
Weight = 3 × Waist + Height
```

This equation is a little more accurate. It's still not really true, but only in the absolute sense of getting exactly the right number for every man. This equation might get within 20 pounds of correctly predicting the weight of 70 percent of all men. That's pretty good. You could probably make it better if you made the formula even more complex:

$$Weight = 2 \times Waist^{1.5} + 0.75 \times Height - 12.1 \times ShoeSize$$

Perhaps this equation would get within 10 pounds of correctly predicting the weight of 80 percent of all men. The perfect equation—the one that correctly predicts with zero error the weight of all men—is impossible to figure out. Perhaps it could be found with enough effort, but it would probably involve thousands of variables put together in the most intricate fashion and be dozens of pages long. For all practical purposes, perfection is impossible.

Perfection is seldom necessary, however. A chair designer needs to know the approximate relationship between the size and the weight of most people, but there's no need for exact numbers; getting within 20 pounds is good enough. An interactive storyteller need not achieve perfection of mathematical description; getting close enough for dramatic fidelity is all that's required.

Modeling as Metaphor

One of the oldest figurative metaphors is Homer's "rosy-fingered dawn." It's a powerful metaphor because it compares the rays of predawn sunlight and the fingers of the hand, suggesting an animation of a natural process. Poets are in the business of creating metaphors. So are most other artists, in at least some sense. The same thing applies to the mathematical modeling required for interactive storytelling. Indeed, this mathematical modeling is the essence of its artistic content—NOT the images, NOT the sounds, NOT the dialogue, NOT even the plot development. Sure, you can have artistic images in an interactive storytelling product, and you can stuff in a symphony or two, mix in a dash of poetry, and so forth, but that's not interactive storytelling. You could create a movie consisting of little more than pictures of great paintings, but would it be a good movie? You could create a movie of a great poet reading poems, but would it be a good movie? You could create a movie showing an orchestra playing a Beethoven symphony, but would it be a good movie? Taking good art in one medium and simply transferring it to another medium doesn't make the end result good art. Indeed, a true artist strives to express content most parallel to the grain of the medium.

This point is immensely important, but sadly, one that many people find difficult to accept. Part of their resistance arises from the passionate attachment that any artist feels for his or her art and its medium. Moviemakers love the cinema; poets adore poetry; writers worship literature. My claim that these magnificent art forms have no primary place in interactive storytelling sounds like a principal telling a parent that her child isn't good enough to attend his school. The same outraged rejection is the inevitable reaction to my claim.

But, hold, friend. I write these words not to belittle your child but to help you find the ideal place for your efforts. In past times, sons were forced to take up their father's trade regardless of their own proclivities. This interactive storytelling medium might not be the best place for your talents or inclinations; if so, don't fight it. Follow your muse.

And don't try to prostitute your muse into a role for which she's ill suited. In the earliest years of cinema, some gifted thespians attempted to force Melponene and Thalia into this new and alien medium. They simply set up the camera in the middle of the audience seating and acted out a play on the stage. These travesties earned the approbation of the better people, but nobody actually enjoyed them; they were inferior versions of the real thing. They were seen as rather like canned fruit: a feeble substitute for the real thing, but adequate for distribution to remote areas lacking access to the genuine article. They were also financial flops, buried by the success of vulgar, sensationalist collections of what were nothing more than carnival sideshows. As a consequence, thespians came to disdain the cinema as a simian medium. It took D.W. Griffith, a failed actor with no emotional attachments to the theater, to approach the cinema without preconceptions. No worshipper of Melponene and Thalia, he conjured up his own muse and succeeded where so many talented thespians had failed.

Therefore, friend, if you have already set your path on the well-trod way up the mountain peaks of other media, I wish you well but urge you not to drag the medium of interactive storytelling along with you. That is another mountain peak, along a very different path. Worse, the path to that mountain peak is unexplored and unmarked; you'll need a machete as much as good hiking boots. Progress up this path will be slower than what you can accomplish in other media. You'll not get there faster by taking the easier path.

If you can jettison your emotional attachments to other media (including games!) and approach interactive storytelling with the naiveté of a child, then you can accomplish something. If you try to force it to fit into your preconceptions, you will fail.

These things said, I shall now explain how to create metaphors using mathematical modeling.

I'll start with a simple example: that overwrought moment in *The Return of the Jedi* when Darth Vader, watching the evil Emperor torture his son, Luke Skywalker, suddenly changes his mind, sides with Luke, and tosses the Emperor down a convenient deep shaft. As the Emperor blasts Luke with his nasty Evil-Electricity bolts, Darth looks at Luke, then at the Emperor, then at Luke, then at the Emperor—this goes on for what seems an eternity. Obviously, he is making a decision. In the film, the decision (and the difficulty of making it) is communicated through the long back-and-forth sequence. But in interactive storytelling, you must determine *how* this decision is made. What forces are at work in Darth's mind?

Obviously, this decision represents a battle between two competing forces: his loyalty to the Emperor and his natural love for his son. But there are secondary forces as well: self-interest, which adds to his loyalty to the Emperor, and idealism, which detracts from it. There's also the empathy that any person feels for those who suffer. These various factors do battle in Darth Vader's mind to decide whether Darth should turn against the Emperor.

You can translate the ideas in the preceding paragraph into mathematical terms, line by line, sentence by sentence:

this decision represents a battle between two competing forces

```
IF (competing force 1 > competing force 2)
```

This formula is the mathematical representation of a simple yes-or-no decision. It doesn't specify what happens in each of the two conditions; it merely establishes the decision's basic form. If the strength of competing force 1 is greater than the strength of competing force 2, then the result is "yes." We'll figure out what "yes" means later.

his loyalty to the Emperor

```
Competing force 1 = Loyalty[Darth, Emperor]
```

This formula simply represents the idea of loyalty with a mathematical variable that's read as "Loyalty of Darth for the Emperor." You specify the two Actors,

Darth and Emperor, because you could just as well worry about Loyalty of Darth for Luke or any other pairing of Actors.

Here's the next term from my descriptive paragraph:

his natural love for his son

```
competing force 2 = Love[Darth, Luke]
```

But there are secondary forces as well

This means you have to adjust the earlier formulas with additional factors, such as:

self-interest, which adds to his loyalty to the Emperor

```
competing force 1 = Loyalty[Darth, Emperor] + SelfInterest[Darth]
```

This new term is read as "Self-Interest of Darth" because it refers to Darth's own self-interest. Again, you might want to use Luke's Self-Interest somewhere else, so you might as well maintain the variable separately for each Actor.

and idealism, which detracts from it

```
competing force 1 = Loyalty[Darth, Emperor] + SelfInterest[Darth] -
➡Idealism[Darth]
```

This formula subtracts ("detracts") Darth's Idealism from his Loyalty to the Emperor. Onward:

There's also the empathy that any person feels for those who suffer

```
competing force 2 = Love[Darth, Luke] + Empathy[Darth]
```

Next:

These various factors do battle in Darth Vader's mind to decide whether Darth should turn against the Emperor.

```
if (competing force 1 > competing force 2)

    then WatchLukeDie

    else TurnAgainstTheEmperor
```

Here `WatchLukeDie` is the verb for doing nothing, and `TurnAgainstTheEmperor` is the verb that leads to Darth shot-putting the Emperor.

Now assemble the whole thing in one fragment of pseudocode (*pseudocode* is a programmer's term for code that's not written in any particular programming language, but is so plain and simple in structure that anyone who knows how to program could understand it):

```
competing force 1 = Loyalty[Darth, Emperor] + SelfInterest[Darth] -
➥Idealism[Darth]

competing force 2 = Love[Darth, Luke] + Empathy[Darth]

if (competing force 1 > competing force 2)

    then WatchLukeDie

    else TurnAgainstTheEmperor
```

This little snippet might look like a gross simplification of human behavior, and indeed it is. It's not about human behavior, but about drama. It is an artistic simplification. One of the most important realizations in mathematical modeling is that there's no such thing as the "correct" model, only models that emphasize different facets of reality with more or less resolution and accuracy. The trick is to let go of a narrow-minded insistence on "correctness"; embrace the realization that the more you learn, the less you know; and regard reality with the playful attitude that every thought in your mind is merely a puppet-like rendition of the infinite complexity of reality. Humbly accept your work as sketches, not photographs. Don't bemoan your failure to achieve photographic perfection in your paintings—revel in the cleanness of line, the clarity of image you can produce.

Now go over the artistic content of the snippet of pseudocode. It says that Darth has just two choices: `WatchLukeDie` or `TurnAgainstTheEmperor`. Yes, there could be a number of other choices: `ProtestToEmperor`, `BegForLuke'sLife`, `LaughAtLuke'sSuffering`, `TurnAwayInSorrow`, `JumpBetweenLukeAndEmperor`, or even `PlayRummyWithAStormTrooper`. Under other dramatic circumstances, these options might be appropriate for Darth, but this moment is the climax of the whole movie (indeed, the climax of the entire six-part series). You don't want to spin this out into interesting sideways curlicues; it's time for Darth to put up or shut up, so you give him a stark choice between two options. Remember, you could give him more choices if, as a storybuilder, you wanted to play the storyworld out further; it's a matter of artistic choice, not an absolute requirement.

Having established the basic nature of the choice to be made, now turn to the criteria by which that choice is made. I have established that the force driving Darth to side with the Emperor is equal to his Loyalty to the Emperor plus his SelfInterest minus his Idealism. This is the simplest possible mathematical combination of those terms. However, I might want to place more emphasis on Darth's SelfInterest, believing that it will play a larger role in the decision than his Loyalty to the Emperor. I can do this with a simple change:

```
competing force 1 = Loyalty[Darth, Emperor] + (2 × SelfInterest[Darth]) -
➥Idealism[Darth]
```

All I've done here is doubled the influence of SelfInterest in the final outcome. I might also want to reduce the influence of Empathy in Darth's decision:

```
competing force 2 = Love[Darth, Luke] + (Empathy[Darth] / 2)
```

Or I could make the influence of Empathy even smaller:

```
competing force 2 = Love[Darth, Luke] + (Empathy[Darth] / 4)
```

My point with these variations is to demonstrate how simple it is to express artistic ideas with arithmetic. There's nothing absolute about these formulas; I don't insist that dividing by 4 in the last formula is the only, or even the best, way to express it. You could have divided by 3 or 5 and still gotten decent results. The important idea is that I, as an artist, decided that Darth's Empathy was a less important factor in his decision than his Love for Luke, so I scaled down the Empathy factor a notch or two.

To summarize, mathematics is just as valid a medium of artistic expression as oil and canvas, stage and actor, or pen and paper. The artist uses the medium to create metaphorical descriptions of the human condition. There's one big difference: Mathematics, more than any other medium, addresses the *choices* that characters make. That's because mathematics is about processes, not data. Other media can show the results of those choices, the attitudes of the characters, the anguish on their faces, but ultimately, the choice must be treated as a black box, like Darth Vader looking one way and then the other. Mathematics can delve right down into the fundamental basis of the choice; no other medium can do that.

Aside: Quantifying Humanity

 The notion that human traits can be represented by a mathematical variable raises my hackles. Human beings are infinitely complex creatures; reducing a person to a set of numbers is dehumanizing. The function of art is not to dehumanize people, but to explore and glorify the wonder of our existence.

Here's my counterargument: Remember, this is drama, not reality. Yes, real human beings are infinitely complex, but much of that complexity is stripped away in drama. Imagine the nastiest real person you've ever known; can that nastiness hold a candle to the Emperor's nastiness? Have you ever known any real person remotely similar to Darth Vader? Anybody as dashing as Han Solo? The characters in movies are not real, complex persons; they are simplifications. A movie that's 100 minutes long can't delve into the infinite complexities of the human condition, so it discards most of that complexity to show a few glimpses of it in shining clarity. Thus, the mere fact that mathematical representation simplifies isn't a significant argument against using mathematical expressions.

 There's still the argument that quantification is intrinsically demeaning.

Is not loyalty a trait you can have more or less of? Are there not degrees of loyalty? If we can agree that loyalty does exist in varying degrees, what's wrong with assigning numbers to those varying degrees? If we can say that Darth Vader's loyalty to the Emperor is greater than Luke's loyalty to the Emperor, is there any fundamental shift in thinking to assign numbers to reflect that?

 But loyalty is a multidimensional concept, one that can't be measured by a single number. There are differing kinds of loyalty: the loyalty to superiors and subordinates, the loyalty for family members, and the loyalty for friends. These different kinds of loyalty can't be represented by a single number.

Are these differences significant to the storyworld you intend to create? Will actors in that storyworld behave differently because they have these different dimensions of loyalty? If so, you must break down the single variable Loyalty into four separate flavors of loyalty, and quantify them separately. But if these differences aren't significant to your storyworld's artistic content, you can dispense with them and use the single factor Loyalty.

 There's a huge difference between talking about "greater" or "lesser" loyalty and "57" Loyalty or "23" Loyalty. The verbal description leaves plenty of room for the approximate nature of appreciation of human qualities, and the quantitative description creates a wholly inappropriate impression of accuracy.

Consider the following list:

▶ Greatest loyalty

▶ Greater loyalty

▶ Lesser loyalty

▶ Least loyalty

▶ No loyalty

Clearly, this list constitutes a verbal description of varying degrees of loyalty. Hence, you could easily assign numbers to it:

Greatest loyalty	4
Greater loyalty	3
Lesser loyalty	2
Least loyalty	1
No loyalty	0

You could readily extend this list by adding more terms:

Greatest loyalty	7
Strong loyalty	6
Greater loyalty	5
Moderate loyalty	4

(continued)

Lesser loyalty	3
Insignificant loyalty	2
Least loyalty	1
No loyalty	0

You could extend this list and achieve better precision if you didn't stumble over imprecise—and, therefore, overlapping—terms such as "insignificant," "strong," and "great." But these are limitations of the vocabulary; how do you know they're intrinsic to the idea of loyalty? I agree that specifying somebody's loyalty as 2,364,198.7349 is ridiculous; you couldn't possibly insist that 2,364,198.7349 is correct and 2,364,198.7348 is wrong. Perhaps specifying loyalty with an integer scale of 0 to 100 is too ambitious; perhaps you should specify it on an integer scale of 0 to 10. The *principle* of quantification is not at issue—only the degree of precision is debatable.

Quantification is not dehumanizing, nor does it trivialize the complexity of the human condition. Finding the right value for a variable is analogous to finding the right word for a sentence. It's just a matter of zeroing in on the precise content you want. The only difference is that the process is numerical rather than verbal. Quantification uses a different vocabulary, but it says the same things. The benefit is that this vocabulary can be used with a computer.

Despite all these arguments, some readers will still choke at the notion of quantifying human qualities. If all my reasoning fails to move you, is it perhaps because of a profound emotional aversion to all things mathematical? If so, I ask you to confront your feelings and determine whether you can set them aside in pursuit of the grand and glorious goal of realizing interactive storytelling. If you cannot, then this field of endeavor is not for you; you will always be unhappy struggling without the proper tools. Go, follow your muse elsewhere.

The Artist's Mathematical Palette

Now explore the palette of mathematical colors available to the artist. What do you have to work with?

The four fundamental arithmetic operators (addition, subtraction, multiplication, and division) provide the starting point. The easiest way to understand them is as extensions of logical operations you're already acquainted with. Start with addition. When you add two variables together, the sum will be large if the first number is large *or* the second number is large. Another way to think of it is to imagine the sum as a criterion for action. It sits inside a formula like this:

```
Heroism = Courage + Selflessness

IF (Heroism > 50) THEN

    DoTheRightThing

ELSE

    SitThereSniveling
```

In this case, the Actor in question will pass the test if EITHER his Courage OR his Selflessness is high. High Courage can compensate for low Selflessness, and vice versa.

Subtraction is really just addition backward; many situations that require subtraction could be handled by inverting the meaning on one term and using addition, as in this example:

```
Heroism = Courage - Selfishness

IF (Heroism > 50) THEN

    DoTheRightThing

ELSE

    SitThereSniveling
```

If you have set up a personality model to record Selfishness instead of Selflessness, you would use subtraction here. If you think about it, almost any kind of variable can be presented in a left-handed version and a right-handed version. Here are some examples:

Selflessness	Selfishness
Courage	Cowardliness
Magnanimity	Pettiness
Empathy	Hard-heartedness

(continued)

Gullibility	Skepticism
Idealism	Cynicism
Intelligence	Stupidity

And so on. In some situations, you need to use subtraction instead of addition, but from a larger viewpoint, the two variables are just mirror images of each other.

The use of multiplication is just a bit more difficult to understand. Multiplication operates like an extension of the logical AND operator; you multiply two numbers together when BOTH the first number AND the second number are crucial to the outcome. For example, suppose an Actor has just been wronged by another Actor and is contemplating taking revenge. Suppose further that the two relevant variables in this case are Anger and Malevolence. The Actor's inclination to take revenge is the product, not the sum, of his Anger and Malevolence because they don't compensate for each other. All the anger in the world doesn't cause a fundamentally benevolent person to seek revenge, and all the malevolence in the world doesn't cause a happy person to seek revenge. That's why multiplication, not addition, is called for in this case.

As with subtraction, division is just multiplication backward. In cases in which you would multiply by Selflessness, you would divide by Selfishness. However, division can blow up in your face. This happens when you divide by a value that turns out to be zero. This situation is bad; no computer in the world can handle division by zero, so your algorithm is bound to fail. You need to refrain from using division unless you are absolutely certain the denominator can never be zero. Sometimes you can guarantee this by simply adding a small constant to the denominator, like so:

```
Courage / (Selflessness + 5)
```

You might ask why I chose the value 5. That brings me to a whole new subject: weighting factors.

Weighting Factors

Rare is the case when the values of variables can be used directly; most of the time you must adjust them so that one variable plays a more important role. This adjustment requires the use of *weighting factors*.

Additive Weighting Factors

The simplest kind of weighting factor is the additive weighting factor. For example, suppose that a female Actor must choose between two men, one of whom she already has a relationship with. Her inclination to leave Boyfriend #1 for Boyfriend #2 would be based on the difference in the degree to which she loves each:

```
Inclination[BreakUp] = Love[Girl, Boyfriend#2] - Love[Girl,
➡Boyfriend#1]
```

For example, if the girl feels 46 Love for Boyfriend#1 and 52 Love for Boyfriend#2, the formula becomes:

```
Inclination[BreakUp] = 52 - 46
```

This formula yields a +6 Inclination to break up. Tough luck, Boyfriend#1!

But this formula has a flaw: We all have a natural resistance to change and tend to stick with what we already have. So the equation should be altered by making it a little harder to break up. You could accomplish this with the following change:

```
Inclination[BreakUp] = Love[Girl, Boyfriend#2] - Love[Girl,
➡Boyfriend#1] - 25
```

So the new formula becomes:

```
Inclination[BreakUp] = 52 - 46 - 25
```

This yields a -19 inclination to break up. Lucky for Boyfriend#1!

Subtracting 25 makes it a little harder for her to break up with Boyfriend #1. Now, if you want to model the decision to break up more precisely, you could throw in factors for her Loyalty, but if you want to keep it simple, this formula works.

Multiplicative Weighting Factors

Suppose an Actor must decide whether to respond angrily to an insult (a Retort), and you have already decided on the two factors that will control this decision: the affection the Actor feels for the insulter, and the anger the Actor feels as a result of the insult. Therefore, the inclination equation looks like this:

```
Inclination[Retort] = Anger[Actor] - Affection[Actor, Insulter]
```

If the Actor's Anger is 18 and his Affection for the Insulter is 28, the formula gives this result:

```
Inclination[Retort] = 18 - 28
```

This yields -10; in other words, the Actor is not going to issue a retort.

But suppose you decide this formula isn't quite right; the Affection component isn't as important as the Anger component. You want to ensure that the Anger component plays the primary role in the decision, and the Affection component plays only a secondary role. To do this, insert a multiplicative weighting factor, like so:

```
Inclination[Retort] = 2 × Anger[Actor] - Affection[Actor, Insulter]
```

Here's how the numbers work out now:

```
Inclination[Retort] = 36 - 28
```

This formula gives you an answer of +8, so the actor using this formula will issue a retort.

This weighting factor doubles the weight that Anger plays in the decision. Of course, you could accomplish almost exactly the same thing by halving the weight of the Affection component, like so:

```
Inclination[Retort] = Anger[Actor] - Affection[Actor, Insulter] / 2
```

See how the numbers work out to the same result:

```
Inclination[Retort] = 18 - 14
```

The result is +4, still positive, so the Actor still issues a retort.

You could also make the Anger component even stronger by using a larger multiplicative weighting factor, like so:

```
Inclination[Retort] = 5 × Anger[Actor] - Affection[Actor, Insulter]

Inclination[Retort] = 90 - 28
```

This means the Actor would retort even if Affection were much greater.

The general rule is that if two factors are being added or subtracted, and one deserves more weight than the other, multiply the more significant factor by a number.

Exponential Weighting Factors

What if two factors are being multiplied or divided? How do you weight one in relation to the other? Using a multiplicative weighting factor won't work because it multiplies both factors equally. For example, suppose that, for some crazy reason, you multiplied the two factors in the previous example. Here's what a multiplicative weighting would yield:

```
Inclination[Retort] = 5 × Anger[Actor] × Affection[Actor, Insulter]
```

Plugging in the numbers, you get

```
Inclination[Retort] = 5 × 18 × 28
```

The result equals +2520.

Suppose the situation is reversed, however. Suppose the Actor's Affection value isn't 28 but 18, and the Actor's Anger is 28. Then the formula would look like this:

```
Inclination[Retort] = 5 × 28 × 18
```

The result equals +2520, exactly the same as the previous example. Multiplying by 5 doesn't do anything to alter the weights of either factor; it just makes the end result five times larger. Therefore, this formula does nothing to distinguish the two factors; you need something else. That something else is an exponentiation, like so:

```
Inclination[Retort] = (Anger[Actor]²) × Affection[Actor, Insulter]
```

Here's the formula with the numbers plugged in:

```
Inclination[Retort] = 18² x 28
```

The result is 9072. This time, however, if you reverse the values of the two variables (making `Anger` 28 and `Affection` 18), the formula gives this result:

```
Inclination[Retort] = 28² × 18
```

This formula yields 14,112—not the same as in the previous example. By squaring the `Anger`, you have doubled its overall weight in the formula. As with multiplicative factors, you can achieve the same effect by applying its opposite to the other factor:

```
Inclination[Retort] = Anger[Actor] × √(Affection[Actor, Insulter]
```

Now run through the same reverse-the-variables test. The first case (18 `Anger` and 28 `Affection`) looks like this:

```
Inclination[Retort] = 18 × √28
```

The result is 95.25.

The second case (28 `Anger` and 18 `Affection`) looks like this:

```
Inclination[Retort] = 28 × √18
```

The result is 118.79.

Here's what happened: When `Affection` went down and `Anger` went up, the answer went up, not down; it followed the `Anger`, not the `Affection`. In other words, taking the square root deemphasizes a variable.

You can achieve more or less weighting by using larger or smaller exponents. However, be careful here: Exponentiation can yield astoundingly large numbers!

How to Set Values

How do you decide how big a weighting factor should be? There's no simple answer to this question; it's fundamentally an artistic decision. How prominently should a painter highlight the nose in a portrait? How many lines of dialogue should a playwright give a character? How close to the camera should a character stand? There are no mathematical answers here; you simply make a first guess and see whether the formula behaves the way you want it to. Again, you don't have to find the perfect formula, just one that's close enough to satisfy your own artistic goals.

There's one major difference between other artists and storybuilders: Other artists can experiment and immediately see the results of their efforts. A film director can position actors and look through the camera to see the frame that results; if it doesn't look right, the director can reposition them. A painter can fiddle with the nose, step back, and evaluate the result; if it doesn't look quite right, the painter can fiddle some more. A storybuilder working on an inclination equation, however, can't step back and look at the formula and determine whether it looks right; the only way to try it out is to run a rehearsal and see how the decision comes out.

The difficulty of fine-tuning inclination formulas is another example of the degree of abstraction required to build storyworlds. It simply doesn't do to write down a formula and leave it at that; the storybuilder must instead think in terms of huge ensembles of rehearsals. If you tell the computer to run through a storyworld a thousand times, what percentage of the time will an Actor reaching this decision choose the Retort option, for example? It's easy if the Actors almost always go one way or the other; clearly, the inclination equation is out of balance and requires adjustment. But what if 25% of the Actors facing this situation choose the Retort option? This could be a good balance if all the Actors choosing the Retort option are fairly hot-headed people and all the Actors rejecting the Retort option are more level-headed. There's no way to know from the single statistic, however. Therefore, the single statistic emerging from multiple rehearsals gives a rough gauge of the inclination equation's performance, but for fine-tuning a storyworld, more detail is required.

You can obtain this detail in several ways. One way is using a statistical analyzer that permits detailed statistical analysis of a database of rehearsals. This technique permits the storybuilder to examine the circumstances under which each decision was made. For example, a storybuilder working on the problem described previously could examine all cases in which the inclination equation was used, the identity of each Actor who used it, and what that Actor's Anger and Affection values were at the moment the decision was made. This detail would give the storybuilder the information needed to perform finer adjustments in the inclination equation.

There's another way to adjust inclination equations, much more tedious but perhaps workable. This technique requires the storytelling engine to run through rehearsals in which the storybuilder can intervene after every decision and provide some correction. In this way, the storybuilder experiences the storyworld directly, and every time an Actor makes a decision, the storybuilder can look at the list of options, check the inclination values the actor produced, and then indicate which inclination values are too low and which ones are too high. The engine would then adjust the weighting factors correspondingly.

The difficulty with this technique is that thousands of rehearsals would be required to get the weighting factors balanced properly. Moreover, because this process would extend over many months, decisions the storybuilder makes late in the process might contradict decisions made early in the process.

I will discuss some of these issues in more detail in Chapter 17, "Development Environments."

Wrapping Up

▶ The two most fundamental components of all languages are nouns and verbs. Nouns are about existence; verbs are about action.

▶ Choice lies at the heart of interactivity. You choose between verbs, not nouns. Therefore, good interactivity design requires verb thinking (thinking about things in terms of what they do, not what they are).

▶ First rule of software design: Ask "What does the user DO?"

▶ Mathematical formulas are a kind of extended syllogism. The mathematical modeling used in interactive storytelling is the essence of its artistic content.

▶ Quantification does not trivialize the complexity of the human condition. Computers use a different vocabulary than people do (numerical rather than verbal).

▶ Mathematics, more than any other medium, addresses the choices characters make because it delves right down into the process of the choice, not its results.

PART III

Strategies for Interactive Storytelling

CHAPTER 7
Simple Strategies That Don't Work

PEOPLE HAVE BEEN EXPERIMENTING with interactive storytelling for years, and many approaches have been tried. Some have proved to be failures; I have mentioned a few of them elsewhere in the book. In this chapter, I shall address these examples in more detail.

Branching Trees

Everybody seems to make the same mistake when they first approach interactive storytelling: They build a *branching tree* structure (see a simple example in **Figure 7.1**). They start off with a beginning ("Once upon a time, there was a handsome young man...") and then attach a choice to it ("and he either a) went off in search of adventure or b) stayed home to care for his sick mother"). Then they attach another choice to each of the first choices, then another set of choices to those, and then more choices, and pretty soon they've got a huge branching tree that consumed many hours of labor. They're proud of their work, but when they show it off, nobody likes it because of the heavy workload involved.

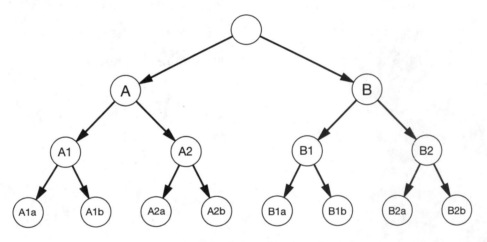

FIGURE 7.1: A simple branching tree structure.

The reason for the failure is easy to understand with a little mathematics. Imagine the smallest, simplest possible structure: Each decision is a choice between just two options and leads to a new situation with a new binary choice. Thus, the first level of choice has exactly two states; the second level has four states, the third has eight, the fourth 16, and so on. Next, say that a productive designer should be able to create a thousand such states—that seems like plenty of work. If you walk through the doubling process, you get to a thousand after just 10 steps. From the designer's point of view, these 10 steps represent a heavy workload. From the player's point of view, however, all this work yields a story that's just 10 steps long. It might read like this:

1. Once upon a time, there was a handsome young man. One day, he set off in search of adventure, and in the forest, he heard a cry and a growl. (Investigate or avoid?)

2. He investigated the sounds and found a maiden being held prisoner by an ogre. (Intervene or ignore?)

3. He told the ogre to release the maiden, but the ogre challenged him to a quest. (Accept or reject?)

4. He accepted the quest and entered a nearby cave. There were two paths: Down one path he could hear water trickling; down the other, he smelled smoke.

5. He went down the path that smelled of smoke. There he saw a dragon sleeping; it was clutching the key the ogre wanted, but there was also a sword lying nearby. (Take the key or sword?)

6. He picked up the sword. Should he use it to attack the dragon, or take it back and attack the ogre?

7. He decided to use the sword to attack the ogre. He went back and confronted the ogre, and the ogre laughed at him and threatened to kill him. (Attack or retreat?)

8. He attacked and wounded the ogre, who fell to the ground. The maiden begged him not to kill the ogre. (Kill ogre or relent?)

9. He went ahead and killed the ogre anyway. When a drop of blood from the ogre splashed onto the maiden, she turned into an ogre and was very angry with him. (Apologize or kill?)

10. So he killed her, too.

Not much of a story, is it? Even it were fleshed out with pretty verbal descriptions and embellishments, it's still skeletal. That's because real stories have a wide array of decisions. Only a few are dramatically crucial, but a myriad of tiny decisions help define character: the way one character addresses another, the degree of impatience or alacrity with which a character operates, and so on. A real story contains hundreds or thousands of these tiny decisions; this kind of fine detail just isn't possible in a branching tree.

Lesson #17
Branching tree designs are always too much work for the designer and not
enough meat for the player.

Foldback Schemes

Some clever people have tried to solve the problem of branching tree designs
by rerouting the consequences of decisions. In the previous example, a clever
designer might have set up the cave decision in the following way: If the player
chooses to go toward the sound of trickling water, he encounters some minor
obstacle that deposits him either at the mouth of the cave or in the dragon's lair.
I call this stunt a *foldback* because it simply folds the storyline back to some predetermined path (see **Figure 7.2**).

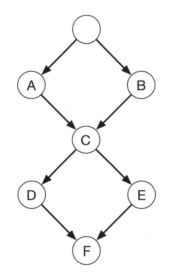

FIGURE 7.2: A simple foldback structure.

A foldback scheme does indeed give players more decisions without requiring a
lot of additional effort from the storybuilder. Alas, it achieves this goal by mendacity. Consider closely the decision a player faces at the mouth of the cave: He
can follow the sound of trickling water or the smell of smoke. That decision has
no significance, however, because both choices ultimately lead to the same result.
In other words, a foldback merely tricks players into thinking they're making a

choice. This scheme is fraudulent interactivity; when players discover the fraud (as they inevitably do when they play the storyworld several times), they feel cheated.

People keep coming up with variations on the foldback scheme, such as combinations of foldbacks with branching trees, hoping to find a magic combination that works. There isn't one. Every single case of foldback renders a player's decision meaningless. If you have only one instance of foldback in your design, your design is only a tiny bit fraudulent; as you add more foldbacks, you create many more meaningless pathways and add to your design's overall fraudulence.

Foldback schemes do work in one situation: when internal variables alter as a result of the difference in pathways. For example, suppose that, in the previous story, the player had taken the path toward the trickling water and found a sleeping potion he could use on the dragon, enabling him to wrest the key away from the dragon without being cooked. Therefore, the player would take the path toward the trickling water, get the sleeping potion, return to the main entrance, take the path toward the smell of smoke, disable the dragon, and so on. In other words, the initial choice between the two tunnels becomes meaningful with the addition of the sleeping potion. Going down the smoky tunnel first isn't as good a choice as going down the noisy tunnel. That's why this design would be a worthwhile use of a foldback scheme.

 But it's still a stupid situation. How is the player to know the difference between the two choices?

You're right; it is a stupid situation. I'm trying to keep it simple to avoid burdening the reader with too much stuff at once, okay?

You can generalize the idea of using internal variables to a foldback system by considering the classic videogame PacMan (see **Figure 7.3**).

In Figure 7.3, PacMan has reached a junction; he must make a decision to go up, down, or back to the right. In terms of design structure, this is the same situation a player has in a storyworld when confronted with a choice. In this situation, PacMan's best choice seems to be to go down; going up would probably lead to an encounter with a ghost, and going to the right wouldn't collect any dots.

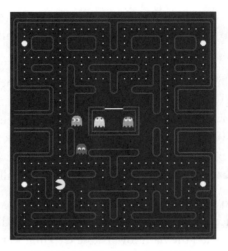

FIGURE 7.3: PacMan at a junction.

Now consider the situation as it might exist a moment later (see **Figure 7.4**).

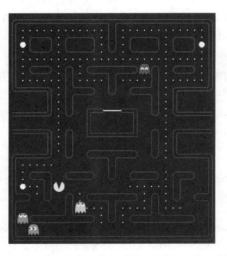

FIGURE 7.4: Same junction, different internal variables

PacMan finds himself back at the same intersection, with exactly the same three choices: up, down, or right. But this time the context is different; the positions of the ghosts indicate that PacMan should go up. Therefore, it's possible to design a network of choices so that the player faces the same choices over and over, but the choices mean something different each time. PacMan offers players exactly 23 such choices (if you reject turning around in the middle of a pathway and reversing course). Of those 23 choices, 19 are binary (if you exclude course reversal as a choice), and 4 intersections offer three choices. That's all there is. Instead of creating a thousand different branchpoints, the PacMan designers created only 23. It's the context that makes those choices variable in meaning. You can actually quantify that context. There are four power pills and 270 edible dots. Each object has just two states: eaten or uneaten, requiring just one bit of information to store. That's 274 bits. Next come the four ghosts and PacMan himself; each has a position that could be stored as just 9 bits of information. That's at total of 45 bits for the five movable characters. Add up everything, and you get a grand total of 319 bits of information. That's the context of PacMan. It might not sound like much, but in fact it amounts to 10^{96} differentiable states. Yes, 10^{96} is a large number—ridiculously large. In other words, the PacMan designers built a system with a tiny number of branchpoints but made it rich by giving it 319 bits of context, which transformed a simple maze into something much more interesting.

Interactive storytelling, however, isn't a mechanical subject that can be handled with simple geometric mazes and up/down, left/right decisions. The systems built for interactive storytelling can't directly use a system as elementary as PacMan's, but storybuilders can use the example of PacMan to guide their efforts. You cannot return players to the same decision point 100 times, but you can return them to similar decision points several times. For example, consider the layout of a romantic storyworld; surely kissing plays a large role in such a storyworld. What's wrong with presenting a potential kissing situation to players several times during a storyworld? The first time, it's a clumsy oaf who wants to kiss the heroine; the next time, it's a smooth operator; the third time, it's the clumsy oaf who has since turned out to be quite sweet. It's the same situation in three completely different contexts.

In general, then, branching stories don't work, even with foldback. If you twist a branching tree system around enough, however, so that lower-level branchpoints can feed back to upper-level branchpoints, you can transform it from a tree into a network. (Computer scientists call it a *directed graph*, which is why computer scientists haven't made any progress with interactive storytelling.) If you then set up appropriately differentiating contexts, you can have your players move through the network of dramatic possibilities, revisiting each point with a different context each time.

Constipated Stories

Another commonly used strategy is the *constipated story*. This little jewel offers a story in fragments, with each succeeding fragment earned by successfully completing a game segment (see **Figure 7.5**). It's rather like watching a movie on DVD, except this DVD requires you to jump through hoops before it shows you the next portion of the story. Sometimes the obstructions are puzzle-like; some are more game-like. The story in these cases is never interactive, however; apparently the designers believe that if they alternate between an interactive game and a noninteractive story fast enough, the game alloys into an interactive story. Right. Despite these problems, purveyors of these software products are always able to find some people willing to pay $40 for them. Most people, however, prefer to pay $15 to get the entire movie without the masochistic encumbrances.

The classic example of this approach dates back to the early 1990s and a game called The Seventh Guest. This game was quite a sensation when it appeared because it featured full-motion video, which was a major technical breakthrough. The gameplay consisted of a series of tricky puzzles; after successfully completing a puzzle, you'd be treated to (Wow!) more full-motion video presenting a little more of the story. Only after solving all the puzzles did you see the resolution of the story.

Kill 'Em If They Stray

I described this approach in my discussion of Dragon's Lair in Chapter 6, "Verb Thinking." The basic idea is to set up a single storyline and make alternative paths available to the player. However, should the player be so insolent as to actually try one of these alternative paths, the game kills the player. "You can have any story you want," says the designer, "so long as it's mine." These products are little more than training mazes for rats who pay for the privilege.

Storified Games

People have been attempting to embellish games with stories since at least 1980. In the early 1980s, stories were put into the game documentation. The story wasn't part of the game; it served as dramatic context for the game. The documentation would present some grandly written tale of action, intrigue, and suspense (the most common line being "THE FATE OF HUMANITY IS AT STAKE!!!!!"). Several of my early games used this technique, although with somewhat more nuance.

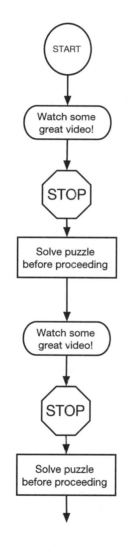

FIGURE 7.5: A constipated story.

Typical games of this time had considerable gaps between the story's dramatic content in the manual and the game on the screen. You'd read grandiose tales in the manual and then confront orange and purple squares buzzing about on the screen.

In the early '90s, CD-ROMs became available, and suddenly multimedia was the rage. Designers used this new capacity primarily for the purpose of inserting a story into the game. One example is Wing Commander, a space combat game that included an overarching story. The Wing Commander series of games were quite a fad in the early '90s. You would go out and fight the bad guys, and then come back to the space base to experience another step in the unfolding story. The story and the game were independent, so the manner in which you played the game didn't affect the story development beyond simple winning and losing, and the story development had little effect on the game. This design is what I call an *interleaved story/game*. You played some interactive game, saw some noninteractive story, and then went back to the game. Somehow the alternation between noninteractive story and interactive game was supposed to blur the two together and create a "kinda-sorta" interactive story.

A variation on this design is the *interleaved story/puzzle*, best exemplified by Myst. This game offered a classic adventure-style puzzle built into a kind of hidden story. The product's popularity was boosted by the use of beautifully rendered 3D imagery. The result was a huge success, but Myst didn't offer anything like true interactive storytelling. Players deduced the story from fragments picked up during their meanderings through the Myst world. The story itself was completely noninteractive, in no way responding to players' actions. The most convincing demonstration of this approach's futility lay in the declining success of the product line. Although each succeeding product in the line offered even higher quality, overall sales dropped off. The Myst concept was a fad, not an enduring solution.

The game Half-Life (1998) produced an even better attempt at an interleaved story/game. The story was presented in the same 3D real-time engine used for gameplay. Previous games had alternated the display between the game screen, with lots of action, and the story screen, with lots of graphics. The dysjunction between the two displays was obvious and intrusive; by integrating story elements into the same display engine as gameplay, this dysjunction was eliminated, and the interleaving of story and game became seamless. But the change was cosmetic only; the basic architecture of interleaving was unchanged. Half-Life triggered a series of emulators that expanded on the interleaving concept. One of the more notable examples is Grand Theft Auto. Its third incarnation generated lots of excitement, but didn't change the basic structure.

Three arguments explain the continuing failure to attach stories to games. The first error lies in subordinating the story to the game. For many game designers, the game is the core of the entertainment, and the story exists to embellish the gaming experience. In many cases, the story is nothing more than a crude justification for the game's mayhem. After all, blasting every living creature you encounter isn't exactly approved by Miss Manners, so some convoluted backstory must be concocted to make this extreme antisocial behavior morally plausible. Subordinating story to the needs of the game, however, inevitably yields handicapped stories.

The second argument concerns the intrinsic subject matter of the two entertainments. Games are ultimately about things, and stories are fundamentally about people. Game designers go to great lengths to dehumanize victims, so the player spends his time gathering things, tracking things, acquiring things, shooting things, being chased by things, and so forth. The gamer plays with things, never people. But stories always have been and must be about people. So long as games are stripped of human relationships, they can never be compatible with stories.

The third fundamental incompatibility arises from the noninteractive nature of stories that are bolted onto games. Attaching a noninteractive story to an interactive game yields a product that's neither a good game nor a good story. When jammed together in a shotgun marriage, story and game don't complement each other; they merely stumble over each other. The public's appetite for stories is so great that it can tolerate such monstrosities, but nothing that has emerged from these efforts has achieved the goal of interactive storytelling. These storified games remain a design bastard with no promise for the future.

Wrapping Up

People have been trying and failing to build interactive storytelling software since the 1980s. They keep repeating the same mistakes: branching trees, fold-back schemes, constipated stories, kill-'em-if-they-stray, and storified games. There are so many more interesting ways to fail with interactive storytelling; try to avoid these boring ways to fail.

CHAPTER 8
Environmental Strategies

GAME DESIGNERS HAVE NEVER given storytelling a high priority. This is not to say they refuse to make some efforts in a storytelling direction. After all, they like to wrap themselves in the glamor and legitimacy that Hollywood enjoys, so they happily claim as much storytelling territory as they can convince others to accept. But their design decisions reveal their true priorities. Game designers put all their money on action, violence, and cosmetic extravagance. They see story as an embellishment they can tack onto their basic design, but certainly not a fundamental component of their products.

Therefore, after the game design is fairly complete, they hire "storytelling talent"—preferably someone with a Hollywood pedigree—to "storify" their games. The Hollywood talent is presented with the basic scenario and game structure and instructed to weave a story into the existing design. The storytellers do the best job they can under impossible circumstances, but their contribution is an embellishment, not a central component of the design. The story goes along for the ride.

An example of the second-class status given storytelling in game design is the classic Deus Ex. Game designers hold this game in high regard because it has such a strong storytelling element. Storytellers look at the same game and ask, "What story?" Sure, there's something within the game that matches the academic definition of the term "story," but Deus Ex sports a thin shadow of the real thing—and this is the game that game designers hail as a triumph of storytelling in games! There's no question that vast talent and energy were devoted to the game side, but the storytelling side comes up short by any normal standards.

Nevertheless, game designers have slowly bumbled toward a conceptual approach to interactive storytelling that merits consideration. I call their idea the *environmental approach*. The basic concept is to create a large three-dimensional world broken up into buildings, rooms, caves, and other regions; equip that world with a variety of weapons, tools, and resources; and populate it with a variety of weakly interactive agents. These agents are seldom given any character to speak of. In general, they're dispensers of information or providers of resources. Players move through this three-dimensional world searching for goodies in pursuit of some simple objective (kill the boss monster, save the princess, acquire the jewel, or some such). Along the way, players must deal with a variety of obstacles and make use of a variety of resources. Agents are placed and equipped to provide these obstacles or resources. Thus, players get the chance to bring all their videogame skills to bear: running, jumping, climbing, shooting, searching, acquiring, and so forth. Occasionally they might need an agent's assistance, which is normally done through some mechanical process, such as presenting the correct gift, giving the right answer to a question, or carrying out a required task. So far, this environmental approach has accomplished nothing significant in the way of storytelling.

Emergent Story

Emergence, a hot buzzword these days, refers to the notion that complex systems can produce behavior that surprises us with its organization. One of the earliest examples of emergence came from the old computer program The Game of Life. This program introduced the concept of *cellular automata*, a map or array of intelligent cells, each of which followed some simple set of rules for its behavior. Cellular automata inspired a generation of research work and led to the creation of that great game SimCity. In the original Game of Life, a simple set of rules for cells produced a system capable of building complex phenomena such as "gliders," moving patterns of activated cells, and "glider factories," stable systems of activated cells that produced gliders at regular intervals. As the theory of cellular automata matured and interacted with ideas from complexity theory, the concept of *emergent phenomena* arose: the idea that sufficiently complex systems can generate even more complex phenomena that the system's original creators never expected.

Most of this research was carried out with computer programs that created artificial systems and then generated their behavior. Although the academics who advance this field of research have developed and refined it considerably, a bastard form of the concept has trickled down to the programmer community as a fervent belief that big complicated systems can be made to produce almost any desired result, if only programmers make them big enough and complicated enough and give them enough time. From this belief the concept of *emergent story* has arisen, the hopeful fantasy that somehow, if programmers diddle around with complicated systems long enough, they'll eventually get a story to emerge.

This isn't the first time the concept of emergence has been eagerly seized upon. Starting about a thousand years ago, a concept that could be called "emergent chemistry" achieved some popularity among Western Europe's intelligentsia. They figured that if only they could mix enough smelly chemicals in complicated enough ways, they'd eventually figure out how to cook up gold. For hundreds of years these people messed around, but they never did get any gold. (Ironically, the same chemical properties of gold that made it so valuable were what foiled alchemists.) Some alchemists gave up on the search for gold and instead searched for something that seemed easier: life. They didn't get far, either. But their spirit lives on; some people simply refuse to learn the basics. You can't just throw together a bunch of bits and pieces and expect wonderful things to happen.

Just as alchemists had to understand the basics of chemistry before they could start cooking up interesting chemicals, storybuilders are just going to have to understand the basics of drama before interactive storytelling works.

Lesson #18
Emergence is not the same thing as magic.

Possible Extensions

Can the environmental approach provide a foundation on which genuine interactive storytelling can be built? To answer this question, consider the conceivable extensions to the design foundation.

Extending the Size of the Three-dimensional World

The obvious approach is to make the world bigger. Add more buildings, rooms, tunnels, caves, doorways, alleys, and bridges. Give the player more space to explore and more places to discover.

Although this approach is popular, it doesn't accomplish anything because the size of the universe has no bearing on the dramatic substance of the experience. Consider, for example, the list of stages in the original *Star Wars* movie:

1. Corridors of Princess Leia's ship

2. Darkened room in Princess Leia's ship

3. Escape pod in Princess Leia's ship

4. Sandy desert of Tatooine

5. Rocky desert of Tatooine

6. Interior of Jawa vehicle

7. Exterior of Luke Skywalker's farm

8. Kitchen of Luke Skywalker's farm

9. Work area of Luke Skywalker's farm

10. Rocky area where Luke finds R2D2

11. Interior of Obi-Wan's home

12. Rocky area where destroyed Jawa vehicle is found

13. Mos Eisley exterior

14. Bar in Mos Eisley

15. Mos Eisley alley

16. Space dock at Mos Eisley

17. Cockpit of Millennium Falcon

18. Corridors of Millennium Falcon

19. Turrets of Millennium Falcon

20. Landing dock on Death Star

21. Control room on Death Star

22. Prison cell on Death Star

23. Conference room on Death Star

24. Corridors on Death Star

25. Prison central room on Death Star

26. Prison corridor on Death Star

27. Trash compactor on Death Star

28. Chasm on Death Star

29. Shield control site on Death Star

30. Site of final battle between Darth Vader and Obi-Wan

31. Briefing room at rebel base

32. Hangar at rebel base

33. Throne room at rebel base

That's it: just 33 stages for the entire movie. I exclude several settings, such as fighter cockpits, because they can hardly be referred to as stages; they're more like backgrounds against which a single actor performs. I also exclude a number of conjoined stages, such as the corridors of the Death Star, the alleys on Mos Eisley, and so forth. Even if you throw in all these secondary stages, you still come up with fewer than 50 stages total. Most exploratory games have more than 50 locations already; indeed, a single level of the old game Doom could boast that many distinct locations. Therefore, games already have all the stage locations you need.

More Props

The 3D games are chock-full of interesting objects: weapons, ammunition, medical supplies, tools, money, sources of energy, keys, books, and so forth. You might think that perhaps you could find a story lurking in an adequately large set of props. If only you add enough items to the object list, perhaps you could end up with something dramatically interesting.

This is wishful thinking with no foundation whatever. Stories aren't about *things*; they are about *people*—that was one of the lessons of Chapter 1, "Story." Adding more things to a game accomplishes nothing in the way of improving its storytelling potential.

More Agents

Agents in many games are notoriously stupid; perhaps their stupidity could be overcome by building a large cast of one-trick pony agents who, taken as a group, can offer players some interesting dramatic interaction. Dramatic interaction cannot be subdivided into tiny fragments, however. You don't provide romance by offering one girl who flirts, a second girl who goes out on a date, a third who kisses, and a fourth who falls in love. Storytelling requires characters with depth, not cardboard cutouts—and adding more cardboard cutouts doesn't help.

Smarter Agents

So why not make agents who are smart enough to handle more interaction? This idea sounds more reasonable, and it could work. Character interaction is certainly central to any kind of storytelling, but that's another strategy, one discussed in detail in Chapter 7, "Simple Strategies That Don't Work." You don't need an environmental shell to provide good character interaction. The character-driven approach is independent of the environmental approaches popular in so many 3D games.

Chapter 11, "Personality Models," also discussed some mechanics of the process of character interaction.

More and Better Puzzles

Some designers have taken this route, hoping that more puzzles will make for a more interesting game. Indeed, more and better puzzles might make a product more entertaining—but as a puzzle product, not a storytelling product. Puzzles aren't central to storytelling; that was another lesson from Chapter 1. Many stories do have something like puzzles—problems that the player must solve or obstacles that must be overcome—but a story is considerably more than a series of puzzles. A goodly number of products over the years have provided a series of puzzles, such as The Seventh Guest (1992) and Myst (1994). Both games were commercially successful, but nobody would claim they point the way to interactive storytelling. They succeeded as puzzles, not stories.

A Journey Structure

Some designers have speculated that the classic "journey structure" of storytelling can be built on top of an environmental base. For example, you could build something analogous to Mark Twain's classic *Huckleberry Finn*. The player, as Huck, starts the story in his home town and can wander about there as much as he wishes, but the only way to push the story forward is to get on the raft with old Jim and head down the Mississippi. As the player travels down the river, he's free to wander around the stages placed along its banks. Each stage can offer an interesting puzzle or spectacle, but the only way to advance the plot is to move farther down the river. Eventually the player, having experienced a variety of adventures, reaches the end of the journey, and the story reaches its conclusion.

This structure has much appeal. Players have plenty of freedom to explore each stage along the river as deeply or as perfunctorily as they like, but the river's gentle flow always pushes them forward. This approach doesn't seem as heavy-handed as some other methods, yet keeps players moving along the intended plotline.

The minor objection to this approach is that the dramatic universe has only so many rivers; you can't solve the problem of interactive storytelling by putting every protagonist on a raft. Sure, you can come up with variations on the theme: wind-powered craft that carry the protagonist, like Odysseus, to a variety of locations on the journey home; train trips that offer stops at intermediate destinations; road trips down Route 66 on the way to LA. Ultimately, however, this approach is an artifice, not a solution; it can be applied a few times, but loses its charm when it's overused.

The killer objection to this approach is that it does nothing, in and of itself, to provide drama. A journey is merely a thread that ties together separate components of a story; the story's success depends on the quality of the components. Therefore, the journey structure begs the question by shifting the problem to the components while doing nothing about the components themselves.

All of the Above

Perhaps if you combined all the previous strategies, some synergy among them might contribute to an overall solution. If this thought has crossed your mind, stamp it out! It's hopeful thinking taken beyond reason. There's no reason to believe that some magical synergy exists. You can expect synergy only among elements undergoing some mutual interaction. None of the previous techniques shows any indication of interesting mutual interactions. Throwing more and smellier ingredients into the pot doesn't get you any closer to cooking up gold.

Storytelling in The Sims

There remains the important and exceptional case of The Sims, Will Wright's brilliant exercise in simulating household life. Much has been made of this game's storytelling aspect. Of course, The Sims could be described as an environmental approach to storytelling, although it offers no explicit storytelling, and Will Wright is quick to point out that it's definitely not an interactive storytelling product. Yet millions of people who play The Sims laud its storytelling content. They perceive story to exist in their characters' behaviors, and they concoct elaborate stories to explain the activities going on in the game. This creates a fascinating theoretical conundrum: There's no story in the product, yet players imagine stories based on its behavior. Are these stories real? Can a product that stimulates the player's imagination to create a story be considered interactive storytelling?

I tend to dismiss such definitional arguments and concentrate on the delivered reality. If customers perceive a story, that's all that matters—it's good enough for me. Yet this answer leaves me unsatisfied. People concoct stories in all manner of situations, for all manner of reasons. Children playing with toys create intricate stories around those toys, but toys aren't storytellers. The enjoyment of players who festoon their play experiences with grand stories of their characters' life histories can't be questioned. The Sims, however, doesn't offer storytelling per se. It is, to use Will's own description, a toy. Like any good toy, it stimulates the imagination, and that imagination proceeds to create stories.

If you look more closely at The Sims, you can see that it falls far short of anything that could be called interactive storytelling. The characters in The Sims have no personality to speak of, and interactions with other characters are shallow and devoid of emotional content. If you apply Crawford's First Rule of Software Design, and ask "What does the user DO?" the answer is even more revealing. Players of The Sims guide their characters in going to the bathroom, taking showers, preparing and eating meals, cleaning the dishes, taking out the garbage, cleaning house, sleeping, and earning a living. This is not drama; this is a housekeeping simulation. Alfred Hitchcock once described drama as "life with the dull bits cut out." The Sims is life with the dramatic bits removed.

I do not offer these cruel observations to denigrate Will Wright's achievement; anybody who throws mud at such a shining triumph besmirches only himself. My intent is to make clear that, for all its greatness, The Sims isn't interactive storytelling. It's a brilliant success—but not an interactive storytelling success.

 Might The Sims lead game designers in the direction of interactive storytelling? Doesn't it offer a solid foundation on which to work?

I don't think so. Six years have elapsed since The Sims first appeared. During that time, Electronic Arts has released a cavalcade of expansion packs pushing the design in many different directions: Livin' Large, House Party, Hot Date, Vacation, Unleashed, Superstar, and Makin' Magic. Yet none of these expansion packs expands the design's dramatic range; they merely add more parts to the simulation. If after six years no progress has been made toward better dramatic interaction, there's little hope we'll see any in the next six years—or the six years after that.

Wrapping Up

The environmental approach is a dead end; it doesn't solve the problem of interactive storytelling. You can set up a gigantic stage, equip it with a cavalcade of fascinating props, create spectacular scenery and magnificent sound effects, and still have nothing. Actors make the stage come alive, actors with talent and perception. A good acting company can make Shakespeare come alive on a plain wooden stage; an army of cardboard figures in a magnificent 3D environment is still just a pile of cardboard.

CHAPTER 9
Data-Driven Strategies

ONE OF THE TIME-HONORED strategies in algorithm design is the use of *data-driven* methods. Sometimes coming up with equations that carry out the required calculations is just too difficult; in some of these cases, using data-driven methods is possible. These methods substitute tables of data for formulae.

A data-driven storytelling engine would require two major sections: a mass of data and a means of assembling that data into a story in response to the player's actions. The data itself is composed of two parts: story components (the basic parts of the story) and connectivity data (how these parts connect with each other).

Story Components

Story components are bits and pieces of stories that the engine stitches together to yield a continuous story in response to the player's input. They can take a variety of forms. The most basic forms are simple nouns: Actors, Props, and Stages. They would be characterized by their dramatic functions, which in turn might form the basis of the connectivity data. For example, an Actor could be characterized not in terms of personality variables, as discussed in Chapter 11, "Personality Models," but in terms of actions. Thus, Snidely Whiplash might be characterized in terms of willingness to do dastardly deeds. If the story calls for a dastardly deed, the engine searches through the Actors and finds Snidely Whiplash ready to perform.

In other words, the connectivity data for noun-based story components would specify the types of verbs those story components require. This in turn requires a classification system for verbs based on noun requirements. For example, verbs might be classified by their "Dastardliness," their "Nurturative Value," their "Humor," and so forth. Then a story component would call for certain combinations of these dimensions. I haven't explored the possibilities of such a system.

Another story component could be more detailed dramatic archetypes (or clichés, if you prefer). Actor instances of these archetypes could be Rebel With a Chip on His Shoulder, Female Detective's Client With Great Legs, Loner With a Dark Past, and so forth. Prop instances might include Fabulously Valuable Archaeological Artifact, Tattered Old Treasure Map, Knife in Boot, or Handy Getaway Vehicle. And for Stages, you have settings such as Dark Threatening Forest, Smoke-Filled Bar, Homey Dining Room, and Shabby Office.

I'm more optimistic about story components based on events: The First Kiss, Escape on Horseback, Hide From Pursuer, Accidentally Reveal Secret, and so forth. Indeed, my Erasmatron technology relies on this concept. However, creating the connectivity data for these story components is a time-consuming task.

Connectivity Data

Connectivity data provides the information the engine uses to decide which story components to stitch together. This data is the yin to story component's yang, so it is difficult to discuss connectivity data in the absence of a specific set of story components. Moreover, connectivity data is more difficult to imagine than story components because it's necessarily more abstract in nature. Connectivity data concerns cause-and-effect relationships, not simple existences. All the ideas I offered for story components are easily recognizable, but the connectivity data for those components is harder to explain. It's simple enough to talk about evil witches, gingerbread houses, or ovens, but declaring the connections among these components takes a lot more work.

A Short Digression

This brings me to a digression: In any project, tackling the most difficult task first is always prudent. Many designers put off the most difficult task, hoping that if they can start off by solving the simpler problems, they will create momentum or credibility for the project that will enable them to bull through the tough parts. This is a mistake, for two reasons.

First, if you can't solve the tough problem, the whole project founders and the time you have spent on the easy problems has been wasted. Better to kill the project early than magnify the failure by putting off the day of reckoning.

Second, every design decision you make constrains all future design decisions. If you're designing a superfast inkjet printer, and you design the case first, the dimensions imposed by that case control the design of the printing mechanism, which could seriously hamper your design efforts. If, however, you design the printing mechanism first, you can easily design a case to fit over that mechanism.

 But automotive designers often design the car's exterior first, and then design the engine to fit into the engine compartment specified by the exterior design.

That's because designing automotive engines isn't as difficult a task as designing appealing exteriors. Automotive engineers have been laying out engines inside engine compartments for a century now; the design trade-offs involved are well understood. Appealing exteriors, by contrast, are considered to be a killer problem in automotive design. The sequence isn't inside to outside; it's more difficult to less difficult.

Lesson #19
Tackle the toughest problems first.

Therefore, the connectivity system should be designed first. What elements make a good connectivity system? I can't offer any clean answers to this question; I can only present some existing sources in the following sections that might be worthy of further exploration.

The Aarne-Thompson Catalogues

Folktales, or "fairy tales," as they are commonly referred to, share many common themes, elements, and plots. Carl Jung studied folktales carefully to determine what they revealed about the human psyche; later, Joseph Campbell carried on Jung's work in a less rarefied style. Campbell showed that common psychological threads do indeed run through folktales the world over.

Similarly, folktales seem to share many common components, or *motifs*, as scholars call them. Evil witches, nasty spells or potions, young innocents, journeys to faraway places—these and other motifs seem to crop up over and over.

In trying to understand all these connections, scholars have attempted to organize the vast database of information about folktales in some fashion that reveals their underlying commonalities. A hundred years ago, a Finnish scholar named Antti Aarne prepared an index of the various types of folktales and their motifs. Later in the twentieth century, an American researcher named Stith Thompson greatly expanded on the index Aarne had created. The result was a sort of Dewey Decimal catalogue of folktales, which a number of scholars have subsequently built on. The resulting index goes by the name of *The Aarne-Thompson Types of the Folktale*. Here is the highest level of the index:

Animal Tales

1–99	Wild Animals
100–149	Wild Animals and Domestic Animals
150–199	Man and Wild Animals
200–219	Domestic Animals
220–249	Birds
250–274	Fish
275–299	Other Animals and Objects

Ordinary Folktales

300–399	Supernatural Adversaries
400–459	Supernatural or Enchanted Husband (Wife) or Other Relatives
460–499	Superhuman Tasks
500–559	Supernatural Helpers
560–649	Magic Objects
650–699	Supernatural Power or Knowledge
700–749	Other Tales of the Supernatural
750–849	Religious Stories
850–999	Romantic Tales
1000–1199	Tales of the Stupid Ogre

Jokes and Anecdotes

1200–1349	Numskull Stories
1350–1439	Stories About Married Couples
1440–1524	Stories About a Woman (Girl)
1525–1874	Stories About a Man (Boy)
1875–1999	Tales of Lying
2000–2399	Formula Tales
2400–2499	Unclassified Tales

Here is an expansion of one of the categories:

460–499	Superhuman Tasks
460A	The journey to God to receive reward
460B	The journey in search of fortune
461	Three hairs from the Devil's beard

465	The man persecuted because of his beautiful wife
465A	The quest for the unknown
470	Friends in life and death
471	The bridge to the other world
473	Punishment of a bad woman
475	The man as heater of Hell's kettle
480	The spinning-woman by the spring

Because so many folktales contain common motifs, this taxonomy doesn't have a satisfying cleanness of separation. Thompson therefore augmented the index of folktale types with the much larger *The Aarne-Thompson Index of Folktale Motifs*. Here's the highest level of the index:

A. Mythological Motifs

B. Animals

C. Tabu

D. Magic

E. The Dead

F. Marvels

G. Ogres

H. Tests

I. Unused

J. The Wise and the Foolish

K. Deceptions

L. Reversal of Fortune

M. Ordaining the Future

N. Chance and Fate

O. Unused

P. Society

Q. Rewards and Punishments

R. Captives and Fugitives

S. Unnatural Cruelty

T. Sex

U. Unused

V. Religion

W. Traits of Character

X. Humor

Y. Unused

Z. Miscellaneous Groups of Motifs

Here is an expansion of one of the categories:

R.	Captives and Fugitives
R11.1	Maiden abducted by monster
R31	Light extinguished and woman stolen
R151.1	Husband rescues stolen wife
R231	Obstacle flight—Atalanta type
R245	Whale-boat
R246	Crane bridge
R261.1	Pursuit by rolling head
R311	Tree refuge

These extracts represent a tiny fraction of the Aarne-Thompson material. The entire dataset is available from the University of Indiana on CD-ROM[1].

Applications

This huge dataset could conceivably be put to use for interactive storytelling. The basic approach would be to stitch together the various motifs in response to player input, assembling a folktale in tinkertoy-like fashion. The algorithms to accomplish this task would rely on some sort of connectivity data associated with each motif.

There are two ways to provide basic connectivity information. The simplest and most direct would be a matrix of boolean values, one column and row for each motif in the catalogue, as shown in **Figure 9.1**.

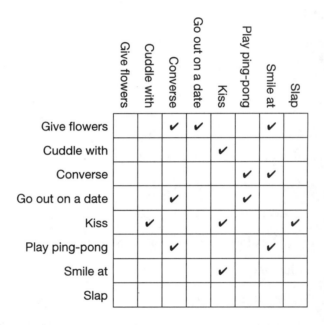

FIGURE 9.1: A matrix of boolean connection values.

Because there are thousands of motifs, this matrix would contain millions of cells. Each cell would be initialized to "False," meaning that the motif in Column X can't be followed by the motif in Row Y. The storybuilder would then set to "True" those cells that constitute reasonable sequences of motifs. This job would be huge, however, and leave many questions unanswered. For example, a boolean value couldn't address the many contextual circumstances that might be required to make a sequence reasonable. For example, "break down door and enter castle" could reasonably be followed by "free the princess" only if some preceding motif had made the princess a captive. This method creates so many complexities that the underlying system of using a matrix of boolean values is called into question.

A second way to provide connectivity data is with a large set of boolean flags associated with each motif. Each flag specifies a particular condition that must be met for the motif to be applied. As the story develops, it builds a kind of "lock" consisting of the pattern of flags that represent the story so far. It then searches for a motif possessing a "key" that fits the lock. Both locks and keys would actually have three states: True, False, and Don't Care. This third state would match either of the first two.

Although this method is clever, implementing it would require a great deal of labor. The storybuilder would need to create hundreds of flags representing a wide range of situations, and each time a new flag was created, every single motif would have to have that flag appended to its existing key. Moreover, the calculation of some keys might be a complex procedure. For example, suppose that one of the motifs is "pursuit by rolling head". To link this motif with, say, "the clever horse" motif, the storybuilder must establish that "pursuit by rolling head" creates a threatening situation requiring escape and that "the clever horse" can provide the means of escape. This linking is possible, but the details of implementing complex situational analysis will be time-consuming.

Despite these problems, the Aarne-Thompson catalogues represent huge sources of information about the most fundamental of all types of stories, the folktale. They provide the raw material for a data-driven storytelling engine—if only a clever designer can figure out how to organize that data into computable form.

Vladimir Propp

In the early twentieth century, a Russian scholar named Vladimir Propp analyzed 100 Russian folktales and figured out that these folktales contained many common elements, which he called *universal functions*. He designed a notation for representing these universal functions and published his work as *The Morphology of the Folktale*[2]. His list of universal functions runs as follows:

α	Initial situation
β	Absentation or departure of elders
γ	Interdiction or command
δ	Interdiction violated or command carried out
ε	Reconnaissance between villain and hero
ζ	Information is obtained
η	Deceit
θ	Hero falls victim to villain
λ	Preliminary misfortune caused by a deceitful agreement
A	Villainy
a	Lack or insufficiency
B	The connective incident
C	Consent to counteraction
D	The first function of the donor
E	Reaction of the hero
F	Acquisition of a magical agent
G	Transference to a designated place
H	The hero struggles with the villain
I	Victory over the villain
J	Branding or marking of the hero
K	The reversal of the misfortune or lack
↑	Departure of the hero
↓	Return of the hero
Pr	Pursuit of the hero
Rs	Rescue of the hero
o	Unrecognized arrival
L	Claims of a false hero

M	Difficult task
N	Solution of the task
Q	Recognition of the hero
Ex	Exposure of the false hero
T	Transfiguration
U	Punishment of the false hero or villain
W	Wedding and accession to the throne
X	Unclear or alien forms
<	Leave-taking at a road marker
Y	Transfer of a signaling device
mot.	Motivations
+	Positive result of a function
-	Negative result of a function
§	Connectives

This notation can then be used to present almost any of the 100 Russian fairy tales in the sample (and a great many more) in codified form. For example, one of the simpler tales presented in the book is, in shorthand form:

> *131. A tsar, three daughters. The daughters go walking, overstay in the garden. A dragon kidnaps them. A call for aid. Quest of three heroes. Three battles with the dragon, rescue of the maidens. Return, reward.*

And in codified form:

βδABC HIK W

Propp's system is considerably more complex than this; there are numbered variations on many of these functions, and some tales require double-threaded codings.

I suspect a useful system could be built based on Propp's work, but considerable modification would be required. The crucial issue concerns the grammar that connects his functions in sequence. Although he does discuss a number of rules for connecting functions into a sequence, Propp doesn't provide a full grammar. As you dig deeper into the details of his system, you find more complications requiring special treatment. Propp achieves generality only at the higher levels of abstraction in the storytelling process; manifesting those abstractions into specific story components lies out of reach of his system. Nevertheless, like the Aarne-Thompson catalogue, Propp's system could form the basis for a storytelling engine. It's not as large as the Aarne-Thompson catalogue, but this factor should reduce the size of the problem. Perhaps a "Russian folktale storytelling engine" would be the ideal precursor to a full-blown Aarne-Thompson storytelling engine.

An Application

Chris R. Fairclough and Pádraig Cunningham of Trinity College in Dublin, Ireland, have integrated Propp's system into a story engine with impressive results[3]. Their software uses a double layer of intelligence to provide the narrative. The lower layer uses agent-based technology to guide individual Actors in the storyworld; the upper layer uses Propp's rules in a case-based reasoning system, which applies old precedents to new problems. The software maintains a library of previously solved problems in the problem domain. Upon encountering a new problem, the software searches through its library of precedents and identifies the closest matching precedent, and then adapts the solution to the precedent to solve the current problem. Propp's ideas are used to supply Actors with roles to play (Villainy, Guidance, Testing of the Hero, and so forth). Actors are capable of gossiping with each other; the authors hope to augment this capability with deception at some future time. Their system isn't complete as of this writing, so we must wait to evaluate their results.

Georges Polti

In 1921, a French writer, Georges Polti, published *The Thirty-Six Dramatic Situations*[4], which reduced the basic storylines of all literature and theater to a core set:

1.   Supplication

2.   Deliverance

3. Crime Pursued by Vengeance

4. Vengeance Taken for Kindred Upon Kindred

5. Pursuit

6. Disaster

7. Falling Prey to Cruelty or Misfortune

8. Revolt

9. Daring Enterprise

10. Abduction

11. The Enigma

12. Obtaining

13. Enmity of Kinsman

14. Rivalry of Kinsman

15. Murderous Adultery

16. Madness

17. Fatal Imprudence

18. Involuntary Crimes of Love

19. Slaying of an Unrecognized Kinsman

20. Self-sacrifice for an Ideal

21. Self-sacrifice for Kindred

22. All Sacrificed for a Passion

23. Necessity of Sacrificing Loved Ones

24. Rivalry of Superior and Inferior

25. Adultery

26. Crimes of Love

(continued)

27. Discovery of the Dishonor of a Loved One

28. Obstacles to Love

29. An Enemy Loved

30. Ambition

31. Conflict with a God

32. Mistaken Jealousy

33. Erroneous Judgment

34. Remorse

35. Recovery of a Lost One

36. Loss of Loved Ones

Although Polti intended this list to be universal, it does reflect the cultural context of his times. For example, Situation #27, "discovery of the dishonor of a loved one," hasn't been much in use in the past 50 years. However, Situation #9, "daring enterprise," covers many of the movies and books now popular.

To give you a better idea of his system at work, here are his categorizations of some famous tales:

▶ *Hamlet*: #4 and #13 (vengeance taken for kindred upon kindred, enmity of kinsman)

▶ *Romeo and Juliet*: #29 (an enemy loved)

▶ *Macbeth*: #30 (ambition)

▶ *Don Quixote*: #2 (deliverance)

▶ *The Purloined Letter*: #11 (the enigma)

▶ *Around the World in 80 Days*: #9 (daring enterprise)

▶ *The Ring of the Nibelungs*: #5 (pursuit)

▶ *The War of the Worlds*: #6 (disaster)

Many of Polti's categories are broken down into subcategories. For example, he breaks down Situation #22, "all sacrificed for a passion," as follows:

A.

1.   Religious vows of chastity broken for a passion

2.   A vow of purity broken

3.   A future ruined by a passion

4.   Power ruined by passion

5.   Ruin of mind, health, and life

6.   Ruin of fortunes, lives, and honors

B.

1.   Temptations destroying the sense of duty or pity

C.

1.   Destruction of honor, fortune, and life by erotic vice

2.   The same effect produced by any other vice

Finally, Polti lists the basic roles necessary to each situation; for #22, he offers The Lover, The Object of the Fatal Passion, and The Person or Thing Sacrificed. I believe this taxonomy could become the basis for an interactive storytelling engine, but at present I have no concrete suggestion to offer.

Wrapping Up

It might be possible to build an interactive storytelling engine using a scheme that breaks stories down into components or categories. Three such schemes have already been built: Aarne-Thompson, Propp, and Polti. Of these three, only Propp has been adapted for computer use.

---

1. www.indiana.edu/~iupress/books/0-253-35994-5.shtml

2. Vladimir Propp, *Morphology of the Folktale* (University of Texas, Austin: 1996; ISBN 0-292-78376-0).

3. www.cs.tcd.ie/publications/tech-reports/reports.03/TCD-CS-2003-43.pdf

4. Georges Polti, "The Thirty-Six Dramatic Situations," in *The Writer*, 1999 (ISBN 0-87116-109-5).

CHAPTER 10
Language-Based Strategies

"IF YOU CAN'T SAY IT, you don't *know* it." That's what one of my English teachers used to say, and over the years I have come to realize how profoundly right he was. It's not just that transcribing an idea from thought into language is the only proof of thought; the thought and the language are deeply intertwined.

Linguists have tussled over this idea for 75 years; it's formally known as the Sapir-Whorf hypothesis. The strong version of this hypothesis declares that language *determines* the nature of thought.

The weak version claims only that language *influences* thought. The strong version has few advocates, but the weak version has attracted a large following. Those who don't like the weak Sapir-Whorf hypothesis spend their time attacking the straw man of the strong version. I accept the weak version: that language influences thought, but you can Google the term "Sapir-Whorf" to find more debate than you'd likely care to wade through.

An Inside-Out Approach

This approach suggests that perhaps something could be accomplished if the problem of interactive storytelling is turned inside out. Instead of trying to model the laws of drama, perform lots of clever processing, and then convert the results into language just before presenting it to players, why not make language itself the core of the process? The belief here— and it's a belief, not a proof—is that language itself contains the core elements of drama.

The notion of designing the language to define the reality is tried and true. As far back as the early seventeenth century, philosophers realized that natural language was too sloppy to enable the kind of precise reasoning they wanted. This realization gave rise to a number of speculations about designing a philosopher's language. It never got off the ground, but mathematics met part of the need for a precise language. Since then, all manner of special-case notational systems have been developed for governing certain classes of thought: mathematics, music, chemistry, nuclear physics, quantum mechanics, and so on. There's the classic fictional example of designing a language to govern thought: NewSpeak, the language appearing in the novel *1984*, was designed to ensure that all citizens had good thoughts because there were no words for bad thoughts.

So I'll ask you to grant, for the purposes of this chapter only, the possibility that a properly designed language could somehow contain the elements needed for interactive storytelling. This possibility leads to the real question: Can such a language be designed?

Language and Reality

Because language and our perception of reality are intimately intertwined, it stands to reason that the size of any language reflects the complexity of our perception of reality. This is the real reason that so many attempts to make computers understand natural language have failed. It's not that computer scientists can't express in algorithmic form the many types and structures of language; no, the killer problem is bringing enough knowledge of the real world into linguistic calculations.

Here's an example: "Johnny, I want you to stop crying and take this pill right now!" What does this sentence mean? A typical computer program would assume that the speaker is demanding Johnny take possession of the pill, but any human knows that the speaker is requiring Johnny to *swallow* the pill. That's because the verb "take" has a special meaning when used with pills. If you don't know this tiny detail about reality, you can't understand the sentence. It also helps to know that children cry when they're reluctant to take their medicine and are usually referred to by diminutives (Johnny) rather than their formal names (John).

Here's an even trickier example: "She flew into a rage when she noticed the lipstick on his collar." You have no problem understanding exactly what that sentence means. But consider all the social information you brought to bear in figuring it out: the relationship between men and women, concepts of faithfulness in marriage, how lipstick can get onto a collar, and so forth. How's a poor computer to keep up with all that knowledge?

Therefore, the dramatic reality that's covered must be tightly defined to make a dramatic language usable. You'll have to dispense with one of the storyteller's favorite tricks: the complexly implicit realization. Lipstick on the collar is a perfect example of the kind of knowledge that no dramatic *sublanguage* (a vocabulary that's much smaller than everyday working languages) could address.

The impossibility of using complexly implicit realizations might lead some storytellers to dismiss the potential of dramatic sublanguages. Lots of stories include elements like the lipstick on the collar—without these elements, how can you build good stories? My answer is that you can still build stories, but they can't share this feature with more complexly crafted stories. That doesn't mean stories built with dramatic sublanguages are crippled; it means they're different. In the early years of cinema, there was no sound track; some old fogies insisted that without sound, storytelling was impossible. Early cinema artists worked out a new visual vocabulary, but they *never* really solved the problem of dialogue. Instead, they created stories that required little dialogue. Interactive storytelling requires something similar. Fortunately, you don't have to create an entire language as expressively powerful as, say, English or Chinese; you can get away with much smaller sublanguages.

Lesson #20
Interactive storytelling requires a sublanguage that both computers and humans can use.

Vocabulary

To be computable, the vocabulary of a dramatic sublanguage must be small—smaller than the average person's working vocabulary (about 5,000 words). Fortunately, a vocabulary of only a few hundred words should be adequate. Even more fortunately, there are numerous lists of the most common words in a variety of languages[1]. Here are the 100 most common English words:

1. the	16. as
2. be	17. not
3. of	18. on
4. and	19. she
5. a	20. at
6. to	21. by
7. in	22. this
8. he	23. we
9. have	24. you
10. it	25. do
11. that	26. but
12. for	27. from
13. they	28. or
14. I	29. which
15. with	30. one

31. would	56. only
32. all	57. new
33. will	58. year
34. there	59. some
35. say	60. take
36. who	61. come
37. make	62. these
38. when	63. know
39. can	64. see
40. more	65. use
41. if	66. get
42. no	67. like
43. man	68. then
44. out	69. first
45. other	70. any
46. so	71. work
47. what	72. now
48. time	73. may
49. up	74. such
50. go	75. give
51. about	76. over
52. than	77. think
53. into	78. most
54. could	79. even
55. state	80. find

81. day	91. through
82. also	92. long
83. after	93. where
84. way	94. much
85. many	95. should
86. must	96. well
87. look	97. people
88. before	98. down
89. great	99. own
90. back	100. just

Here are the English words in the frequency range 2,100–2,200:

2,100	sometime	2,114	pearl
2,101	applaud	2,115	ray
2,102	underneath	2,116	lazy
2,103	hello	2,117	limb
2,104	pretense	2,118	grammatical
2,105	descent	2,119	beast
2,106	conquer	2,120	monkey
2,107	framework	2,121	jewel
2,108	confidential	2,122	persuasion
2,109	adoption	2,123	obedience
2,110	disgust	2,124	sock
2,111	waist	2,125	vowel
2,112	momentary	2,126	hammer
2,113	receipt	2,127	inn

2,128	chimney	2,153	complication
2,129	dissatisfaction	2,154	right
2,130	annoyance	2,155	indoor
2,131	ornament	2,156	lower
2,132	honesty	2,157	actress
2,133	outward	2,158	congratulation
2,134	sharpen	2,159	ounce
2,135	handkerchief	2,160	fry
2,136	greed	2,161	everlasting
2,137	heavenly	2,162	goat
2,138	thirst	2,163	ink
2,139	niece	2,164	disappearance
2,140	spill	2,165	reproduction
2,141	loaf	2,166	thicken
2,142	wheat	2,167	avoidance
2,143	worm	2,168	spoon
2,144	secrecy	2,169	strap
2,145	rude	2,170	deceive
2,146	heighten	2,171	lengthen
2,147	flatten	2,172	revenge
2,148	loosen	2,173	correction
2,149	cheese	2,174	descendant
2,150	rivalry	2,175	hesitation
2,151	royalty	2,176	spade
2,152	discontent	2,177	basin

2,178	weed	2,189	discomfort
2,179	omission	2,190	enclosure
2,180	old-fashioned	2,191	attentive
2,181	bicycle	2,192	paw
2,182	breadth	2,193	overflow
2,183	photography	2,194	dissatisfy
2,184	coward	2,195	multiplication
2,185	mat	2,196	whichever
2,186	rejoice	2,197	tidy
2,187	cheat	2,198	bribe
2,188	congratulate	2,199	mend

Note two observations about these lists. First, many words in the first list are function words, such as articles and prepositions, which can often be discarded in a sublanguage. Second, many words in the second list aren't truly necessary for interactive storytelling. You could build a perfectly good sublanguage for interactive storytelling without using such words as "handkerchief," "photography," or "ray." This means your vocabulary can be smaller than 2,000 words—a large but achievable goal.

Moreover, your vocabulary can be extended by a variety of means. All languages sport a set of prefixes and suffixes that extend the meaning of a root word in many directions. Here are just a few of the common prefixes and suffixes commonly used in English:

▶ bak<u>er</u>

▶ fond<u>ness</u>

▶ nation<u>hood</u>

▶ king<u>dom</u>

▶ <u>re</u>sharp<u>en</u>

▶ terror<u>ize</u>

▶ fort<u>ify</u>

- ▶ mandat<u>ory</u>

- ▶ <u>un</u>fortun<u>ate</u>

- ▶ <u>anti</u>dote

- ▶ <u>contra</u>dict

- ▶ <u>inter</u>ac<u>tive</u>

- ▶ <u>non</u>sensi<u>cal</u>

- ▶ <u>predic</u>tion

- ▶ <u>pro</u>du<u>cing</u>

- ▶ <u>trans</u>form

- ▶ <u>sub</u>langu<u>age</u>

A small set of these extensions to your sublanguage could increase its vocabulary without taxing players.

Grammars

Language equals vocabulary plus grammar. That's a bit of a simplification, but for the purposes of sublanguage construction, it's adequate. A grammar specifies the rules for putting words together into a sentence. Natural-language grammars are horridly complicated: The conjugations, declensions, voices, moods, and gender overwhelm the beginner, and then there are all the exceptions! English has, for example, sink-sank-sunk and drink-drank-drunk but wink-winked-winked. Clearly, you want to design a sublanguage with a clean grammar.

But what's the best grammar to use? A cleaned-up version of English grammar? Spanish has a particularly clean grammar; perhaps it would be a better starting place. Fortunately, a clean, simple grammar already exists, and it appears to be wired into our brains. Throughout history, a number of revealing linguistic experiments have been carried out as the unintended consequence of immigration. If a large body of immigrants occupies a new territory, not as conquerers but as laborers, the first generation of their children finds itself handicapped by the incompatibility of the language spoken at home and the language of their playmates. In this social context, where neither language can assert itself as dominant, the children invent a new language called a *creole*. This new language borrows vocabulary from both parent languages, but its grammar is always the same, no matter where or when it's created. The core structure of creole grammars is simple: There are no conjugations, declensions, voices, moods, or genders. All these functions are handled with *auxiliary words*. For example, a hypothetical creole based on English might include statements such as:

I go store.	I am going to the store.
I been go store.	I went to the store.
I gwanna go store.	I will go to the store.

Auxiliary words are simply tacked onto the existing words to modify their meaning. As Mr. Spock would say, "crude, but effective."

A completely different approach relies on creating a square matrix with vocabulary words along the top and the left side. Each cell in the matrix represents one pairing of a column-word with a row-word; if that cell is marked True, the column-word is permitted to follow the row-word; otherwise, it is not. In **Figure 10.1**, for example, the row-word "Go to" can be followed only by the column-word "the house." This approach to grammar is even cruder than a creole grammar, but it's simpler to understand and implement.

A word connection matrix's worst problem is its inadequacy to address contextual factors that might change the word sequence. You can partially address this problem by including special-case rules for these contextual factors. A clean sublanguage might have only a few such special-case rules, but as the language grows, the number of special-case rules explodes.

Meaning

Interactive storytelling demands a sublanguage that both computers and humans can use. The program must be able to read any valid expression in the language and understand what it means. But what does "understand" mean in this context? Surely a computer can't understand language in the way that people do. What it can do in response to a sentence is change a storyworld's components. Each sentence must somehow generate changes in the values of variables in the storyworld; presumably these changes will then trigger responses from other Actors.

FIGURE 10.1: A word connection matrix.

Thus, "meaning" in the narrow sense I'm using here is nothing more than the changes engendered in the storyworld triggered by a verb. The verb "make" means a new prop will be entered into the database of props; its properties can be partly derived from other components of the sentence containing the verb. For example, "Joe makes a box" means that a new box is placed into the Prop database owned by Joe, and that the components used to make the box are removed from the Prop database.

This example, however, is simple because it's merely mechanical. Verbs with more dramatic import demand more complex treatment. For example, consider the verb "to love." It takes an Actor as its direct object. Carrying out this verb requires a change in the relationship between subject and direct object. It could also affect the relationships of each Actor with other Actors.

But it gets worse: What about verbs whose significance depends wholly on the context? The verb "invite home" provides an example. If this event takes place on the schoolgrounds where little Molly invites little Tommy over to her house, it means one thing; if Molly and Tommy are unattached 20-somethings, it could mean something entirely different. You can solve this problem by carefully choosing the vocabulary to ensure that no ambiguities of this kind result. You can also tighten your storyworld to make sure it's not populated by both school-children and young singles.

Inverse Parsing

People automatically speak natural language in complete sentences. You frame the sentence in your mind, and then speak it as a unit. So when computers came along, programmers just naturally assumed people should talk to computers the same way they talk to each other—except they then designed abstruse languages too difficult for people to remember. There's no reason that sentences in dramatic sublanguages must be created in their entirety; a sentence can just as easily be assembled word by word.

 Why does it matter whether you construct sentences word by word or as entire units?

The difference lies in players' interactions with the computer. If they compose sentences as complete units, they must be certain that every single word in the sentence is perfect. Suppose that a player is only 90% certain of each word in a seven-word sentence; the odds are even lower that the sentence as a whole will be correct. Requiring players to submit sentences in their entirety compounds the uncertainties.

The biggest benefit of word-by-word composition is that the computer can present players with a menu of all appropriate words that can be entered at that point in the sentence. Instead of guessing from memory, players need only select from a menu—a much simpler task.

 But menus are so slow to use!

Pull-down menus are slow because they require three actions for each selection: click on the menu title, drag down to the menu item, and release. Menus for this kind of interface (which I call an *inverse parser*) can be kept front and center. The player looks directly at the menu choices, identifies the best choice, and clicks on it—just one action instead of three. The inverse parser then recalculates the sentence and, using the sublanguage's grammar, determines all the words that might fit into the next open slot. It displays those words in a new menu that replaces the previous menu.

What if there are so many words that they don't fit into the available space?

Then you make the menu a scrolling window. This occurrence will be rare; with a vocabulary of less than 2,000 words, it's unlikely that more than a dozen will fit into most slots. Indeed, the context of the situation often narrows down the choice to but a single word, which the inverse parser can fill in automatically for players.

Suppose you're playing as Tom, occupying a Stage with just one other person: Diane. You enter "Tom" as the first word in the sentence (after all, Tom is the only Actor you control), and then you choose the verb "asks." The inverse parser can figure out that Diane is the only Actor the question can be directed to, so it fills in "Diane" as the direct object of the sentence. This kind of one-word choice happens all the time with inverse parsers.

Every sublanguage must have grammar, and every sentence must be contextually appropriate. If you use a regular parser, you must write code that analyzes the grammatical and contextual appropriateness of players' input—but you'll have to disappoint players with error messages explaining that their sentence input makes no sense. With an inverse parser, you use the same code that analyzes grammatical and contextual appropriateness, but you execute that code *before* players make their decisions, not *after* they've made their mistakes. With an inverse parser, grammatical and contextual errors are impossible.

Semantic Networks

Realizing the problems inherent in language comprehension, computer scientists have been assembling a variety of *semantic networks*, which are data structures that connect words by their various meanings. The most advanced semantic network is WordNet[2], also known as a *lexical database*: a huge database of more than 150,000 English words with all their logical connections. Each word is connected to each of its synonyms, antonyms, hypernyms, hyponyms, meronyms, and holonyms. You already know what synonyms and antonyms are. A *hyponym* is a specific instance of the word in question; thus, "spaniel" is a hyponym of "dog." A *hypernym* has the reverse relationship, so "mammal" is a hypernym of "dog." A *holonym* is an object that includes the word in question as one of its parts; thus, "body" is a holonym for "toe." The reverse case is that "toe" is a *meronym* of "body."

WordNet includes additional information, such as classes of words (nouns, verbs, adjectives, and so forth) and some additional relationships among words. The project continues to develop as researchers expand the database to include ever more useful information.

Another example of a semantic network is the Visual Thesaurus[3], it presents the synonyms of a word, and their synonyms, as a three-dimensional structure. It's visually striking and screams with potential.

Many researchers are exploring the potential of semantic networks. Elizabeth Figa and Paul Tarau at the University of North Texas, for example, have explored the possibilities of using semantic networks for interactive storytelling.

See Chapter 19, "Research," for more on Figa and Taura's work on using semantic networks for interactive storytelling.

 Wouldn't you need a superpowered machine to parse all that data?

Nope. WordNet is distributed in a form that runs on a modern PC. Its operation isn't optimized for speed, but it still runs plenty fast for our purposes. Remember, inverse parsing takes place one word at a time, between player inputs. The code can fiddle around with the parsing problem for, oh, half a second before a player would notice the delay. Half a second represents a billion machine cycles on a modern PC. A computer can parse of a *lot* of information in a billion steps.

Graphical Languages

A sublanguage for interactive storytelling has one gigantic advantage over natural language: It's visual rather than auditory. Auditory expressions are one-dimensional, but visual expressions have multiple dimensions (horizontal, vertical, color, texture, and animation). The visual expression of natural language, writing, remains one-dimensional in structure even on a two-dimensional page.

Failure to take advantage of the computer's multidimensional capability would be a mortal sin against the Muse of Design. I first used a graphical language in 1986 with my game Siboot. My sublanguage used icons that were linked into sentences, as shown in **Figure 10.2**.

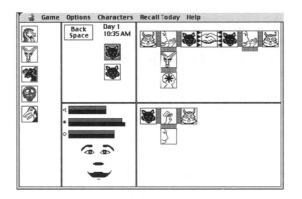

FIGURE 10.2: Linking icons in Siboot.

In this screenshot, the lower-right pane shows a short sentence: "Wiki greets Vetvel pleasantly." Wiki is the catlike icon, and Vetvel is the horned icon. The verb "greet" is in the center, and the adverb "pleasantly" modifies the verb.

Player input is handled in the upper-right pane; it shows a complex sentence the player has almost completed. (This is an example of an inverse parser at work.) The almost complete sentence says "Vetvel offers to tell Wiki what Gardbore's shial-value is if in return Wiki tells Vetvel…" The notion of the deal is communicated by the central handshake icon. The verb "tell" shows up in two places. Vetvel's "tell" is modified by the icon for Gardbore (the long-eared creature), which in turn is modified by the value for "shial" (a critical quantity in the game). On the right side of the sentence, Wiki's "tell" hasn't yet received its modifier and so has a hanging connector. A list of icons shown at the far left could be used as modifiers; each icon represents a character.

An important concept used in this sublanguage is the notion of *autofilling*. The sublanguage's software is intimately connected with the game's database (as it must be if it's to be useful). The software knows what words fit into which situations, so it can prune the menu of available words to display only permissible words. In the preceding example, the software has restricted the set of choices to include only those secrets that Wiki has available to trade. It can even exclude secrets Wiki has to trade that Vetvel already knows, so wouldn't be interested in.

The big benefit of sublanguages is that they focus players on what's possible and make it impossible to conceive of utterances that aren't permitted. The sublanguage contains the rules as well as the substance of the storyworld—a powerful feature.

 But wouldn't it be difficult for people to learn a new language just to play a storyworld?

Don't underestimate the facility with which people pick up languages. The average tourist can start picking up the rudiments of the local language after only a week. If people can begin learning complex natural languages so readily, imagine how easy it would be to learn a narrowly defined sublanguage.

The sublanguage in Siboot has a vocabulary of about 80 words—too skimpy for interactive storytelling. Larger vocabularies require more complex software. Fortunately, computers' graphical powers have improved dramatically in the 17 years since I designed Siboot's sublanguage. It's no problem to use word icons that are 64 pixels wide rather than the 32 pixels I had to use for Siboot. Doubling the icon's size quadruples its theoretical expressive power. In addition, I had to use black and white for my icons, but now you can use 24-bit color; that alone increases icons' theoretical expressive power by a factor of 24. In other words, 64-pixel icons on modern computers are about 100 times more expressive than the icons I used for Siboot.

Basic English

Basic English was created about 80 years ago in an effort to provide a simple, easy-to-learn variant of English[4]. It uses a small, carefully selected vocabulary design to cover all situations and contains about 1,000 words, with only 18 verbs: come, get, give, go, keep, let, make, put, seem, take, be, do, have, say, see, send, may, and will.

With this system, many more verbs can be assembled by combining verbs with nouns. Thus, the verb "attack" becomes "make an attack"; "cry" becomes "have a cry." By reducing verbs to the absolute minimum, the designers of Basic English were able to simplify the language. Unfortunately, the system makes heavy use of prepositions to extend the meanings of verbs in ways that make sense to people but aren't so easy for a computer to understand. "Dedicated" is translated as "given up to"; "die" is "go to death." I suspect that a reworked version of Basic English could be developed into something useful for interactive storytelling, but first someone must build a better system for handling verbs. With that done, the next task would be creating a large semantic database defining what all the words mean. This is a huge task, but certainly not an impossible one—and after the system was built, it could be used in a wide variety of products.

Pictorial Languages

A lush garden of resources on pictorial languages flourishes on the Web. Some of the more interesting are discussed in the following sections.

Bliss

Bliss is a symbolic language developed over several decades in the mid-twentieth century[5]. It was applied as a language for handicapped children in an experiment in Canada, with impressive results. It has since been expanded, revised, and refined. The language is built from 120 "key symbols," which then combine into more than 2,000 words. **Figure 10.3** shows a sample.

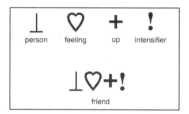

FIGURE 10.3: In Bliss, "much good feeling person" equals "friend."

The Elephant's Memory

Timothee Ingen-Housz has created a beautiful graphical language called The Elephant's Memory[6]. It uses a brilliant set of icons that work well together.

There's a catch: Although the language is a tour de force in graphic design, Mr. Ingen-Housz's genius is not all-encompassing. The language has 156 words, and there seems little chance of it growing beyond that. Words that are easily drawn, such as "elephant" or "rabbit," are present, but the language lacks many crucial words.

Conlangs

The delightful term *conlangs* is a contraction of "constructed languages" (as opposed to languages that evolved naturally). Believe it or not, plenty of people love creating their own languages. Few of these languages have any relevance to the problems you face in creating a sublanguage for interactive storytelling, but these efforts will certainly broaden your thinking. To find out more, just search the web for "conlang" or visit `http://www.langmaker.com/`. Another resource for pictorial languages is at `http://vlado.fmf.uni-lj.si/seminar/28jul99/PicLang.htm`.

Wrapping Up

One way or another, your interactive storytelling engine must communicate with your players. Every computer program creates a tiny sublanguage that it uses for communication with its users. You could cobble something together with menus, dialog boxes, pushbuttons, and so forth; after all, this is what people have been doing for decades. But for interactive storytelling, the range of expressions your players will require is so great that it's worth your while to go whole hog and create a formal sublanguage.

---

1. John B. Carroll, Peter Davies, and Barry Richman, *The American Heritage Word Frequency Book* (Houghton Mifflin, 1971; ISBN 0395135702).
2. WordNet: www.cogsci.princeton.edu/~wn.
3. Visual Thesaurus: www.visualthesaurus.com/index.jsp.
4. Basic English: http://ogden.basic-english.org/basiceng.html.
5. Bliss: http://home.istar.ca/~bci/.
6. The Elephant's Memory: www.apple.com/education/LTReview/spring99/elephant/.

PART IV

Core Technologies for Interactive Storytelling

CHAPTER 11
Personality Models

WRITERS MOVE BETWEEN TWO POLES: plot and character. (These poles, by the way, correspond to process and data.) Plot-style writing aims to develop an interesting plot and then create the characters to make the plot work. The other strategy is to create interesting characters and then see how they interact, expecting a plot to arise from the characters' natural interactions. The plot-style approach is described in Chapter 12, "Drama Managers." This chapter explains the character-driven approach.

The first step in this effort is creating a *personality model*, which is a data structure containing all the information needed to define a character. Differentiating between personality modeling as it's used in psychology and interactive storytelling is important. In psychology, personality modeling is a scientific endeavor to determine the elements of human personality; it can be used to evaluate real people. The needs of interactive storytelling are quite different, however, so the use of psychological personality models is limited. There have been some attempts to apply psychological personality models to interactive storytelling, but they have yielded dull results because real people aren't as highlighted in their personalities as actors in drama. They make prudent decisions where characters in stories make bold ones; they hedge their bets where story characters throw caution to the wind; they stay well within the envelope of socially acceptable behavior where the characters in stories deliberately push the edges of that envelope to explore the human condition.

Factors in Developing a Personality Model

The factors used in a personality model for interactive storytelling must meet four crucial criteria: They must be complete, concise, and orthogonal, and they must be tied to behavior.

Completeness

The factors that make up a personality model must completely address all the behaviors you want to evoke in your storyworld. If your storyworld is to include sexual behavior, you must have factors such as lust and sex appeal. If your storyworld is a children's storyworld without any sexual elements, you can dispense with these factors. If your storyworld is a macho-guy action world with lots of action and only a token sexy chick, you need only one or two factors concerning romantic interaction; in a chick-flick storyworld, you'd need many more romantic variables.

Lesson #21
The personality model must cover the behavioral range of your storyworld.

Conciseness

Some storybuilders are tempted to develop a huge personality model containing every possible factor and trait imaginable. Whenever a design problem arises, they throw a new personality trait into the model, and poof! The problem is gone. This approach ultimately comes back to bite them because as more personality traits are added, determining which traits should be applied in any given situation becomes more difficult. A good personality model must be small enough to keep inside your head at all times. If you have to consult it every time you use it, you've made it too big.

Lesson #22
Keep the personality model as small as possible.

Orthogonality

Variables in a personality model must not overlap; if they do, you'll always face difficulties in knowing which one to apply. Suppose you have built a personality model with the variables Good-Humored and Friendly. These two factors aren't identical, but they do overlap somewhat. That overlap can cause endless problems. Suppose an Actor with these traits encounters a stranger under inauspicious circumstances. In calculating the Actor's reactions to the stranger, the storybuilder needs to take both factors into account. It's difficult to imagine any situation in which one factor would apply but the other factor wouldn't. If you can't imagine such a situation, then there's no functional difference between the two factors. They should be collapsed into a single variable.

A simple geometric analogy might help those who never endured vector analysis. Imagine getting around in a city with streets laid out in a regular rectangular gridwork, with numbered avenues running north to south and lettered streets running west to east. If you are at the corner of 3rd Avenue and B Street and you need to get to 8th Avenue and D Street, you know you must go 5 blocks south and 2 blocks east. That's the only combination that will work.

Now suppose you live in a city with a three-way street grid, as shown in **Figure 11.1.**

You could get from one point to any other point by a number of combinations. For example, you could go from the corner of 1st Avenue and A Street to the corner of 4th Avenue and C Street by going 2 blocks east along γ Road and 1 block southeast along C Street or, if you don't want to travel along Greek-lettered roads, by going 2 blocks northeast along 1st Avenue and 3 blocks southeast along C Street.

Of course, no city is organized in this way because it's silly. You don't need three sets of roads when there are only two main sets of directions (north-south and east-west). You want to collapse those three sets of roads down to two sets. In the process, you get roads that are at right angles to one another, and that's what I mean by *orthogonality*.

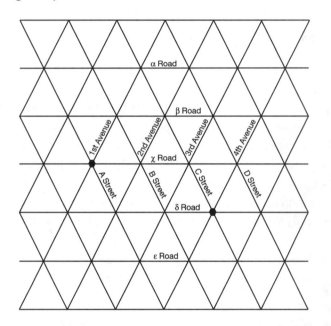

FIGURE 11.1: Three dimensions of streets on a two-dimensional surface.

This idea of orthogonality is just a formalization of the concept of conciseness. If two variables are orthogonal, they have nothing whatsoever in common. Hence, orthogonality is really a means to achieve conciseness.

Lesson #23
Achieve conciseness through orthogonality.

Tied to Behavior

Personality models aren't built as an academic exercise; they're used for the pragmatic purpose of determining Actors' behaviors. Every personality trait in the model must be created with an eye toward the behavior it might control. Spirituality might seem like an important personality trait, but if your storyworld doesn't include spiritual behavior, this trait is useless and doesn't belong in the personality model. The personality model must be created after determining the storyworld's basic content. After storybuilders have answered the question "What does the user DO?" by creating a list of verbs accessible to the Actors, they can start to build a personality model that permits Actors to discriminate among those verbs.

Lesson #24
The personality model mirrors the behavioral universe of the storyworld.

Overspecificity

It's possible to take Lesson #24's admonition too far, however. Some behaviors can be so difficult to define that it's tempting to create custom traits that directly control the behavior, even though you have no idea what that trait might mean. For example, suppose you need to decide the behavior of Actors who might engage in kissing. What factors would determine their proclivity to kiss somebody? The wrong answer is to create a special variable called `Proclivity_to_Kiss`. Instead, look deeper into the human soul; think more abstractly. What fundamental personality traits lead to a proclivity to kiss? Sensuality seems like a good choice; affection for the other person should be another factor. You're better off controlling behavior with these fundamental variables than tossing in a special-case variable every time you feel stumped.

If you can't derive behavior from fundamental personality traits, either you don't understand the human condition well enough to design storyworlds, or your personality model is incomplete.

Lesson #25
Don't create special-case personality variables for individual verbs.

Types of Personality Variables

Five broad types of variables could be used in a personality model: *intrinsic, mood, volatility, accordance,* and *relationship.* The first type includes the intrinsic personality traits associated with any character: greed, lust, pride, and so forth. The second type, mood, includes the variable emotional states people are subject to, such as anger or joy; these personality traits change with time. Volatility variables govern the readiness with which mood variables can change; accordance variables govern the readiness with which relationships change. The last variable type includes the relationships each Actor has with all the others.

I call the first four variable types *first-person variables* because they are represented in many data structures as entries in a one-dimensional array of Actors: Greed[ThisActor], Anger[ThisActor], and so on. The fifth type (relationships) I refer to as *second-person variables* because they are represented with two-dimensional arrays, such as Affection[ThatActor, ThisActor] or Trust[Joe, Fred].

This notion of first-person and second-person variables might strike you as odd, but in fact it makes a great deal of sense when you approach it in a larger context. For example, in a relationship such as trust, couldn't you say that trust is really one person's perception of another's honesty? Could you call fear one person's perception of another's potential to wreak damage? This way of thinking about personality variables offers a remarkable benefit: It can be extended usefully to three dimensions. A third-person variable would then be one person's perception of another's perception of a third person. Although that might sound like an mouthful of egregious indirection, third-person statements are made every day: "No, Joe wouldn't ever trust Marcie." The speaker is expressing his perception that Joe holds a negative perception of Marcie's honesty.

Accordance variables represent the degree to which an Actor readily perceives high values of another's intrinsic variable. The most obvious example is the concept of gullibility—the willingness to accord trust to another. Its opposite, suspiciousness, is a proclivity to accord small amounts of trust to others. Another example would be timidity, the degree to which one Actor accords power to another Actor. The concept of accordance might seem abstruse, but when you write formulae for relationship changes, the need for these variables leaps out at you. If Actor A insults Actor B, how angry will Actor B become? Some people have thick skins; some people are easily antagonized. Storybuilders need some means for expressing this important personality difference, and accordance variables fill that need. Every relationship variable needs an associated accordance variable.

This way of organizing a personality model imposes some constraints on a system of variables, but these constraints clarify the operation of any personality model. Thus, if you have a personality trait of Honesty, the second-person perception of that trait in another is the relationship known as Trust.

What other personality traits could be considered? The obvious choice is love. A bewildering array of terms are available: love, affection, caring, friendship, warmth, and many others. For reasons that will become clear later when I present my entire system of variables, I prefer to use Virtue as the intrinsic variable, AccordVirtue as the accordance variable, and PerVirtue as the relationship variable.

 Just a minute, here. These terms you're using don't fit the concepts. Affection, love, or whatever you call it is motivated by much more than virtue. Kinship matters, as does parallelism of goals and interests.

True, but the fact is there are no ideal words for what I'm seeking. Here's a long-winded example of the problem: Consider the terminology for defining colors. That terminology is completely arbitrary; in fact, different colors slice up the color spectrum in different ways. Some cultures merge what we call blue and green into a single color. Some cultures define just a few colors, and other cultures recognize many colors. The words and the concepts are all completely arbitrary. However, in terms of the human eye, there are three basic colors. That is, any color distinguishable by the human eye can be defined in terms of three numbers. A common system for defining color is RGB, for red, green, and blue. Any color can then be defined as some combination of red, green, and blue values. Or there's HSB: hue, saturation, and brightness. Again, any color distinguishable by the human eye can be defined in terms of those three numbers. I suppose hundreds of different three-dimensional systems could define color, but here's the rub: No color terms correspond precisely to the mathematical elements of these color systems. The term "red" covers many colors, but "red" in the RGB system is a precisely defined color. For conversational use, the sloppy term "red" works fine, but for mathematical use, the term "red" in the RGB system has a much narrower meaning.

In the same fashion, my use of terms such as Virtue or Power is mathematical, not conversational. I capitalize terms that have a special meaning in my models to differentiate them from common usage. These terms in my system don't correspond precisely to their meanings in normal language. They are storybuilding-specific versions of common terms; they suggest the concept in use but don't properly define it. Accordingly, I must supply precise behavioral definitions of how these terms work. Rather than argue about the semantics of the terms, in the following sections I show how they actually operate in a personality model. If you don't like my usages, you're welcome to create your own. Good luck; English words never quite fit into mathematically neat slots.

Polarity of Variables

One of the more confusing problems in personality modeling concerns the polarity of variables. *Unipolar* variables have a maximum value and a minimum value of zero. In other words, Actors can have lots of Integrity or zero Integrity, but they can't have negative Integrity. Similarly, Actors can have positive Wisdom or zero Wisdom, but they can't have negative Wisdom. That's the unipolar model.

In the *bipolar* model, variables have a maximum that's positive and a minimum that's negative. The value of zero indicates a middling or neutral quantity of that variable. Thus, in the bipolar model, an Actor with zero Integrity is average, a dishonest actor has negative Integrity, and an honest actor has positive Integrity.

The choice between unipolar and bipolar variables brings up a variety of tricky considerations. In some cases, a variable that makes perfect sense as a unipolar variable is nonsensical when treated as a bipolar variable. For example, it's easy to understand a high value of greed, but what would a negative value of greed imply: charity or generosity? If you wanted to build an inclination formula representing the intensity of an Actor's desire to obtain some trinket, you would naturally multiply the value of the trinket by the Actor's greed. In this case, you would expect that a saint would simply have zero desire for the trinket. But using a bipolar value for the greed variable would make the saint's desire for the trinket negative—is that reasonable?

My own experience has led me to the conclusion that bipolar variables are, in general, more practical to use than unipolar variables. However, I am certain that a clever designer could create a perfectly workable personality model using unipolar variables. And nothing prevents mixing unipolar variables with bipolar variables, so long as you keep them straight.

The problem that drove me to using bipolar relationships was rather messy. I wanted to determine the reaction of one Actor to another's behavior toward a third. To make this easier to follow, here's an example: How is Mary to react if she observes Fred do something to Tom? Will her overall reaction be positive or negative? That depends on two factors: how nice or nasty Fred's action was, and how much she likes or dislikes Tom. In other words, there are four possible variations:

▶ Fred does something nice for Tom, and Mary likes Tom: Mary is pleased.

▶ Fred does something nice for Tom, and Mary hates Tom: Mary is displeased.

▶ Fred does something nasty to Tom, and Mary likes Tom: Mary is displeased.

▶ Fred does something nasty to Tom, and May hates Tom: Mary is pleased.

Now, to model this behavior in arithmetic relationships, you need to multiply niceness/nastiness with affection/hatred, but you *also* need to ensure that both niceness/nastiness and affection/hatred are bipolar values. In other words, both nastiness and hatred have to be negative numbers. Here's the same set of statements using arithmetic values:

▶ Fred does something +2 for Tom, and Mary feels +4 for Tom: Mary is pleased +8.

▶ Fred does something +2 for Tom, and Mary feels -3 for Tom: Mary is pleased -6.

▶ Fred does something -4 for Tom, and Mary feels +4 for Tom: Mary is pleased -16.

▶ Fred does something -4 for Tom, and Mary feels -3 for Tom: Mary is pleased +12.

This example shows why relationships need to be bipolar. And because a relationship is nothing more than a perceived intrinsic variable, these variables must be bipolar, too.

Moods

Another aspect of character that could be included in a personality model is mood. As with intrinsic personality traits, mood is difficult to define precisely. Fortunately, the task of including mood variables isn't so complicated. My own personality model uses three moods: Anger/Fear, Arousal/Revulsion, and Joy/Sadness. Note that each mood is bipolar.

But anger is not the opposite of fear.

I think it is. Think in strictly behavioral terms: How are anger and fear manifested? The classic answer is "fight or flight," and the brains of most animals have a basic mechanism for gearing up for one or the other. Adrenalin pours into the bloodstream, heart rate soars, breathing becomes deeper and faster: You're ready for action. Whether that action is fight or flight doesn't matter. Inside the brain, fight and flight are just two sides of the same coin, and they can't share the same coin unless they're opposites.

Mood spontaneously diminishes. No matter how angry you become, the passage of time will surely diminish that anger. Although the actions of others can both intensify and diminish moods, these moods can nevertheless diminish all by themselves. The storytelling engine, therefore, must examine each Actor's mood at regular intervals and relax it toward zero. This is most easily accomplished by multiplying the mood at regular intervals by some value less than 1.00. The smaller the number, the more quickly the mood decays.

Including fatigue or even hunger as a mood is also possible, but as these states require specific actions to ameliorate, I treat them separately from moods. Moreover, because they're more physical in nature than emotional, I prefer to minimize their role.

My Preferred Personality Model

I offer for your consideration the personality model I have ended up with after many years. I do not claim this model to be the best of all possible models—just the one I have found most workable.

Intrinsic Variables

Integrity: This variable is close to the common use of the term. Actors with high Integrity always keep their word, never tell lies, and never reveal secrets. Actors with low Integrity break their promises, lie, and reveal secrets.

Virtue: This is the degree to which an Actor takes other Actors' needs and desires into account when making decisions. Actors with high Virtue make choices based on what's best for other actors (themselves included). Actors with low Virtue are selfish, self-centered, and egotistical. They always place their own interests ahead of other considerations.

Power: This variable represents the ability to wreak physical, financial, or social injury upon others. Actors with lots of Power have the capacity to do harm, but not necessarily the motivation.

Intelligence: This variable represents the ability to make correct decisions. Actors with high Intelligence tend to make the most efficacious and pragmatic choices. Actors with low Intelligence often make incorrect judgments.

Attractiveness: This variable represents an Actor's physical appearance. A female Actor with high Attractiveness is pretty; a male Actor with high Attractiveness is handsome.

Mood Variables

Anger/Fear: Positive values denote anger; negative values denote fear.

Joy/Sadness: Positive values denote joy; negative values denote sadness.

Arousal/Disgust: This pairing counterbalances arousal, normally thought of in its sexual manifestation, with disgust, normally associated with smell and taste. In this case, however, arousal is used to indicate any heightened sensuality. Licking your lips before digging into a meal constitutes arousal.

Volatility Variables

Adrenaline: Think of this variable as "the speed with which adrenaline pours into the bloodstream." It controls the rate of change of Anger/Fear. High values describe an Actor who angers or runs quickly.

Manic/Depressive: Actors with high levels of this variable soar to peaks of joy or plunge to depths of despair every time they look at the mail; controls Joy/Sadness.

Sensuality: This variable controls the rate of change of Arousal/Disgust. An Actor with a high value of Sensuality is readily aroused and easily disgusted.

Accordance Variables

`AccordIntegrity`: This variable is close to what's known as gullibility; its negative sense would be close to suspiciousness.

`AccordVirtue`: This variable represents the willingness to see the good in other people. An Actor with high `AccordVirtue` would be more sympathetic and not respond as harshly to another Actor's evil actions.

`AccordPower`: This variable might be called timidity. An Actor with high `AccordPower` overestimates the power of others. An Actor with low `AccordPower` underestimates the dangers of any social situation.

`AccordIntelligence`: No simple English term adequately captures this concept. An Actor with high `AccordIntelligence` more readily defers to others' judgments, thinking them wise. An Actor with negative values of `AccordIntelligence` thinks everybody else stupid and rejects their suggestions.

`AccordAttractive`: This variable also has no ready translation into English. Behaviorally, an Actor with high values of `AccordAttractive` sees everybody else as beautiful. This variable makes more sense in terms of self-image, in which case you might call its negative value vanity. `AccordAttractive` might also translate into something like lust.

Relationship Variables

`PerIntegrity`: This variable is very close to what's known as trust. An Actor who has high `PerIntegrity` for another acts on the belief that the second Actor will honor his promises, keep secrets, and not tell lies.

`PerVirtue`: This variable represents the `Virtue` of one Actor as perceived by another. `PerVirtue` toward another substitutes for `Virtue` in oneself. In other words, one person's `PerVirtue` for another operates in exactly the same way he would behave if he had a similar amount of `Virtue`. Indeed, it might be best to add `Virtue` and `PerVirtue` together in calculations.

`PerPower`: This variable indicates the relationship engendered by `Power`; it's close to fear. High values of `PerPower` induce an Actor to defer to the judgment and carry out the wishes of the powerful one. An Actor with little `PerPower` toward another is less inclined to carry out the second Actor's wishes. However, true fear is more precisely a combination of `PerPower` and `PerVirtue`. In other words, an

Actor doesn't fear another unless he perceives the second Actor to be powerful and amoral.

PerIntelligence: This variable represents one Actor's perception of another's Intelligence; it's close to the concept of respect, although respect can also represent high perceived Virtue or even high perceived Power. An Actor with high PerIntelligence for another defers to the other's judgment more readily. An Actor with low PerIntelligence for another doesn't give much weight to the other's recommendations and wishes.

PerAttractive: This variable indicates the degree to which an Actor perceives another as attractive. This value might be heightened by PerVirtue, and vice versa.

But these traits and relationships aren't orthogonal. You could make a good argument that PerIntegrity *and* PerVirtue *are correlated—do you really trust somebody you don't like? Doesn't this break your rule for orthogonality?*

Well, yes, there's some overlap. This system's orthogonality is not perfect. Orthogonality is an ideal to strive for, not an absolute requirement. This model has what I consider an acceptable degree of orthogonality.

Nor is this set complete: It doesn't address traits such as greed or pride.

Both greed and pride can both be approximated through the existing personality set. For example, an Actor with negative Virtue puts his own interests ahead of others' interests, and so tends to be greedy. Similarly, pride is a combination of negative Virtue and negative Intelligence.

There's no question that this personality model has its weaknesses. Human beings are messy creatures, and I don't think we'll ever find something as neat and clean as the RGB system for color. That's what makes storybuilding an art form—you simply have to make artistic judgments about the system you use. I'm sure there are lots of other ways of slicing the cake. In designing a personality model, you must treat orthogonality as a desideratum, not an absolute rule. You also want completeness and conciseness, but will never truly achieve them. Perhaps one day some genius will come up with a system that's perfectly orthogonal, complete, and concise. When that day comes, we can all rejoice. Until then, we just have to make the best approximations we can.

Automatic Relationship Adjustment

Every Actor's reaction to an event must include two elements: a choice among the verbs available to the Actor and an emotional reaction that's an alteration of the Actor's perceived values. Specifying the inclination formulae for verb choices is an onerous task; specifying the emotional reactions adds to the workload. Fortunately, there's a way to automatically derive the emotional reactions. The reacting Actor need merely consult the decision script that led to the original verb choice.

Suppose that Fred is considering his options with respect to James, who has just called him a mumbling moron. For simplicity, give Fred just two options: Call James a nattering ninny, or punch James in the face. Suppose further that Fred's decision is based primarily on his Virtue: If this variable is negative, he'll punch James, but if it's positive, he'll merely return the insult. Suppose that Fred decides to punch James. Anybody witnessing the event (including James) could examine the inclination formula Fred used to make his decision and infer that Fred's Virtue must have been negative for him to have decided to punch James. Therefore, witnesses can adjust their PerVirtue for Fred (that is, their perception of his Virtue) in keeping with this information.

To see how this works, assume that the inclination formulae Fred used in his decision looked like this:

```
Inclination[Punch] <= Anger[Fred] - Virtue[Fred]

Inclination[Insult] <= Anger[Fred] + Virtue[Fred]
```

The only difference between the two formulae is the Virtue variable. You can infer from the formulae that Virtue[Fred] must be less than zero, but how much less? There's no way to know—and this is perfectly compatible with dramatic reality. Observing a single case of a person losing his temper doesn't prove a lot about that person. Therefore, you apply only a gross approximation. In this case, the simplest assumption is that Anger[Fred] = -5.

Come on! There's no foundation for that assumption!

Yes, there is. You know that -10 < Anger[Fred] < 0. I chose the middle value in that range. As I said, it's a gross assumption, but it's still a reasonable one given the paucity of data. Besides, I don't simply substitute this new value for the older value of PerVirtue[James, Fred]; I average it in with the existing value. I could use a simple averaging:

```
PerVirtue[James, Fred] <= (PerVirtue[James, Fred] + (-5) ) / 2
```

Hence, if James's original PerVirtue for Fred was -3, the new value of PerVirtue would be:

```
PerVirtue[James, Fred] <= (-3 + (-5) ) / 2

                       <= (-8) / 2

                       <= -4
```

Or I could use a weighted average representing the fact that this new observation about Fred is only one of many (it uses a 3:1 weighting ratio):

```
PerVirtue[James, Fred] <= (3 × PerVirtue[James, Fred] + (-5) ) / 4
```

In this case, James's PerVirtue for Fred calculates to:

```
PerVirtue[James, Fred] <= (3 × (-3) + (-5) ) / 4

                       <= (-14) / 4

                       <= -3.5
```

Or I could get snazzy and keep some sort of weighting factor for each perceived value, denoting the amount of information that has gone into the value. To make it work, I'd have to keep track of the reliability of the current value of PerVirtue; this is most easily done by counting the number of observations of Fred's behavior that have gone into the value of PerVirtue. That reliability factor (PerVirtueReliability) then replaces the weighting factor of 3 used in the preceding formula, as shown here:

```
PerVirtue[James, Fred] <= (PerVirtueReliability[James, Fred] ×
➡PerVirtue[James, Fred] + (-50) ) / (PerVirtueReliability
➡[James, Fred] + 1)
```

For this calculation, say that James has observed Fred's behavior just twice before; then `PerVirtueReliability` is only 2 and the calculation looks like this:

```
PerVirtue[James, Fred] <= (2 × (-3) + (-5) ) / (2 + 1)

                       <= (-11) / 3

                       <= -3.66
```

I would follow up with an increment of `PerVirtueReliability[James, Fred]`.

I could get even snazzier by using variable increments to an observation's reliability. When I actually witness an event, I assign high reliability to the value arising from that event. When I am told of an event by another, I give that report a weight proportional to my `PerIntegrity` (trust in) the reporter. I could give a different weight to a second- or third-person evaluation of Fred's `Virtue` (as in "Mary thinks that Fred is an odious cad.")

The significance of this technique is that it relieves storybuilders of the burden of specifying Actors' emotional reactions to each event they witness. The act of specifying motivations automatically reveals the character traits that are at work. As Aristotle said, character is revealed by the decisions actors make. This technique is simply the mathematical realization of Aristotle's dictum.

Calculating with Personality Variables

"My love for you is without measure; it is deeper than the deepest ocean, higher than the tallest mountain, as numberless as the very stars." So says the romantic lover. Unfortunately, in the world of interactive storytelling you can't be this poetically extravagant; you have to carry out calculations with these numbers, so you need normal, workable numbers. Each variable you use must have a maximum value and a minimum value.

 Okay, so what should the maximum be? A thousand? A million? A billion?

The only consideration in setting a maximum is that you should use a scale most people can easily appreciate. For the average person, thinking in terms of 453,287 love points, for example, is hard. I recommend a maximum value of 1.00, which enables storybuilders to think in terms of percentages, should they be so inclined.

As soon as you create a maximum, you must devise a means of enforcing that maximum. After all, if you decide that the maximum value of Affection is 1.00 and then discover that somehow an Actor ended up with an Affection of 1.20, that will certainly wreak havoc with your algorithms. Ergo, you need some means of enforcing your maximum, which is made difficult by most alterations in these values being incremental in nature. That is, if Fred has Affection of 0.38 for Jane, and Jane smiles sweetly at Fred, you need to increase Fred's Affection by some small amount. You don't merely set it to some absolute value because you could end up jerking poor Fred's emotions all over the map.

Suppose, for example, that Jane smiles sweetly at Fred, which you hold to be worth 0.30 Affection, so you set Fred's Affection to 0.30. A moment later, Jane fails to laugh at Fred's lame joke, so you set his Affection down by -0.10. Then she puts her hand on his shoulder to reassure him, and poor Fred's Affection jumps back up by 0.50. You need to blend all these events together to integrate them emotionally. You could use a differential system, like so:

Event	Intrinsic Change	Fred's Affection
Start	-	0.38
Jane smiles sweetly at Fred.	+0.30	0.68
Jane doesn't laugh at Fred's joke.	-0.10	0.58
Jane places hand on Fred's shoulder.	+0.40	0.98

This simple additive system won't work, however, because it can violate your maximum and minimum values. Suppose you extend the table with a few more events:

Event	Intrinsic Change	Fred's Affection
Start	-	0.38
Jane smiles sweetly at Fred.	+0.30	0.68
Jane doesn't laugh at Fred's joke.	-0.10	0.58
Jane places hand on Fred's shoulder.	+0.40	0.98
Jane laughs at Fred's joke.	+0.10	1.08
Jane holds Fred's hand.	+0.30	1.38

Oops! What now? The solution is to apply a stimulus-response relationship that follows an S-curve, as shown in **Figure 11.2**.

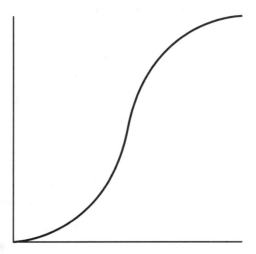

FIGURE 11.2: A simple S-curve for stimulus-response relationships

To do this, you replace simple addition and subtraction with "end-weighted" addition and subtraction. End-weighted addition looks like this:

```
NewValue = CurrentValue + (MaxValue - CurrentValue) ×Increment /
➥(MaxValue - MinValue)
```

End-weighted subtraction looks like this:

```
NewValue = CurrentValue - (MaxValue - CurrentValue) ×Decrement /
➥(MaxValue - MinValue)
```

There's an additional requirement: The increment or decrement can never exceed the MaxValue or MinValue. In other words, your increment can never be greater than 1.00, nor can your decrement be less than -1.00.

Here's an example of how end weighting works in practice. Suppose you start with an initial Affection of 0.00 and a maximum value of 1.00, and then carry out end-weighted addition of 1.0 five times. With simple addition, adding 1.0 five times would yield a result of 5.0, but with end-weighted addition, the results look like this:

Original value:	0.00
After first end-weighted addition:	0.50
After second end-weighted addition:	0.75
After third end-weighted addition:	0.875
After fourth end-weighted addition:	0.988
After fifth end-weighted addition:	0.994

This algorithm ensures that the result always stays under the maximum. It also ensures that every increment to the value has some effect, however tiny it may be.

Putting a Personality Model to Work: An Exercise

Building a personality model can be a huge task, but it's only the beginning. A personality model by itself is useless; the whole point of personality modeling is to equip Actors with the means to make reasonable, understandable decisions.

Decisions are choices between options. You don't decide "27" or "banana"; you decide to execute one option or execute a different option. You might decide to buy 27 screws, or you might decide to eat a banana, but remember that the real options are the verbs: buy and eat.

Therefore, designers must create a system that links the personality model to the verbs. This linkage takes place through mathematical statements (the "inclination formulae" I've mentioned in this and other chapters) that use personality and relationship variables to make choices. One way or another, a personality model must eventually feed its numbers into some sort of mathematical formula that makes decisions. This is a more difficult problem than personality modeling.

To get a clear idea of the difficulties involved, I challenge you to concoct your own personality model. The personality model I have presented in this chapter is certainly not the best possible model, but it reflects my personal artistic sensibilities. There are plenty of other perfectly reasonable personality models, so try your hand at creating one. Remember the basic goals: completeness, conciseness, orthogonality, and tight behavioral linkage. How well can you meet them? The result of your work should be a list of all the variables used in the model, with complete descriptions of their behavioral implications, as I have done earlier in this chapter.

When you're done, evaluate your model with the following questions:

▶ How many variables does my model use? (The fewer, the better.)

▶ What kinds of behaviors can't be discriminated by my model? For example, can it decide whether the girl should kiss the guy passionately or just normally? Can the variables it offers be used to determine whether the sidekick will stand by the hero at the moment of truth, or bolt and run?

▶ If a storybuilder were using your model, would it always be obvious in any situation which variable should be used, or can you imagine situations in which the storybuilder might be torn between two related variables? Might the storybuilder feel a need to use lots of different variables in some complicated mess?

▶ Is your model fine-tuned for a particular type of storyworld, or is it a general-purpose model that could be used in all storyworlds?

Wrapping Up

Building personality models is the least formidable of all the challenges in interactive storytelling. It's not difficult to design a simple personality model, but optimizing one demands considerable finesse. The requirements of completeness, conciseness, orthogonality, and tight behavioral linkage are impossible to satisfy to perfection; designers must make difficult compromises to optimize personality models.

CHAPTER 12
Drama Managers

A MAJOR MENTAL LEAP REQUIRED to understand interactive storytelling is the realization that it concerns storytelling, not story. The most common mistake of beginners is to think in terms of "story plus interactivity." As I have explained earlier, a story is a data structure, and you cannot interact with data; you can only interact with a process. Story is data but storytelling is process. Therefore, we must always think in terms of storytelling, not story.

Storytelling implies a storyteller; interactive storytelling presumes the existence of some kind of algorithmic storyteller built into the software. That storyteller might be called an engine, a system, or an agent, but the term most commonly used is drama manager. Quite a few schemes for interactive storytelling rely heavily on this concept, although the specific implementations of drama managers vary.

Brenda Laurel pioneered this concept nearly twenty years ago with her 1986 doctoral dissertation on the potential of computers in theater. She used the term "Playwright" instead of "drama manager", but her approach laid the groundwork for all subsequent drama managers. Dr. Laurel prepared a list of thirteen basic functions that a Playwright must be able to carry out. Because she was blazing new trails, she sought completeness of coverage rather than economy of definition; her list therefore contains considerable overlap in its entries. With hindsight, we could probably boil the list down to perhaps five or six more abstract entries. Here is her list of required functions[1]:

1. Model the plot in progress.

2. Specify the formal characteristics of upcoming events.

3. Change the storyworld.

4. Modify the goals of actors.

5. Access proposals for future actions of actors.

6. Simulate these proposals to determine their impact on the plot.

7. Evaluate the results of the simulations.

8. Mandate future events.

9. Formulate the script for the next event.

10. Direct the actors.

11. Control its own operation.

12. Remember past events.

13. Learn from past results.

Sadly, Laurel didn't offer any ideas for how these functions would actually be carried out; it's a wish list, not a plan. Still, her work represents the first major attempt to consider the problems of interactive storytelling. A number of researchers have accepted the challenge of actually building this technology, although nowadays they use the term *drama manager* to refer to a software agent that oversees story development and somehow guides it in desirable directions. Chapter 19, "Research," offers a description of this research work.

Laurel's laundry list is also overlong. Although all these functions are desirable, just three fundamental steps are required for a drama manager, all of which spring from my basic definition of interactivity in Chapter 2:

> *A cyclic process between two or more active agents in which each agent alternately listens, thinks, and speaks.*

Listen

The drama manager must monitor the story's progress. This step is simple listening—but listening is not the same thing as hearing. To hear another person speak, you must be able to interpret the noises in terms of the language used. All those squeaks and grunts must be translated into words and sentences, which must then be analyzed to determine their meaning. In the same fashion, a drama manager must interpret the raw material of the developing story (its events) in terms of an abstract drama language. It must recognize the patterns of behavior that differentiate drama from tedium.

The simplest means of accomplishing this step relies on *overview variables*, which are numbers the storytelling engine calculates to assess the storyworld's overall state. For example, you could calculate the sum of all affections held by all Actors for each other; this number would indicate the overall level of "good feeling" in the storyworld system. A low value means that everybody hates each other; a high value indicates universal love and brotherhood. The drama manager monitors this value to determine what to do. If everybody is too happy, maybe it's time to toss something ugly into the mix. If the storyworld has degenerated into a dog-eat-dog jungle, perhaps it's time to bring some balmy sunshine to the cast.

Creating overview variables is a central creative challenge in interactive storytelling. The database for a storyworld will be large: perhaps a megabyte of numeric information. All those numbers can be put together in a staggering number of ways. Here are just a few possibilities for overview variables:

▶ **Gross trust:** The sum of all the trust that all Actors feel for each other; at low values, this variable signals a complete breakdown of social cooperation.

▶ **Acceptability of violence:** A running sum of violent actions; as this sum grows, Actors' inhibitions against violent behavior lower.

▶ **Dullness:** The sum of verb Import values (see Chapter 13, "Verbs and Events") for recent events. If the sum becomes too small, the cast has settled down into a dull period and the storyworld needs some spicing up. Inject some sensational or divisive event.

▶ **Storyworld exploration:** Have all the verbs in the storyworld been used at least once? Has the player spent most of the time using a small set of verbs?

Think

Having developed a coherent dramatic interpretation of the events so far, a drama manager must then determine how the story should progress from that point forward. A number of schemes have been tried for drama manager computations.

A well-designed set of overview variables makes this task easier, as each overview variable indicates some significant factor in story development. The overview variables listed previously suggest some action the drama manager should take. Conceivably, a good drama manager would consist of nothing more than a large set of overview variables, each controlling some action by the drama manager. For example, if the Storyworld Exploration overview variable indicates that the player hasn't used many of the verbs in the storyworld, the drama manager could search through the unused verbs, looking for those verbs that tend to precede the unused verbs. Having identified these *leader verbs*, the drama manager could then generate events using them; this might get the player to travel down some previously unused paths.

Another approach uses *dramatic templates*. The storybuilder generates a large set of templates, each of which constitutes a well-formed story. Then the drama manager matches the story generated so far with each template, searching for the one that best fits the story so far. That template then becomes the guide for action by the drama manager.

A third approach assumes the existence of a *story grammar*, which is a set of rules governing the sequencing of events in a story; it's analogous to grammar in linguistics, but it concerns the connections between narrative components in a story instead of the connections between words in a sentence. This story grammar then provides the basis for calculating story development. Although much has been written about story grammars, precious little has actually been accomplished. Vladimir Propp's work described in Chapter 9, "Data-Driven Strategies," is often cited as an example of a story grammar.

Speak

A drama manager's final task is translating its determinations into some form that will actually change the storyworld in a manner that helps the story evolve in the desired direction. You can use any or all of the following schemes to influence story evolution.

Environmental Manipulation

The most overbearing technique is making environmental alterations in the storyworld. If a player attempts to go over the mountain pass, and your drama manager determines that she should instead be traversing the tunnels underneath the mountains, the drama manager need only throw a few snowstorms and avalanches at the player. If that doesn't work, have the trail end abruptly at the top of a cliff. All manner of physical constraints can be applied to force players into the intended course of action. These devices, however, are often transparent and insulting to players. Use them only as a last resort to save the developing story from catastrophe.

In a different set of circumstances, using environmental manipulation is more satisfying:

It's the climax of the movie. The hero has driven the villain out of his stronghold and pursued him up the craggy mountaintop. The trapped antagonist turns and fights, and the two struggle as the wind tears at their capes and the rain lashes at their faces. A rock gives way under the hero's feet and he slips, nearly plummeting into the yawning chasm below, but somehow his fingers find a handhold and he dangles helplessly at the feet of the delighted villain. The villain sneers and picks up the hero's own sword, raising it high over his head to deliver the deathblow. Suddenly, a bolt of lightning strikes the villain, who plunges off the mountain peak, his final scream echoing off the cliffs. The hero picks himself up and gazes down at the still-falling villain.

The difference between the two examples (snowstorm versus lightning bolt) lies in the matter of free will. In the former case, environmental manipulation is used to foil the player's intentions. The storybuilder has assumed an antagonistic stance with respect to the player. This will never do; storyworlds aren't tests of will between storybuilders and players. In the latter case, the environmental intervention is an integral part of the narrative, not a blatant attempt to block the player. Indeed, there are actually two environmental interventions in this example: the rock giving way beneath the player's feet and the lightning bolt striking the villain. This could be interpreted as a one-two punch delivered by a drama manager who has already determined the story's outcome. The player, having driven the villain out of his stronghold, has successfully concluded the story, and now the only remaining task is to finish off the villain. The drama manager wrings one last bit of drama out of the situation before concluding the story.

Lesson #26
Use environmental manipulation to heighten drama, not foil the player.

Goal Injection
A more subtle scheme is instilling some new goal into an Actor. This new goal, however, must of course be compatible with the Actor's personality; it simply won't do to have Gandalf suddenly decide he wants to make whoopee with Galadriel. This new goal should also be of a temporary nature so that its effects are localized to the immediate situation. If your player as Frodo is just about to do something seriously wrong, make Samwise cross his legs desperately, rock back and forth, and insist that he absolutely *must* go urinate. Then get Samwise into serious trouble, diverting Frodo from his intended course.

Lesson #27
Use goal injection to divert the player toward a better course.

Shifting Personalities

The most elegant solution is altering the personalities of other Actors in such a way as to induce them to make decisions that influence players in the desired direction. This scheme is the most indirect; the drama manager makes changes that will cause events that will change the player. That's what makes it so elegant—but it also makes it difficult. To continue with the *Lord of the Rings* examples, altering Samwise's personality can indirectly influence the behavior of the player as Frodo. If Frodo persists in an obviously futile course, increase Samwise's exasperation with Frodo until Samwise explodes in anger. If Frodo seems unwilling to commit himself to action, increment Samwise's pluck and optimism so that Samwise will encourage Frodo.

Lesson #28
Use a companion with an alterable personality to guide the player.

The Ticking Clock of Doom

The simplest scheme is simply the passage of time. It's easy to set up a sequence of timed plot points that force the story forward. For example, in my Arthurian storyworld, Mordred steadily moves toward rebellion, regardless of player-Arthur's actions. Early in the story, Mordred confronts Arthur and suggests that he step down in favor of Mordred. Arthur, of course, refuses. Some time later, Mordred begins fomenting discord within the social group at Camelot. Later still, Mordred raises the flag of rebellion and begins recruiting an army to attack Arthur. All these events lead inevitably to the climactic battle resulting in the vanquishing of Mordred, the Long Walk Down the Short Spear, or the utter defeat of Arthur. This simple time-based scheme forces the story forward regardless of the player's actions. The player is kept busy reacting to Mordred's actions and striving to retain the loyalty of other Actors. This kind of scheme certainly serves its purpose well, but it must be camouflaged properly lest it appear heavy-handed. No explicit clock should appear; events should simply move forward regardless of the player's actions.

Lesson #29
The Ticking Clock of Doom is effective but must be camouflaged.

Dropping the Fourth Wall

I've saved the worst for last. The crudest scheme is to drop the fourth wall and advise players as to actions that are inhibiting satisfying development of the story. I used this technique rather miserably in my game Trust & Betrayal (1987), so I suppose I can lay a feeble claim to having built the first "interactive" drama manager. Here's an example of a typical response when the game detected a player problem; the following text appeared in a new window onscreen:

> *Chris Crawford is waiting outside, dressed in a zoot suit, swinging a pocket watch by a fake gold chain. "Struck out again, huh, baby?" he taunts. "Maybe you haven't figured it all out yet. Let Uncle Chris give you some advice." He sidles up to you, blocking the escape path you were eyeing. "I bet you just walk in on somebody and start offering them deals, right? Well, maybe you can get away with that kid stuff in the Beginner Level game, but in the Expert Level game, you gotta use your head. Look, how would you feel if somebody came barging into your house talking serious deals about tattling on other people? You'd be pretty reluctant, wouldn't you? Especially if they jumped right into it without so much as a howdy-do? You gotta break the ice first. You walk into somebody's house, you say 'hello.' It's a courtesy thing, you know what I mean? Then you make a little small talk, to sorta warm things up. You can really warm up the conversation by offering some free information about somebody betraying somebody else. Just don't pop the first deal-offer until you've got 'em warmed up and ready. So, baby, the name of the game is…" The sound of a big band playing softly fades into the scene; Chris begins a little soft-shoe and starts singing "Getting to Know You." By God, is he bad! You stand dumbfounded as he dances to the left, disappearing behind a small shed. A clatter of garbage cans terminates the music.*

As you can discern, my claim to fame isn't a particularly proud one.

Lesson #30
Dropping the fourth wall is heavy-handed; use it only for comedic effect.

"Correcting" the Player

Hold on! Didn't you maintain earlier that players should have free will? Don't some of these drama manager ideas tread on that free will?

Well, er, yes, I did say that free will can be maintained, and it's true that some of these ideas abuse the player's free will. Certainly the very notion of "correcting" the player implies imposing the storybuilder's will onto the player.

I have already explained in Chapter 5, "Abstraction," that reconciliation between plot and interactivity can be achieved only by moving to a higher level of abstraction. Therefore, the notion of "correcting" the player derives from an obsession with plot at the concrete level; it's fundamentally misguided and doomed to failure. Storybuilders who assume an adversarial role with players ruin their relationships before they even begin.

Good software designers take full responsibility for their creations. If a user perceives that a problem has arisen, it's not the user's fault; it's the designer's fault. Users can never be in error; if the system consisting of user and software fails to carry out the user's desires, the blame falls entirely on the software design.

That's not fair! What if the user is a mumbling moron who doesn't read the manual?

The degree to which a manual is required is indicative of poor design. A truly brilliant design needs no explanation; its operation is transparent. Of course, this grand ideal is never achieved in practice, but it's certainly a goal of good software design. Mere mortals will never achieve such divine perfection, but inasmuch as designers are playing God every time they create software, they must acknowledge how far short of true divinity they fall—and not blame their users for these shortfalls. To begin the design process with the assumption that the user will make errors betrays the user. The initial assumption should be that the user is always right, so the software must focus on how to respond should the user's wishes deviate from what was anticipated.

But what if players want to do something idiotic? Must the design go along with their idiocy?

If that's what players want, by all means! Remember, they're paying for the software. If they want to jump off a cliff, behave boorishly, squash Bambi, befriend Darth Vader, or pick their noses, who are you to defy them?

But I am the storybuilder, the artist who creates this artistic expression! I'll not be party to perversion and ugliness.

Consider the following text:

;oaiuhoisfhga;/gohnwdgsoiwei;'/oisdgshsd;li 'jwkjs;iowensd;gthwoi

Evil is beautiful.

Murder is nurturing.

2+2 = 5

All this text was created with Microsoft Word. It includes gibberish, outrageous lies, and factual errors. Bill Gates can be considered the creative force behind Microsoft Word; are we to accuse Bill Gates of the aesthetic, intellectual, and moral crimes I have perpetrated with his word processor? Is he an accessory to those crimes? Of course not. The software allows me, the user, to do anything I want, so if I exercise my own free will, is there anybody to blame other than me?

But I have no desire to create a soulless storyworld in which any form of depravity is treated as morally neutral.

You don't have to. If a player chooses to jump off a cliff, kill him. If he behaves boorishly, ostracize him. Your design doesn't have to be morally or aesthetically valueless; it need only *address* all reasonable player options, not *reward* them.

But must I waste my time arranging responses to all manner of crazy player activities?

No, only the reasonable ones. The fact is that no reasonable player will want to jump off a cliff (except in contrived situations), so you don't need to provide for that option. The point I make here concerns the difference between your *preferred* options and *reasonable* options.

Lesson #31

Do not impose your preferences *on players; permit them all reasonable options and then impose the* consequences *of their choices.*

What's the difference between blocking the option to jump off a cliff and killing the player if he does so? Isn't it really the same thing?

Not at all. In the first case, you treat him like a child; in the second, like an adult.

But then the player will have an unsatisfying experience with my design, which will reflect badly on me.

No, it doesn't. Someone who leaps over the barrier rail at the Grand Canyon and jumps off the cliff knows perfectly well whom to blame for the consequences. True, there are immature people who try to blame others for their own errors, but in an interactive experience, the player can always go back, do it differently, and enjoy the improved results—thereby demonstrating beyond any doubt exactly where the original error lay.

If correcting the player is a bad idea, then aren't all drama managers bad ideas?

Only drama managers that oppose the player's wishes are bad ideas. The storybuilder who's creating a drama manager is a guide, not a parent. A guide's role is less obtrusive than a parent's. The feedback a guide provides isn't a black-or-white prohibition or command; it is instead communicated in degrees of encouragement or discouragement. These degrees could be quantified, although most human guides don't express their feedback in numeric form because most people are more literate than numerate. Storybuilders, however, work through the computer as their medium, and the digital medium is unquestionably numerate. Therefore, the feedback drama managers should provide must take numeric form: a score.

 What!? You want to turn stories into games?

No. In the first place, I'm talking about storyworlds, not stories, and storyworlds are larger, more abstract structures than stories. Second, "game" is an overly broad term that can mean many things to many people. I am not proposing to transform *King Lear* into Doom or *The Odyssey* into PacMan. The crucial factor to consider here is the wisdom of the scoring system.

Scoring Systems

Scoring systems, be they for exams, sports, or games, have always been constrained by the computational weakness of the people doing the scoring. For generations, teachers, umpires, and boardgame players had limited computational facilities; hence, scoring systems were clean and simple. The computer blasted away all those limitations, yet scoring systems remain as mathematically primitive as they were in the days of Monopoly. There's no reason for basing scoring on body count or the number of jewels a player has collected.

Example: An Arthurian Storyworld

To illustrate, I'll build an example based on an Arthurian storyworld. The storyworld begins with Arthur married to Guinevere and ruling a land at peace. Arthur's primary concern is his legacy; he would prefer to have an heir and a stable, happy kingdom on his departure. Unfortunately, Guinevere is barren, and Mordred, his illegitimate son, is completely unacceptable as an heir. Therefore, Arthur's first priority is to prevent Mordred from gaining control of the kingdom. This priority is easily reduced to mathematical form:

```
IF (Mordred becomes king)

    THEN Score = -100

    ELSE Score = +100
```

Arthur's second concern is for the kingdom's political stability, which is based on the overall sense of community the other Actors share. A simple way to reduce this idea to numeric form is to calculate the sum total of everybody's good feelings toward each other:

```
GoodFeelingScore  = 0

FOR (all Actor pairings except those including Mordred or Arthur)

    GoodFeelingScore = GoodFeelingScore + Affection[ActorA, ActorB] +
➥Trust[ActorA, ActorB]

Score = Score + GoodFeelingScore
```

Here's an important dramatic point: Death holds no terror for Arthur. He knows he has to die someday, and all that matters is leaving his kingdom in the best possible shape. There's one other loose end he must take care of: Excalibur. The sword is his personal symbol of royal authority; if he cannot find a proper heir, Excalibur must be returned to the waters from which it came. Here's how to express that idea:

```
IF (Arthur dies and Excalibur is returned)

    THEN Score = Score + 20

IF (Arthur dies and Excalibur is not returned)

    THEN Score = Score - 20
```

You could also throw in additional points for dealing with a possible romance between Lancelot and Guinevere: point losses for a romance, small point gains for a reconciliation with Guinevere after an affair. These considerations can just as readily be addressed in the GoodFeelingScore; after all, if the queen cuckolds the king, people are going to get upset with one or all of the three characters and take sides in the dispute. Ultimately, this will have negative effects on the GoodFeelingScore.

You might also want to include some consideration for the Grail search, but I shall ignore that factor here, just to keep things simple.

Here's how this scoring system might evaluate a number of different scenarios:

▶ **A:** Arthur maintains a happy kingdom. Lancelot and Guinevere keep their pants on, everybody loves Arthur, Mordred revolts and is killed in a lopsided battle, Arthur dies in bed, and Lancelot throws Excalibur in the lake. Score: high.

▶ **B:** Arthur keeps the peace, but Lancelot and Guinevere have their romance. Arthur somehow holds things together, sending Guinevere off to a nunnery and banishing Lancelot. Mordred exploits the ill-feelings these events generate to raise an army and revolt, but Arthur defeats and kills Mordred. Excalibur slips beneath the waves on Arthur's death. Score: moderate.

▶ **C:** Guinevere and Lancelot get it on, Arthur executes one or both of them, much fighting ensues, and Mordred reaps all the benefits, kills Arthur, grabs Excalibur, and seizes the throne. Score: negative.

The point of this example is that the scoring system provides strong motivations for the player to behave in a manner consistent with your aesthetic goals, yet it doesn't mandate or prohibit any behavior. The player of this Arthurian game must pursue your intended goals to gain points. People can accept the impositions of a scoring system, but arbitrary constraints on behavior don't go down as well. You can build scoring systems to reflect any dramatic consideration; complexity is not a problem with computers. The only constraint is your discomfort with algorithms.

Lesson #32
Use scoring systems to guide players instead of mandates and prohibitions that constrain them.

Tragedy

Many of literature's greatest stories are tragedies; we shed a tear for the hero who dies in the end, but we know it just wouldn't be right if he lived to a ripe old age and died after tripping over a stool. Shakespeare didn't have to kill Hamlet to resolve the story's core conflict; killing off Claudius would have provided closure. He didn't have to kill Juliet, either; with Romeo out of the picture, the romance was over and the story could have been wrapped up then and there. But, no, he had to finish her off. This brings us to an ugly little problem: How do you reflect this situation in a scoring system? Imagine a Romeo and Juliet storyworld, complete with all the Montagues and Capulets and their conflicts and intrigues. Imagine that it happens to wind up following something like Shakespeare's version, and Romeo does himself in on discovering Juliet's comatose body. The player, as Juliet, wakes up to find Romeo's bloody corpse at her feet. Should the player kill herself or shrug her shoulders and walk away?

Here drama diverges from gameplay. A traditional gamer would certainly not commit suicide; she'd walk away. Drama places a higher value on Juliet's death than on her life, however, so the scoring system must accordingly reward Juliet for suicide and punish her for selfish survival.

 This will never work! Nobody's going to commit imaginary suicide.

The source of the problem lies in the historical happenstance that games have always been comedies (in the dramatic sense that they have happy endings). We think of games ending in victory or defeat, winning or losing. There's no fundamental reason for this association; it's just the way things have always been. For the time being, we must respect the audience's aesthetic expectations. As interactive storytelling develops as a medium, artistically minded storybuilders will expand the audience's aesthetic horizon. This happened with literature in the sixteenth century; originally confined to devotional topics and casual entertainment, writers such as Erasmus and later Jonathan Swift used literature for social commentary. The cinema was initially used for spectacle and sensational material; over the course of several decades, artists such as D.W. Griffith expanded the medium to address serious storytelling. In the same fashion, storybuilders will push the medium so that someday, tragedy will be possible.

 But what possible mechanism could encourage a player to commit virtual suicide?

The trick lies in shifting the player's self-perception as the protagonist. An actor playing a role simultaneously lives inside the character and outside the character. Consider an actress playing the role of Juliet. She must surely identify with Juliet to do her job. She must feel something like the intense love for Romeo and the agony of losing him. To be "in character," she must also feel the emotional logic that drives Juliet to suicide and appreciate the dramatic forces that require her death. This is immersion at its deepest level. A player in the role of Juliet in an interactive storyworld should come to precisely the same decision. The player doesn't have to come to that conclusion, of course. The storybuilder can only reward, not control.

 And how does the storybuilder reward the suicide?

The same way an actor is rewarded: with applause. The storyworld should end with curtains coming down, the words "The End" appearing on the screen, and an auditory virtual audience reaction. If the curtains descend upon a dead Juliet, the virtual audience should erupt in thunderous applause; if she saunters away, boos and hisses should be her reward. Therefore, the player's true role is to perform for a virtual audience; the drama manager evaluates the player's performance with a scoring algorithm and expresses that score with varying degrees of applause.

Lesson #33
In tragedy, the reward is applause, not victory.

Wrapping Up

▶   Drama managers must listen, think, and speak. They listen with overview variables. They think with scoring algorithms, story templates, or story grammars. They speak with environmental manipulation, goal shifting, personality alterations, temporal pressures, or by dropping the fourth wall.

▶   The storybuilder is a guide, not a parent.

▶   Don't block the player from error; reward the player for success.

▶   Express your aesthetic values with your scoring algorithms.

▶   In tragedy, the reward is applause, not victory.

---

1. Brenda Laurel, *Computers as Theater* (Addison-Wesley, 1991; ISBN 0201510480).

CHAPTER 13
Verbs and Events

ONE OF THE IMPLICATIONS OF applying verb-based thinking to interactive storytelling is that the central data structure should be the *Verb*. The answer to the classic question "What does the user DO?" is "The user does Verbs." Because verbs define the nature of any software, it's only natural that defining the Verb data structure is the central problem in all software development.

A Verb, in this context, is not quite the same thing as a verb in a sentence; it's functionally similar but a bit more abstract. A Verb is anything a user can tell the computer to do. The most obvious Verb is clicking a button, but contextual changes can create new verbs.

Thus, if I push the mouse button while the cursor is on the Delete button, I'm specifying an entirely different Verb than pushing the mouse button on the Save button.

Verb Counts

Verb counts in most software have always been low, but with the passage of time, those counts have risen inexorably. MacWrite, the first true consumer WYSIWYG word processor, didn't have a great many verbs. Aside from the obvious verbs for text entry, there were verbs for setting font types, sizes, and styles; verbs for justifying text and indenting paragraphs; verbs for inserting images; and verbs for setting and clearing tabs. All in all, I'd guess there were fewer than 100 verbs in MacWrite. But nowadays, Microsoft Word has so many verbs that when I assign students the task of counting them, they lose count somewhere around 300. What with style sheets, footnotes, index entries, tables of contents, and so on, there are just too many verbs to keep track of.

The same goes for games. The verb counts for games of the early 1980s were generally lower than 10, perhaps because of the simple nature of the joysticks used for input. The only inputs possible were left, right, up, down, and the "fire" button: five verbs. Since then, games have become more complex and verb counts have grown, but in general, the verb counts of today's games seldom exceed 30 and usually average about 15.

No matter how you design it, interactive storytelling requires hundreds or even thousands of verbs. Consider the verb count in this bit of fiction:

> Alas, poor Yorick! I _knew_ him, Horatio: a fellow of infinite jest, of most excellent fancy; he hath _borne_ me upon his back a thousand times. And now how abhorred in my imagination it _is_! My gorge _rises_ at it. Here _hung_ those lips that I have _kiss'd_ I _know_ not how oft. Where _be_ your gibes now, your gambols, your songs, your flashes of merriment that _were_ wont to _set_ the table on a roar? Not one now to _mock_ your own grinning–quite chap-fall'n? Now _get_ you to my lady's chamber, and _tell_ her, let her _paint_ an inch thick, to this favor she must _come_; _make_ her _laugh_ at that.

This single short soliloquoy, just eight lines of text, has 12 different verbs. It constitutes less than half a percent of the entire play; clearly the play as a whole boasts hundreds to thousands of different verbs. Interactive storytelling engines must be capable of handling such large verb counts.

Lesson #34
Interactive storytelling requires thousands of verbs.

Specific Versus Generalized Verb Handling

With low verb counts, designers can craft each verb individually, writing custom code for each one. This method worked fine when you could count your verbs on your fingers, but when you start needing your toes to count, things became more difficult. A program such as Microsoft Word is an intricate maze of code, requiring the efforts of hundreds of programmers, yet its complexity causes it to break with depressing regularity. The difficulty of managing hundreds of custom-coded verbs has restrained software designers. Storybuilders, however, cannot evade the monster; their work requires managing thousands of verbs. You simply must dispense with the notion of custom-designing every verb. You need a more generalized approach, something more abstract that allows you to create, design, and program thousands of verbs.

The first step in creating a generalized system of verb handling is to design a data structure for Verbs. You need a general-purpose table of properties that define each Verb. Here are some variables that might belong in such a table:

Note: Henceforth, I'll be contracting "Direct Object" to "DirObject."

▶ **Name:** A simple text label for the Verb.

▶ **Import:** A number indicating how newsworthy this Verb is.

▶ **TimeToPrepare:** The amount of time required to elapse from the time the Actor decides to execute the Verb until execution begins. Although most Verbs require zero TimeToPrepare, a few might require some. For example, if an Actor decides to poison someone, some time might be required to get the poison. An Actor wanting to hop into bed with another Actor requires a moment to remove clothing.

▶ **TimeToExecute:** The amount of time required to carry out the Verb. Again, most Verbs require just a moment to execute, but a few have extended execution periods—for example, `GoJogging`, `BakeCake`, or `BuildBoat`.

▶ **Audience:** Every Verb has certain requirements for the presence or absence of other Actors. Most of the time, the DirObject must be located with the Subject, but in a few cases the reverse is true. For example, should the Subject be hatching some dark plan aimed at the DirObject, the Subject most definitely wants to carry it out without the presence of the DirObject. `MixPoison`, `DigGrave`, or `DonWeddingDress` are three Verbs that require the absence of a DirObject.

Some Verbs require the privacy of Subject and DirObject and, therefore, the absence of others. Verbs used in romantic situations are often like this. A few Verbs require the presence of a third party, either as a witness or as party to the action. And of course, there are also specifications for whether other Actors present can witness a Verb being carried out. All told, I have identified 10 specific situations that require particular combinations of people present or absent:

▶ **MentalState:** This situation represents an action inside the Subject's mind; others can be present but won't be able to witness it.

▶ **AnyAudience:** The most common situation; the Actor executing the Verb doesn't care about the presence or absence of any other person.

▶ **RequireWitness:** The Subject will not execute the Verb unless some third party is present to witness the Event.

▶ **SubjectOnly:** The Subject wants to carry out the Verb in secret and must be alone.

▶ **SubjectAndDirObjectOnly:** The Subject and DirObject both must be present, but must have privacy.

▶ **AllAudience:** This is a special case for an Event so sensational—the 9/11 attacks, for example—that it is, in effect, instantly made known to all Actors.

▶ **ThreeParty:** An Event requiring the presence of three parties: Subject, DirObject, and a third Actor.

▶ **FourParty:** An Event requiring the presence of four parties: Subject, DirObject, and two other Actors.

- **CheekByJowl:** This is a special case in which two Actors are together in a public place, whispering together. Their actions can't be witnessed by anybody except a person deliberately spying on them.

- **AnybodyBut:** Another rare case, it requires Subject and DirObject, but a specified third Actor may not be present. This situation would arise when, say, Subject is insulting the third Actor to DirObject.

These are the variables most likely to be of value in any verb-based interactive storytelling engine. My own engine uses many more variables, but they are specific to that engine and not worth exploring in this general discussion.

Events

When a Verb is executed, it's part of an *Event*. My use of the term "Event" is very close to its normal use, except that, for purposes of interactive storytelling, Events must be reducible to computer expression. The real world is full of complex and tricky events that defy computational expression, so the requirement of making Events fit inside a computer expression does seem to restrict your creative freedom. But if Michelangelo had to fit his work on the ceiling of the Sistine Chapel, you can work within the constraints of the computer, right? The data structure for Events looks something like this:

```
something or other, something or other VERB something or other,
➥something or other
```

What are all those "something or others"? It should be pretty obvious from the way I've written it that they are things like subjects, direct objects, adjectives, adverbs, and prepositional phrases. For the moment, I'll keep it as simple as possible:

```
Subject Verb
```

This data structure is clean and simple, but it's too constrained for most use. Yes, in a few situations this structure works adequately, as in these examples:

- Sammy slept.

- Mary fretted.

- The fruit ripened.

Face it, however: This kind of sentence just won't handle most situations, but it does bring out an important point. The first two sentences look fine, but that third sentence has "fruit" for a subject. That's a tad peculiar. Yes, we use sentences like this all the time, but for the purposes of drama, requiring that the subject of every sentence be an Actor is more appropriate. In other words, inanimate objects can't do things.

 But how would you say "The fruit ripened" if fruit can't be the subject? Doesn't this make it impossible to record events that are outside the control of any Actor? What about natural events, acts of God, or accidents?

The trick is to use an all-purpose character I call "Fate" to handle these events. Thus, the sentence becomes "Fate ripened the fruit." Actually, I go even further in my engine: I require that every Event take an Actor for Subject and an Actor for DirObject. This forces the peculiar sentence: "Fate ripened Fate the fruit." In other words, Fate does this verb to itself, and the fruit is an indirect object. The principle is simple: Subjects and DirObjects must be Actors. It's occasionally clumsy, as in this example, but then again, how much drama is there in ripening fruit?

I have more to say about Fate in Chapter 18, "The Erasmatron."

Getting back to the sentence structure, expand it one step:

```
Subject Verb DirObject
```

This looks more like a regular sentence. It enables you to handle a broad range of events, such as:

▶ Joe greeted Tom.

▶ Tammy missed Jeanette.

▶ Mordred laughed at Lancelot.

 Just a minute, here! In the third sentence, Lancelot is not the direct object; he's the object of the preposition "at."

Grammatically, you're correct. But is there any functional difference between "Mordred laughed at Lancelot" and "Mordred derided Lancelot"? Aside from some slight differences in nuance between the two verbs, the two sentences say the same thing. Mordred did something to Lancelot. For storyworld purposes, the Verb of the sentence is "laughed at."

 But that's not the way English grammar works!

True, and if you hew to the hard lines set down by the grammarians, you'll never get anywhere. The fact is, language is immensely complex, and you can't model all that complexity. What's needed is a gross but functional simplification of the structure of a sentence. You can't afford to compute with real sentences, so you need Neanderthal sentences that primitive algorithms can handle. As part of this, you'll be simplifying away much of the richness of language. However, reducing "laughed at" to a single verb is fairly straightforward; it doesn't wreak havoc with language. Besides, how do you know that a hundred years from now, people won't have contracted it down to "laftat"?

 But what about "John gave Mary the book"?

You could use an indirect object to handle this problem, but lots of other bits and pieces can get tacked onto the basic Subject-Verb-DirObject sentence structure. Here are some examples:

► Fred met Jane in the parking lot.

► Veronica kissed Toby in front of Anthony.

► George traded his decoder ring to Meredith for her marble.

Or how about this monster:

► Jeanette warned Mika not to be around when Paul arrived.

And there are tons of other even messier sentences you can imagine. You can dismiss many of the complex constructions on the grounds that you couldn't compute with them anyway. At the same time, however, you have to admit that the simple Subject-Verb-DirectObject structure is inadequate. So how do you expand it neatly?

Chomskian, or Recursive, Data Structures

The common solution to the problem of not having the complex constructions you need is to structure sentences in the manner always used in computational linguistics. Each sentence consists of a *noun phrase* and a *verb phrase*. A phrase is a compound structure containing a main word and any modifying phrases. A noun phrase is composed of a noun plus phrases that modify it; a verb phrase is composed of a verb plus phrases that modify it. In many cases, there are no additional modifying phrases, but each modifying phrase can contain its own phrases. Thus, the Chomskian sentence is a *recursive data structure*, containing phrases nested inside phrases.

This data structure makes any programmer's mouth water. Recursive data structures are elegant, powerful, and frigorific. All computational linguistics use such data structures, but are they useful for interactive storytelling? I think not. They're too messy. Every one of those nested phrases has to be interpreted within the context of the sentence. Now, programmers in computational linguistics have succeeded in building programs that accomplish this task, so it isn't technically impossible; indeed, it really isn't that difficult. The problem lies in applying all those nested meanings in a dramatically significant fashion. Sure, you can write a program that can figure out something like "The man with the broken arm gave the dog from around the corner a bone that he had purchased from the Armenian butcher that morning." But figuring out the semantic relationships between all those words is considerably less difficult than figuring out the impact each word has on the event's dramatic significance. Someday, storybuilders will be able to handle this kind of sentence. For now, you have to crawl before you can walk, and I advise you to stick with simpler sentence data structures.

Flat Data Structures

I prefer to use *flat data structures* for sentences. This sentence structure handles the majority of all sentences you'll need to use in interactive storytelling:

```
Subject Verb DirObject IndirectObject
```

Unfortunately, handling the majority of sentences you'll need to use isn't good enough; a few special sentence structures always need to be included. They're rare but essential. Here are a few of them:

```
Subject Trades X (to) DirObject (in return for) Y.
```

```
Subject Tells DirObject (that) (he/she) likes ThirdPerson.
```

Things really go to hell when you nest clauses:

```
Subject Asks DirObject (to) give (him/her) X.
```

```
Subject Tells DirObject (to) go (to) Y.
```

```
Subject Tells DirObject (that) ThirdPerson hates FourthPerson.
```

```
Subject Tells DirObject (that) ThirdPerson told (him/her) (that)
➥FourthPerson (did) Verb (to) FifthPerson.
```

The sad truth is that language is infinitely extensible, and without recursion, you can never hope to handle every reasonable sentence structure. The only recourse is to constrain the storytelling engine to handle a limited subset of all such sentences. This is one of the most painful concessions you must make to technological limitations. Indeed, it's so painful that time and again I have returned to the problem of recursive sentence structures, hoping to find a way to make them work. Perhaps you'll be able to see what I can't and solve this wretched problem. In any case, my own solution is to add two *secondary objects* (SecObjects) to the sentence structure:

```
Subject Verb DirObject SecObject1 SecObject2
```

This structure handles even more of the situations I have found necessary in my engine, but it's not quite as simple as it appears. The Verb defines the precise meaning of each SecObject, so the sentence "Subject trades SecObject1 to DirObject for SecObject2" would be represented as:

```
Subject Trades DirObject SecObject1 SecObject2.
```

The algorithms for the Verb Trades must specify that SecObject1 indicates the item given by Subject, and SecObject2 indicates the item given by DirObject.

The same structure is used very differently in the sentence "Subject asks DirObject to give him SecObject2":

```
Subject Asks DirObject SecObject1 SecObject2.
```

Here SecObject1 supplies the Verb that Subject is asking DirObject to perform, and SecObject2 supplies the item to be given. Again, the algorithms specific to the Verb Asks must indicate the meaning of SecObject1 and SecObject2 in this context.

Having the Verb provide the context under which SecObjects are interpreted is entirely reasonable; this is certainly the case in normal language. However, it does impose additional expectations on the designer as well as the storybuilder; somehow those interpretations have to be built into the algorithms for the Verb. Moreover, the storybuilder must keep those contextual requirements in mind while using the Verb. Misunderstandings between designer and storybuilder here can be the source of many difficulties.

There's no reason that you couldn't use three or more SecObjects; the only problem is that when building a storyworld, you can quickly get lost keeping track of all of them.

 What about all those other elements of a sentence, such as time and place?

I attach a number of housekeeping variables to my sentence structures. For example, a variable called When records the exact time the Event took place, a variable called Where records the Stage on which the Event took place, and several other variables keep track of information required for my Gossip system, which I'll explain in Chapter 14, "HistoryBooks and Gossip."

Wrapping Up

The first step in reducing stories to computable form is to reduce options to Verbs and actions to Events. The ideal structure for an Event is a sentence, although some liberties must be taken to make sentence structure easily computable.

CHAPTER 14
HistoryBooks and Gossip

DRAMA IS DRIVEN BY MORE than just Events; the knowledge or lack of knowledge of Events is just as important. If Romeo had known that Juliet had taken a potion to make her appear dead, he wouldn't have killed himself. Mystery stories always include a pile of facts that different actors provide to the protagonist. Comedies often contrive hilarious situations by giving an actor more or less information than they need. Information, or the lack of it, is central to drama.

HistoryBooks

As the player and Actors move through the storyworld, they generate Events that sometimes influence future decisions. Therefore, you must keep track of every Event that takes place during a single playing of the storyworld. I call this record a *HistoryBook*. In its simplest form, a HistoryBook is nothing more than a temporal record of Events that have taken place in the storyworld.

This information can be useful in preventing repetitive behavior. If Bob wants to insult Fred by insinuating that Fred's mother wears military footwear, Bob doesn't want to diminish the witticism's power by repeating it. The only way to determine whether a player has already used an insult is to consult a HistoryBook. In like fashion, consulting a HistoryBook can prevent other forms of repetitive behavior.

The HistoryBook can also ensure that an Actor has met various preconditions for carrying out an action. For example, suppose the hero seeks to rescue the princess by finding the error in the corporate books. If he has taken his accounting course, he'll be able to locate the error; otherwise, the princess is doomed. In programming, the traditional way to handle this problem is to set up a global flag indicating that the hero has in fact taken his accounting course. With a HistoryBook, setting this flag is unnecessary; the software need only search the HistoryBook for the Event in question.

 This technique is incomparably more complicated than simply storing a flag!

True, but a flag requires custom code, whereas using a HistoryBook is a general solution. The HistoryBook can record whether the hero took a pottery course, a thermodynamics course, or a Chinese language course. It can record whether he cut down the oak tree, obtained the silver key, or destroyed the dragon's diapers. A HistoryBook records everything that has happened, so it can keep track of everything that matters. Instead of looking up special-case conditions, the storytelling engine simply searches the HistoryBook. Sure, it costs more machine cycles, but it saves brain cycles—which is more valuable?

The simplest addition to a HistoryBook is including causal information that establishes the sequence of Events in logical form *and* temporal form. This is easily done by working backward; each Event merely records the index number of the causal Event immediately preceding it (the *proximate* cause).

Take a look at an example of a sequence of Events in a HistoryBook (see **Figure 14.1**). The sequence begins with Event #12, Tom spilling soup on Mary at time 20. Mary pokes Tom in the eye (Event #13), and Tom puts a pie into Mary's face (Event #14).

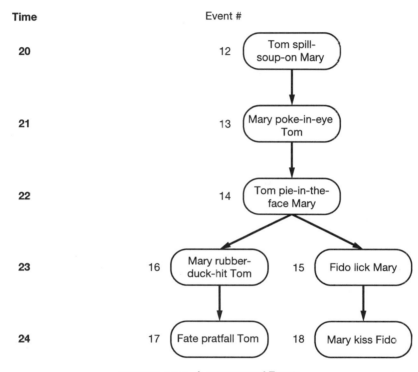

FIGURE 14.1: A sequence of Events.

These three actions are simple; the causal Event is simply the preceding Event. But then the action splits. Fido licks the cream pie off Mary's face (Event #15) while Mary blindly swings a rubber duck at Tom (Event #16). The causality isn't linear now; the causal Event for Event #15 is Event #14, but the causal Event for Event #16 is also Event #14. Fate's action (Event #17) is caused by Event #16, but Mary's action (Event #18) is caused by Event #15. Therefore, you'd need to keep a separate record of the causal Events for each Event in the HistoryBook.

In this example, the record would look like this:

Event	Causal Event
12	---
13	12
14	13
15	14
16	14
17	16
18	15

Forward causation is more difficult to record because of its branching nature. Every event in drama has but one causal Event, but it can have several consequent events. It's technically possible to keep track of forward causation with the proper data structures, but in practice these design contortions are unnecessary; simple brute-force searches of a HistoryBook can run quickly enough, given its small size and the high speed of current processors. For example, to find the consequent Events of Event #14 in the preceding example, you'd simply search through all Events, looking for those with a causal Event #14.

Gossip

Drama seldom relies solely on the direct experience of actors; often crucial dramatic information is communicated indirectly through the statements of intermediary actors. Sometimes this technique is used to heighten the dramatic impact or to give the recipient of information the freedom to declare a reaction to the event by describing it in judgmental terms. Any adequate interactive storytelling system must provide for transmitting information among Actors. I refer to information transmission systems as *Gossip* systems. Such systems are inescapably complicated. I shall first outline the procedure used in the Gossip system of my own interactive storytelling technology; then I shall discuss some of the finer points and possible variations on the basic structure.

Recording Events

When an Event takes place, it's recorded in the HistoryBook. A limited number of Actors are privy to the Event: usually those who populate the Stage on which the Event takes place. This is reflected in an array labeled IKnow that I attach to the Event data structure. Whenever an Actor witnesses an Event, the IKnow flag for that actor is set to true. But that's not all—the Actor also keeps a list of the juiciest bits of gossip, called the *headline list.* There's no reason you couldn't make the headline list for each Actor long enough to include every single Event he or she is privy to, but in practice such thoroughness would be wasteful. Most Actors need only 10 or 20 Events as grist for gossip. I suppose you could get away with only one Event for use in Gossip, but I think it prudent to keep more to ensure that an Actor doesn't run out of material to gossip about.

Each Event in the headline list is prioritized according to its Import (the value assigned to each Verb specifying the degree of dramatic intensity associated with carrying out the Verb). For example, the Import of an insignificant Verb such as ChatWith might be only 1; the Import of a sensational Verb such as Murder might be 10. The engine can then sort Verbs in the headline list by their Import values, with higher Import values placed at the top of the headline list. If a new Event has a higher Import value than the lowest Event in the headline list, it replaces that Event.

Constructing Tales

A headline is not a story; it's the peak event of the story, the most salient event in the story. Having established which headline to reveal, the storytelling engine must then flesh in the Events that are dramatically proximate to the headline. For example, if a newspaper headline is "John Shot Tom," it won't do to simply announce that fact—readers will demand to know the events that immediately preceded and followed the headline. In a storytelling system, that sequence of events is what I call a *Tale.* Thus, you require an algorithm that can isolate Events surrounding the headline from the overall list of Events in the HistoryBook.

By itself, this task isn't particularly difficult. You start at the headline Event's entry in the HistoryBook, working backward through the causal chain of Events. You stop when there's a temporal or spatial break in the Tale. In other words, you keep stepping backward in the HistoryBook until you reach a causal Event that took place on a different Stage or a long time ago. For example, suppose you have the headline Event "John Shoots Tom" and the following Events just before it in the HistoryBook:

Tom enters the bar.

John beats Dick in the poker game.

Gus orders a whiskey from the barkeep.

Tom orders a sarsaparilla from the barkeep.

John makes fun of Tom.

Tom ignores John.

John confronts Tom.

Gus moves out of the way.

Tom shoves John.

John punches Tom.

Tom hits John over the head with a whiskey bottle.

John shoots Tom.

It's not difficult to step backward from the headline Event to the Tale's initiating Event: "Tom enters the bar." Nor is it difficult to skip over the events involving the poker game and Gus. The resulting Tale is clear:

Tom enters the bar.

Tom orders a sarsaparilla from the barkeep.

John makes fun of Tom.

Tom ignores John.

John confronts Tom.

Tom shoves John.

John punches Tom.

Tom hits John over the head with a whiskey bottle.

John shoots Tom.

Stepping forward from the headline Event to trace its consequences is trickier business because there can be several consequent Events. Consider the following sequence of Events subsequent to the shooting:

John shoots Tom.

Dick draws gun and jumps behind bar.

Jane screams for help.

Tom dies.

John laughs over Tom's body.

Dick shoots at John.

Jane screams for help again.

John shoots back at Dick.

Dick ducks under cover.

Jane cries over Tom's body.

John shoots at Dick again.

Dick shoots John.

John dies.

The process of Tale construction creates a new and particularly difficult problem for which I have developed no ideal solution. What happens if the gossiping Actor is unaware of the entire Tale? For example, what if Mary walks into the bar just after Tom orders his sarsaparilla? Worse, what if she walks into the bar just as John shoots Tom? Her version of the Tale is incomplete. Yet Mary does indeed know about the headline Event, so no other Actor will be tempted to tell her the complete story.

My solution is to lock the Stage doors while any activity is taking place onstage, so that nobody can enter or leave until the activity has died down. This solution is the most dramatically reasonable one; in stories or movies, you rarely see a character wander in or out of a scene in the middle of some important action. However, this solution imposes a severe and arbitrary constraint. What if John tries to escape from the bar but can't leave because Jane is still crying over Tom's body? That's a silly situation.

Another solution is to permit Actors to witness only fragments of a Tale, but fill in the empty portions automatically after the action ends. For example, if Mary walks into the bar just as John shoots Tom, she watches the action unfold and then, after the activity in the bar stops, she's magically made aware of the Events preceding the climax she witnessed. It's as though she asked the others present "What happened before I walked in?" and they filled her in.

Another troubling situation is exemplified by this familiar story:

> *Fiona tries to grab the arrow in Shrek's butt. Shrek evades her. She lunges for the arrow and Shrek jerks away; the two topple to the ground, Fiona on top of Shrek. Donkey enters the stage. Donkey sees Fiona on top of Shrek and draws incorrect conclusions as to the reason for Fiona sending him away.*

Here, Donkey's entrance partway through the tale is central to the dramatic meaning. Later in the movie, Shrek reaches the windmill just in time to hear the end of Fiona's confession to Donkey and completely misinterprets the meaning of her words. Clearly, partial knowledge of a Tale can be of great dramatic utility. Unfortunately, most cases of incomplete knowledge lead to chaos, not drama. I haven't succeeded in devising a scheme for winnowing the dramatic from the chaotic.

Finding a Gossip-Mate

The end result of all these calculations is a headline list for each Actor and a means for constructing a Tale for each of those headlines. The next task is to start moving the gossip around—that's when the fun begins!

Initiating Gossip

There are several ways to initiate Gossip. It could be an autonomous process, driven by the engine. If an Actor has nothing better to do, the engine searches for a likely Gossip-mate. It could be prioritized according to the Gossip's value; an Actor who has just come across a particularly juicy item of Gossip sets aside low-priority plans and scurries off looking for somebody to regale. It could also be a consciously chosen course of action: An Actor must actively declare an intent to Gossip in order to do so.

With the Erasmatron, I chose to make Gossip an autonomous process for all actors. It happens automatically, like breathing. I did so because I found that presenting options to Gossip was a tedious burden on the player. Gossip in the Erasmatron system is automatic, requiring no action on the player's part.

Why People Gossip

Before you can build a Gossip system, you need to come up with a model of why people gossip. I could get into a lot of psychology here, but remember, this is drama, not real life; the goal is not to model reality but to come up with a dramatically useful model of gossip.

Therefore, the primary purpose of a Gossip system is to move information through the cast of Actors. Information is interesting only so long as some people know it and other people don't; after everyone knows it, gossip's dramatic value evaporates.

An Actor is motivated to share Gossip by its value to the listener. If I tell you a choice bit of gossip that interests you, your attitude toward me will improve. You'll trust me more because I have taken you into my confidence by revealing the gossip, and you'll feel more affection toward me for granting you this small boon. And you'll likely heighten your estimate of my overall power because you'll believe I have access to all manner of useful information. From my point of view, sharing gossip is advantageous.

But Actors must share their information parsimoniously. Giving information to a blabbermouth guarantees that the information will quickly spread through the cast, robbing the original source of the value of telling it directly to other Actors. The ideal situation from the original source's point of view is to inform the least loquacious Actors first, and then spread the news further. The blabbermouths should be the last ones to know; that way they can't steal the originating Actor's thunder.

A secondary consideration is the degree of affection the originating Actor holds for the listener. Affection motivates the originator to spill the beans.

The Mechanism

The Gossip process begins when an Actor enters a Stage. The entering Actor considers in turn each Actor on the Stage, evaluating the desirability of gossiping with him or her. This decision turns on such factors as the trust and affection the entering Actor has for other Actors. The loquaciousness of the Actor under consideration is also a factor, as mentioned in the preceding section.

The entering Actor chooses the most likely Actor with whom to Gossip, and then determines whether that Actor is good enough to share information with. In other words, the first calculation establishes the *relatively* best Actor of all the others on Stage, and the second calculation decides whether that Actor is good enough in *absolute* terms to be trusted with Gossip. The first calculation depends on the other Actor's characteristics; the second calculation depends on the entering Actor's loquaciousness. Gabby Actors share information with anybody; actors with low loquaciousness are less likely to do so.

Having decided *whom* to Gossip with and *whether* to Gossip with that Actor, the entering Actor must now determine *what* information to share. Obviously, the Actor wants to start with the most important headline, but the importance of an Event to a particular Actor isn't merely a matter of the Verb's intrinsic importance. The importance (that is, the Import value) is modulated by the Actor's closeness to the Subject and DirObject of the Event. In other words, learning about the murder of some nameless person on the other side of the planet probably won't evoke much interest from you, but your brother murdering your wife would be intensely interesting to you. Hence, the personal Import of any Event is the product of that Event's Verb Import multiplied by the magnitude of the relationship variables the Actor feels for the Subject and the DirObject.

Which relationship variables should be used for this calculation?

This question breaks down into two subordinate questions: Which variables should be used, and should their absolute values or signed values be taken into consideration? (Absolute values are only the size of a number; signed values keep track of whether that number is positive or negative. For example, the absolute value of -27 is 27, and the absolute value of 27 is 27.) You could confine your considerations to a single salient relationship variable, most likely Affection; this is certainly justifiable. My preference is taking all relationship variables into consideration because people remain interested in gossip even about those for whom they feel no affection. For example, if a company executive is caught in a compromising situation, employees gossip about it, even though they might have no affection or disaffection for that executive. The power the executive holds over employees creates a relationship that might not involve affection, but nevertheless commands their personal interest.

The second subordinate question is easier to answer: You should use the absolute values, not signed values, of relationship variables. In other words, people are just as interested in gossip about those they hate as about those they love. Gossip is rendered boring by the *lack* of a relationship with its subject, not whether that relationship is negative. Here's the result of these deliberations in mathematical form:

```
Value of telling Event A to ActorB = Import[Verb[Event A]] ×
➡(AbsoluteValue(PerVirtue[ActorB, Subject] × PerVirtue
➡[ActorB, DirObject]) + AbsoluteValue(PerIntegrity[ActorB, Subject] ×
➡PerIntegrity[ActorB, DirObject]) + AbsoluteValue
➡(PerPower[ActorB, Subject] × PerPower[ActorB, DirObject])))
```

`PerVirtue`, `PerTrust`, *and* `PerPower` *are explained in Chapter 11, "Personality Models."*

A few other considerations go into the process of deciding which headline Event to talk about. One is whether the listener already knows the information. This consideration provides a perfect example of the difference between physical reality and dramatic reality. In physical reality, you don't know what events another person knows, which leads to all those boring and pointless sequences of "Did you hear that…" "Oh, you did? Never mind." You don't need this kind of clutter in your storyworld, and you don't have to put up with it because the computer can look inside Actors' minds and establish what they already know. Therefore, your Gossip system should automatically eliminate from consideration any information the listener already knows.

After all these momentous calculations, the actual consummation of Gossip is disappointingly simple: The engine sets the `IKnow` flags for all Events in the Tale to be true for the listener, and the listener can enter these Events into his headline list. There's no need for explicit conversation to take place between the Actors, unless one of the Actors is the player.

Lies

In terms of drama, the yin of information demands the yang of disinformation. Where would storytelling be without the protagonist misled by some dastardly lie? Any Gossip system must include provisions for lying.

In terms of the data structures I have presented, a *Lie* is nothing more than an Event that never happened. It contains all the same data: Subject, Verb, DirObject, and so forth. But one tiny addition must be made to the Event data structure to accommodate lying: a Truth boolean flag indicating whether the Event is true or false. Normal Events have this flag set to true, meaning that the Event is real and true, but Lies will have this flag set to false.

Creating a Lie is simple to implement but difficult to plan. First, the liar has to make the decision to lie. Several motivations, discussed in the following sections, might apply.

Intent to Harm Relationships

The simplest motivation for lying is to wreak some injury upon the victim with a besmirching lie. The first task is to determine whether the goal is damaging the victim's relationship with a particular Actor or damaging the victim's overall reputation with the overall cast. In each case, the liar selects the most salient relationship (that is, the relationship with the highest value) to attack. Next, the liar must search through the storyworld vocabulary to find inclination formulae requiring the desired perceived value of the intrinsic variable (Integrity or Virtue, for example) the liar wants to sully. The best of these inclination formulae (that is, the inclination formula with the strongest reliance on a negative value of the target intrinsic variable) identifies the Verb that should form the basis of the Lie.

Here's an example. Suppose that Al wants to hurt Oecolampadius with a Lie. The values of Oecolampadius's personality traits are as follows: Virtue 27, Integrity 81, and Power 19. Integrity has the highest value, so that's the one to attack. Al next searches through all the scripts of all the Verbs, looking for an inclination formula using Integrity in a negative sense (that is, low Integrity increases the chances of selecting that Verb). He discovers an inclination formula for the Verb Betray that looks like this:

```
Inclination[Betray] <= PerVirtue[You, Subject] - Integrity[You] / 2
```

This inclination formula indicates that only a person with very low Integrity would chose the verb Betray. Hence, Al chooses Betray as the verb for the Lie.

Having decided on the Verb, the only remaining problem is to select an appropriate DirObject. The danger here is that the DirObject will almost certainly know that the Event never happened, so the liar must select a DirObject who is remote from the overall cast or isn't trusted. The simplest solution is for the liar to use himself as the DirObject—if this accomplishes the relationship alteration the liar wants. For example, a female liar could easily besmirch a male victim in the eyes of that victim's girlfriend by claiming that the male victim slept with her. However, the liar can't use himself as the DirObject in some situations. For example, if the liar wants to impugn the victim's benevolence, but everybody knows the victim hates the liar, then circulating the lie that the victim insulted the liar will accomplish little.

After the DirObject has been selected, the liar need merely create the falsehood as an Event with Subject (the victim of the lie), Verb, and DirObject. The liar then inserts the Lie into the HistoryBook, setting the Truth boolean flag to false and the IKnow flag for himself to true. At this point, the liar can simply let the normal Gossip mechanism take over, trusting it to spread the word to the appropriate people as opportunity permits.

Gain Benefit Through Misdirection

A more common motivation for a Lie is to misdirect its victim in some manner that causes beneficial Events for the liar. Drama usually requires that the lie induce its victim into some undesirable situation. For example, Princess Fiona tells Donkey to go into the forest and find a blue flower; she does so to dismiss Donkey, not for medicinal reasons. Sad to say, these lies require complex inference engines. The technology exists, but integrating an inference engine into a storytelling engine is not a first-generation problem. (Indeed, the entire issue of Gossip might be fairly characterized as second-generation technology. After all, it's entirely possible to deliver decent interactive storytelling without any Gossip systems.)

I address the possible uses of inference engines in Chapter 15, "Anticipation."

Defensive Denial

A liar might want to deflect suspicion from himself for some improper action by explicitly denying it. The question is, what is the probability that the Lie can be exposed by external means? This in turn depends on how many people know the truth and whether they can be trusted to keep it secret. A high probability of exposure suggests that it's best to own up to the crime; otherwise, make like a politician and lie, lie, lie!

Secrets

Another form of mal-information is revealing a Secret, which is a true Event that the Subject wants to remain unknown by others. Jane tells Mary "Don't tell anybody, but I'm pregnant by Fred!" Mary then tells Adrienne, who tells Marcy, who tells someone else, and pretty soon everybody knows the news—much to Jane's chagrin. Telling, keeping, and revealing secrets are crucial elements of drama, yet managing the mechanics of this behavior is complex.

I attach to each Event a boolean flag labeled, amazingly enough, Secret, that indicates whether the Event is expected to be kept secret. The Secret is "owned" by the Subject of the Event, and an Actor's respect for the Secret is determined by his or her relationship with the owner.

Here's another interesting example of the distinction between dramatic reality and physical reality: If Fred and Jane have sex and Jane gets pregnant, the physical reality might be reported as "Fred impregnates Jane" because the active role is normally attached to the male. But if the story context makes Jane's pregnancy the important factor, the Event should be recorded as "Jane becomes pregnant by Fred." Jane is, in terms of the drama, the more important Actor, so she should be treated as the Subject. Moreover, this way, she owns the Secret.

Any Event worthy of secrecy will be known by only a few at first, perhaps just the Subject or DirObject. Indeed, for some Events (for example, "Mike decided to kill Adam"), only the Subject has knowledge of them. What causes the Secret to spread?

Realistically speaking, most people would keep these secrets to themselves. But this is drama, not reality, so it's important that the Secret's owner divulge it to somebody else. That's how you get the dramatic pot bubbling. Perhaps nothing will come of it—but it could just as well lead to all sorts of dramatic mayhem. What fun!

This dramatic effervescence arises from a kind of "trust gradient." Jane trusts only Mary, but Mary trusts Adrienne, so Mary tells Adrienne, who trusts and tells Marcy, and so forth. In each case, the bean-spiller advises the recipient to keep it a secret, but the recipient divulges the information to a trusted friend to gain the benefits of sharing Gossip.

Of course, eventually everybody knows, and when the Secret's owner discovers this, there's hell to pay. But what are the accounting details required to pay hell? How can the Secret's owner respond to the betrayal?

The Grapevine

What prevents people from telling every lie and divulging every secret? Answer: the likelihood of sanctions if discovered. The key issue here is discovery; people lie and blab secrets because they believe they won't be caught, but sometimes they *are* caught. Therefore, you need a mechanism that permits improper gossip to be discovered—but only sometimes. In other words, there must be a chance of getting caught, but not so high as to make it overly risky. My solution to this is the *Grapevine* (as in "I heard it through the grapevine").

The basic idea is to keep track of who told what to whom. For each item of Gossip, you have to maintain a record of every transmission of that item. In other words, if Larry concocts the lie that John slept with Margaret and then tells that lie to Dave, and Dave tells Fred, who in turn tells both Mary and Sam, and Mary tells Jane while Sam tells Agnes and Tabitha, and Tabitha asks Margaret why she slept with John, then Margaret has to be able to deny the lie and demand that Tabitha reveal her source for the lie. **Figure 14.2** makes this complicated mess easier to understand.

Assembling the data structure required to keep track of this tree isn't difficult. Its value is that Margaret, upon learning of the lie being told about her, can demand "Who told you that?" Tabitha can then choose to spill the beans about Sam or lie, depending on how her attachment to Sam compares to her attachment to Margaret. If she does reveal that Sam was her source, Margaret can go to Sam and make the same demand. In this fashion, Margaret could trace the lie all the way back to its source. This is cumbersome, of course, but the existence of this possibility is the best deterrent to lying.

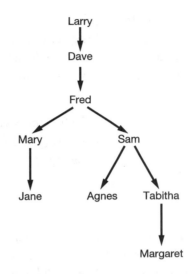

FIGURE 14.2: A typical grapevine.

One possible objection is that this system would quickly spawn an impossibly large pile of meaningless data. Most events aren't worthy of this treatment; why waste computer resource on such a low-priority task?

The trick is that the Grapevine system doesn't consume much RAM. It keeps track of the tree for every Event, but after every Actor has learned of the Event and carried out his or her reaction to it—if any—the storytelling engine dismisses the information. If everybody has heard the news and nobody has anything left to do about it, there's no longer any point in storing the information.

A more serious objection is that successfully tracking the falsehood all the way back to its source is most unlikely. For Margaret to nail Larry, she needs the cooperation of Tabitha, Sam, Fred, and Dave. Should even one of those people decide to protect Larry, Margaret will be stumped. But the real value of this situation lies in the element of suspicion. Suppose, for example, she traces the lie as far back as Sam, who insists that he can't recall who told him (or maintains that he didn't tell Tabitha). This adds grist for the dramatic mill, creating tension between Sam and Tabitha: "Why did you tell Margaret that I told you about her? Now Margaret's on my case!" It also reduces Margaret's trust in Sam. Moreover, she can try to guess Sam's possible informants based on her third-person trust relationships, thereby getting a step or two closer to the source. Thus, Margaret is able to develop suspicions she can then act on—and the plot thickens.

Despite these possibilities, the clinching argument for the Grapevine system is the need for some fair and workable deterrent to lying. Accountability, which the Grapevine system makes possible, is that deterrent.

Wrapping Up

Rare is the protagonist who doesn't stumble at some point in the story over a lack of information, some misinformation, or an unfortunately revealed secret. Information transfer among members of the cast is always an important component of most narrative. Accordingly, any storytelling engine must include provisions for recording information and for Actors manipulating that information.

CHAPTER 15
Anticipation

I LEARNED A HARD LESSON in my early work with interactive storytelling. I was building my engine around an Arthurian storyworld that included Arthur, Guinevere, and Lancelot. In keeping with the conventions of the basic story, I provided for the possibility of Lancelot falling in love with Guinevere. While I was running one of numerous tests on the storyworld, Lancelot did indeed fall for Guinevere, and the two of them consummated their love in the forest.

Now, this verb `MakeLoveTo` had a high `Import` value, and of course the Gossip section of the engine calculated that, because Lancelot was Arthur's best friend and Guinevere his wife, Arthur would have high interest in any event involving both of them. Accordingly, when Lancelot next encountered Arthur, he searched through his headlines and found the one that would most interest Arthur: "Arthur, did you hear? I had sex with your wife!"

Lesson #35
It's difficult to recognize how astoundingly stupid an apparently reasonable algorithm can be.

Including Anticipation

The factor I had left out was anticipation: Lancelot should have anticipated Arthur's likely reaction to the news that he had slept with Guinevere and, accordingly, held his tongue. But the algorithm for anticipation, it turns out, was far more difficult to design than most other algorithms in the engine.

There are two fundamental problems. First, to anticipate another's reaction to something, you must put yourself in that person's place. Lancelot must, in effect, pretend he's Arthur, and then imagine how he would feel in Arthur's shoes. This task requires a considerable amount of computational legerdemain. The second problem is that you're attempting to determine Arthur's reaction in a subjunctive sense: *If* Arthur knew of the event, how would he react?

I had already built into the engine the capability for Actors to have emotional reactions to Events, so I had code in place to ensure that if Arthur discovers Lancelot's betrayal, he would become very angry. The problem was that this emotional reaction was part of the *real* reaction to the Event. In other words, the only way to figure out how Arthur would react was to have him actually react, in which case, he'd kill Lancelot. The whole point of anticipation is to see these things coming *before* they happen. I needed to create a virtual world *inside* the virtual world of the storyworld, a temporary imaginary world inside Lancelot's head where Arthur could react to the news, and Lancelot could observe his reaction in safety and then act accordingly in his real world.

This example illustrates a general problem known in computer science as *recursion*. When a calculation must be carried out inside itself (Lancelot's reaction anticipates Arthur's reaction inside itself), you must use this exotic and confusing method. Unfortunately, recursive code places stringent requirements on program design, and those requirements would have forced me to completely rewrite most of the engine code, so I had to find another way.

There are two possible approaches you could use. In the first, you calculate the listening Actor's likely reaction (that is, the Verb the listener will likely choose upon hearing the news), and then determine whether that reaction is desirable from the speaker's point of view. I rejected that approach for my own engine because it simply defers consideration of the emotional reaction, which is the factor that really matters here. You could follow an endless logical tree of possible reactions, but the further you go down that tree, the hazier your calculations grow and the messier everything gets.

In the second approach—the one I settled on—you go directly to the emotional reaction. The engine calculates the listener's emotional reaction and determines whether it's desirable from the speaker's point of view. This approach requires specifying an emotional reaction for every Verb. When Actors witness or learn of an Event, they must be able to calculate their emotional reaction. Moreover, Actors should react only to Subjects, not DirObjects of Events. The Subject is the Actor actually performing the action; the DirObject exercises no free will in being acted upon. This method saves storybuilders the trouble of specifying the target of the reaction.

For example, Lancelot's problem would be tackled by presenting the Event "Lancelot sleeps with Guinevere" to the virtual Arthur and running him through the calculations of his emotional reaction to Lancelot. The engine obtains those emotional reaction values and feeds them back to Lancelot, who can then use them to determine whether he wants to tell Arthur.

Most Verbs give you no problem with this restriction on reactions, and those few Verbs that might cause trouble are easily dealt with. In the case of Lancelot sleeping with Guinevere, you need only precede that Event with an Event by which Guinevere explicitly agrees to sleep with Lancelot. Arthur can react to this first Event (Guinevere agreeing to sleep with Lancelot) in forming his reaction to Guinevere and react to the second Event (Lancelot sleeping with Guinevere) in forming his reaction to Lancelot. This strategy keeps reaction calculations simple: The Actor reacts to one person at a time. Of course, it requires that Gossip be communicated by Tales rather than by single Events.

For more information on Tales, refer back to Chapter 14, "HistoryBooks and Gossip."

Therefore, when a speaker considers whether to reveal information to a listener, the speaker merely evaluates the listener's emotional reaction to make his decision. The speaker adds up the changes in PerVirtue, PerIntegrity, and PerPower toward him. A positive sum means that the listener, upon hearing this news, will be more favorably inclined toward the speaker, so the speaker will reveal the Gossip.

However, this calculation applies only when the speaker is also the Subject of one or more Events in the Tale. When the Tale contains Events in which other Actors are the Subject, the speaker should take into account the listener's emotional reaction toward those Actors. Even if Lancelot were, by some odd fluke, unconcerned with Arthur's reaction toward him, he would still want to consider Arthur's likely reaction toward Guinevere. The loss of PerVirtue, PerIntegrity, and PerPower that Arthur would feel toward Guinevere would be bad for Guinevere, and because Lancelot retains high PerVirtue for Guinevere, this outcome is undesirable from Lancelot's point of view. Therefore, you must add a factor to the calculation for the desirability of revealing the Event to him; that factor includes the cost to Guinevere of telling Arthur about the tryst. It should be similar to the first factor: the sum of changes in Arthur's PerVirtue, PerIntegrity, and PerPower for Guinevere upon learning of the tryst. However, this sum should be weighted in proportion to Lancelot's PerVirtue for Guinevere. If his love for her is the maximum possible value, Arthur's reaction toward Guinevere should be just as important to Lancelot as Arthur's reaction to Lancelot himself. If his love for Guinevere is, say, only half the maximum, Arthur's reaction to Guinevere should receive half-weight.

Moreover, these calculations have a negative side. Suppose Mordred is the one who possesses the information about Guinevere's adultery. His calculation shows that Arthur will have a negative reaction toward both Lancelot and Guinevere. Because Mordred hates both Lancelot and Guinevere, he calculates that Arthur's reaction to the news will be harmful to both of them, so he's highly motivated to reveal the news.

This approach boasts high emotional acuity. Suppose, for example, Arthur beat Guinevere and is now considering telling Lancelot about the beating. Arthur knows that Lancelot likes Guinevere, so revealing that he hurt her could damage Lancelot's relationship with him. Conversely, if Arthur thinks that Lancelot hates Guinevere, he'll calculate that revealing this information will ingratiate him to Lancelot.

There's another complicating factor to consider. Suppose that Lancelot prudently declines to mention his adultery to Arthur, but then he encounters Mordred. Mordred's reaction is of no concern to Lancelot, so he might be tempted to reveal the fatal truth—which of course Mordred would be eager to learn so that he could use it to weaken the bonds that tie the trio together. Conceivably, the same factors that would make Lancelot unwilling to talk to Mordred about anything would protect him in this case. But unless this problem is handled explicitly, the engine might produce foolish use of Gossip.

The solution to this problem lies in calculating the likelihood of information reaching Arthur from the listener. This calculation can be tricky, but it makes use of the same algorithms that underlie the Gossip system, so no new algorithms need be developed. The only new factor is considering the likelihood that an Actor will betray a Secret; this factor is calculated from that Actor's loyalty to the Secret-holder in relation to his loyalty to the listener he's considering telling the Secret to. Be warned: These calculations can become quite intricate.

For example, if Lancelot is considering telling Galahad about his affair with Guinevere, he needs to determine whether he can trust Galahad. Is Galahad loquacious? Is Galahad's PerVirtue toward Lancelot higher than his PerVirtue toward Arthur? If the first PerVirtue is higher than the second, that means Galahad likes Lancelot more than he likes Arthur, which suggests that he'll keep the Secret.

Lesson #36
Calculating anticipation behavior requires complex algorithms.

Choosing Verbs

Anticipation can also be applied in any decisions Actors make. After all, Lancelot and Guinevere should have taken Arthur's likely reaction into account when they first decided to bed down, not just when they decide whether to talk about it. The basic approach is to add an automatic factor to the inclination formula for the Verb in question. That factor is similar to the factor for determining the desirability of revealing information, but there are two additional considerations. First, in the Gossip system, you're considering one person's likely reaction; for a Verb option that an Actor is considering, every other Actor's likely reaction must be taken into account. In other words, when Guinevere decides whether to sleep with Lancelot, she must consider the reaction of every Actor in the cast. She must then weight (not weigh: *weight*) each Actor's reaction by her own relationship with that Actor. All those reactions should then be added up to produce an overall assessment of how unpopular the decision might make her.

Here's a simplified example of the process: Guinevere is considering whether to sleep with Lancelot. She needs to figure out whether people will react favorably or unfavorably to this decision. For simplicity, I'll boil down the reaction to a single variable called PersonalEvaluation. This variable measures how favorably or unfavorably an Actor would regard Guinevere's decision to sleep with Lancelot. Remember that Guinevere doesn't want to treat all Actors equally; she cares more about how her friends react than how acquaintances react. So the algorithm she would use looks like this:

```
OverallValue = 0.0

For every Actor in the cast:

    OverallValue = OverallValue + PersonalEvaluation(ThatActor) ×
➥PerVirtue[Guinevere, ThatActor]
```

Each PersonalEvaluation is weighted by Guinevere's emotional attachment to that Actor. People she cares about are given more weight in the calculation; their opinions count for more. Conversely, people Guinevere doesn't like are given negative weight; if they don't like her action, so much the better, as far as she's concerned.

Second is considering the probability that the Event can be kept secret. If, for example, Guinevere is contemplating adultery with Lancelot, she knows it's very much in her interest as well as Lancelot's to keep it secret. If they carry out their affair in secrecy, she can be confident that Lancelot will not reveal the Secret and Arthur will never know—in which case the consequences of the choice need not apply. This calculation is made using the algorithms described previously for determining the likelihood that a Secret can be kept.

Including Logical Inferences

The toughest problem in anticipation is including logical inferences. Suppose, for example, that Guinevere tells Arthur she's going to spend the night at her mother's house, and Arthur later discovers that Guinevere didn't do that. In your mind and mine, that's immediate grounds for suspicion. So how do you equip Arthur with the logic he needs to infer the possibility of hanky-panky?

Inference Engines

Artificial intelligence (AI) researchers have developed a technology known as an *inference engine* to deal with this kind of problem. An inference engine is a general-purpose program that can take statements about reality that have been coded in the proper form and use those statements to draw inferences. In its simplest form, an inference engine does little more than arrange syllogisms into sequences. Advanced inference engines can carry out extensive logical calculations and collate many factors to draw surprising conclusions.

In practice, inference engines require a great deal of information to be coded into their databases before they can do anything useful. Take the example of Guinevere failing to spend the night at her mother's house. How would the inference engine come to the conclusion that something fishy was afoot?

The starting point would be these two statements:

1. Guinevere said she would spend the night at her mother's.

2. Guinevere did not spend the night at her mother's.

The inference engine must first detect the discrepancy between the two statements, not too difficult a task. Having established that discrepancy, the inference engine must next attempt to explain it. To do this, it must have at its fingertips a wealth of information about human behavior, such as the following axiom:

3. When there is a discrepancy between what somebody says and the truth, that discrepancy is due to a lie or an extraordinary event.

So now the inference engine must examine two paths: Was it a lie or an extraordinary event? To determine which is more likely, the inference engine must make use of a statement rather like this:

4. People readily gossip about extraordinary events.

And then add in this observation:

5. Guinevere did not gossip to Arthur about any extraordinary events.

Using these two pieces of information, the inference engine can conclude:

6. Guinevere was not prevented from spending the night at her mother's by an extraordinary event.

Combined with #3, this statement leads to the conclusion:

7. Guinevere lied about spending the night at her mother's.

With this example, my point should be obvious: To carry out the calculations necessary for an inference engine, a prohibitively large amount of information about the world must be entered into the inference engine's database. And in fact, AI researchers have learned that inference engines are practical only in special cases in which the domain of applicable knowledge is small and tightly defined. For general-purpose use such as interactive storytelling, too much information is required to build a proper inference engine. Nevertheless, it remains an important field of effort; someday, when we can afford to build large databases of human behavior, inference engines will play a role in interactive storytelling technology.

Lesson #37
Someday inference engines will be useful in interactive storytelling—
but not yet.

Tree Analysis

Another approach to inferring the behavior of others is to explore the tree of possibilities an Actor could follow. If the storytelling engine uses a definable system of links between Events, it should be possible to trace through those links to determine what might happen. This process will likely entail a considerable amount of programming effort; in overall structure, it's similar to the tree-searching methods used in chess-playing programs. The good news is that this kind of tree-searching usually requires fewer branches at each branchpoint; the bad news is that each decision is intrinsically more complex than a decision in a chess game because so many more variables are involved.

At each point in a chess game, there might be dozen pieces that could move, and each piece might be able to move in, say, five different ways. That means a chess-playing program would have to consider at least 60 possible moves for each move. On the other hand, each move is fairly easy to evaluate: there are only so many pieces on the board and so many geometric relationships to consider.

The tree for interactive storytelling is much messier. Each Actor might have only half a dozen options at each stage in the tree, but the basis for evaluating those options is far more complicated than the basis for evaluating chess moves. Personality traits, relationships, roles, historical factors, and moods must all be taken into consideration. These calculations pose a stiff challenge to designers.

Moreover, the decisions made at each juncture must be based on the calculating Actor's perception of the relevant variables, not their true values. For example, if Mordred is unaware of the budding love between Lancelot and Guinevere, he won't be motivated to attempt to further their affair as a ploy to damage Arthur. All this complexity makes tree analysis immensely difficult; I suspect that the first generation of interactive storytelling engines will refrain from using this technique.

Wrapping Up

Endowing Actors with anticipation is a maddeningly difficult task; at heart it requires recursive programming, in which one Actor attempts to think like another, and then uses that anticipatory information to make decisions. Extended anticipation, in which an Actor tries to follow a chain of likely decisions by other Actors, is even more difficult. For the moment, anticipatory behavior lies on the frontiers of interactive storytelling.

CHAPTER 16
Roles and Sequencing

THE BASIC TASK OF ANY storytelling engine is to figure out, after an Event takes place, what happens next; this task is referred to as *sequencing*. Common sense and dramatic logic restrict the number of appropriate reactions to an Event. After all, if Romeo discovers Juliet dead in the tomb, he shouldn't have the option to play ping-pong; that's just not dramatically appropriate. Indeed, for most Events, the range of dramatically reasonable options is quite narrow.

But why shouldn't I be able to play ping-pong or do whatever I want during the course of the story? It's my story, after all.

No, it isn't; it's *our* story. I as storybuilder define the *reasonable* options available to you as player; you choose among those options. (See Lesson #31 in Chapter 12, "Drama Managers.") That's the division of responsibility within the medium of interactive storytelling.

But what if I don't like the options you offer me? What if I want that third option?

If you don't like the options I offer, there are two possible interpretations. Perhaps I'm a failure of a storybuilder, lacking the talent to do my job properly. In that case, you should walk away from my work the same way you would walk away from a writer whose novels you don't care for. The other explanation is that you're a perverse player who revels in contrariness, in which case I recommend you go write your own damned storyworld and see whether you can provide for every contrary player.

Selecting Options

I've been using the term "option" in the somewhat loose sense that's common, but now it's time to formalize my usage of it. An *option*, for the purposes of this book, is a Verb offered to an Actor as a possible reaction to an Event. Because an Event is most precisely characterized by its Verb, in practice I assign options to Verbs, not Events. When an Event takes place, Actors refer to its Verb to determine their options.

Hard-wired Versus Soft-wired Approaches

You have two ways to assign options to each Verb: *hard-wiring* and *soft-wiring*. The hard-wired approach is easier to imagine. For each Verb, the storybuilder builds a list of those Verbs that constitute reasonable reactions to the originating Verb. For example, for InviteToParty, only three Verbs are reasonable reactions: AcceptInvitation, RejectInvitation, or DeferResponse. The storybuilder lists these three Verbs, and the work is done.

The hard-wired approach does seem inelegant because every single item must be specified by hand. It's unavoidably tedious, especially with large sets of Verbs. A more elegant solution is the soft-wired approach: programming the storytelling engine to calculate the appropriate reaction Verbs. To carry out this computation, each Verb must be assigned a set of characterizing traits that the algorithm can examine to determine each Verb's appropriateness for each situation. For example, Verbs could be characterized by such adjectives as violent, physical versus mental, two-party, three-party, four-party, nasty, beneficent, romantic, sexual, angry, sad, confrontational, evasive, intense, and so forth. Each Verb would also have some adjectival specifications for its options. For example, the Verb DiscoverJulietsBody would prefer a sad and romantic Verb as an option rather than a confrontational or beneficent Verb.

However, I believe this soft-wired approach is unlikely to work, at least for the short term. There are simply too many factors that must be taken into account to differentiate every Verb from all the others. The range of reactions available in storyworlds is so broad, the Verbs so varied, that only a huge and complicated taxonometric system will suffice for these computations. Someday, perhaps, interactive storytelling will develop to such an advanced level that the soft-wired approach can be made to work. For the time being, given the primitive nature of interactive storytelling technology, prudence suggests deferral.

For now, the hard-wired approach is more practical. To reduce the tedium of specifying Verbs manually, you need to limit the number of reactions available to players. In addition, you don't want to offer a long laundry list of reactions that would only burden them. You want the reaction list no longer than, say, seven items. In many cases, such as InviteToParty, the reaction list will be even shorter. With such a short reaction list, specifying the Verbs manually is simpler than calculating them algorithmically. The subsequent discussion presumes using the hard-wired approach to selecting options.

Roles

Although options are assigned to Verbs, there's the additional constraint that some options are confined to certain Actors. For example, one of Romeo's male friends, upon discovering Juliet's inert body, might conceivably have some sort of necrophiliac option, but Juliet's mother would surely not. Therefore, the options available to an Actor who's reacting to an Event depend entirely on the Actor.

To put it more visually, here are two lists, Verbs and Actors:

Verbs	Actors
Walk away in tears	Romeo
Commit suicide	Juliet's mother
Collapse in tears	Romeo's buddy
Vow revenge	
Necrophiliac option	

How do you decide which options are available to which Actors?

My preferred solution makes use of *roles*. My use of this term is somewhat similar to its common meaning. A role has four components:

▸ A means for selecting an Actor who can react to an Event

▸ A list of options available to an Actor playing that role

▸ Inclination formulae for choosing the best option

▸ Specifications of physical and emotional changes resulting from the originating Verb

The storybuilder defines roles for every Verb. Each role specifies a dramatic relationship that an Actor might have to the Event in question. For example, if the Verb in question is Punch, you could imagine three obvious roles for it: Victim, BuddyOfVictim, and GirlfriendOfVictim. Each role has its own specifications and its own set of options. The first role, Victim, is the easiest to specify: The Victim is simply the DirObject of the Verb Punch. That role might have as reactions such Verbs as ReturnPunch, BreakBottleOverHead, Shoot, or BackDown. The next role, BuddyOfVictim, is a little trickier. This Actor must be a guy who directly witnesses the event and is a good friend of the Victim. Reactions for this role might be InterveneVerbally, IntervenePhysically, or Ignore. The GirlfriendOfVictim role is about as complex as the BuddyOfVictim role: The Actor must be female, a direct witness of the Event, and romantically attached to the Victim. This role might include reactions such as RestrainVictim, BurstIntoTears, or ScreamAtAttacker.

The process by which roles are used is straightforward. When an Event takes place, the storytelling engine goes through all Actors present on the Stage. It tests the requirements of each role against each Actor. If an Actor satisfies a role's requirements, that role is activated and the engine then considers the reactions available to the Actor. The role contains the inclination formulae for determining which reaction the Actor will choose. After the choice has been made, the storytelling engine need only construct the resulting plan with its Subject, Verb, DirObject, and any SecObjects, and then enter that plan into a plan list. (Plans and plan lists are explained a little later in "From Plan to Execution.") Last, the engine must implement the physical and emotional changes that arise from this role. For example, if the `GirlfriendOfVictim` role is activated, presumably the Actor would have a negative emotional reaction toward the Subject of the originating Event, which was `Subject Punch DirObject`.

What if an Actor fits several roles for a single Event?

This is a nasty problem. It arises rarely, but when it does, it can produce unacceptable situations in which an Actor responds to a situation in multiple (and perhaps incompatible) ways. For example, suppose you have the Verb `BabyCries`. You want to have a Verb for any women to respond, but you also want to have a Verb for the baby's mother to respond. However, the mother is both a mother and a woman, so it's conceivable she would respond twice—first in the role of mother and then in the role of woman. To prevent this problem, you could define the woman role to exclude the mother, but it's exactly the kind of problem that generates bugs in programming. It will surely generate bugs in storyworlds if left to the storybuilder's assiduousness. I therefore restrict every Actor to a single reaction; after an Actor finds a role that fits, that Actor abandons all further examination of roles—even if he or she subsequently takes no action.

But what if you require the Actor to react with multiple actions?

In this case, you can break up the reaction into a sequence of multiple actions. If Joe punches Fred and Fred's girlfriend, Anne, wants to react by screaming at Joe and then approaching Joe's girlfriend to request her intervention, you organize Anne's reaction as a two-step process:

1. Anne screams at Joe.

2. Anne reacts to her own action (the screaming) with a role specifying `RequestIntervention`, the second action in the sequence.

By the way, this notion of having a role for the Subject of an Event is counter-intuitive but handy. Why should Subjects react to their own actions? We tend to think of reactions as something done in response to somebody *else's* actions, not our own. Subject reactions are useful, however; they permit sequential events and multiple behaviors. For example, if Fred shoots and kills Joe, you could have lots of reactions to that one Event. Joe clutches his chest and falls to the ground; Joe's girlfriend screams and kneels over his body, sobbing. A witness runs to fetch the sheriff. Fred turns and runs. These are all reactions to a single Event, and with roles they are easy to organize. This complicated sequence of events is diagrammed in **Figure 16.1**.

What if one Actor's reaction obviates another Actor's reaction?

Yes, this is another little gotcha. If Fred punches Joe and Joe's buddy Clem steps in and intervenes, you can't have Joe return the punch; Clem's intervention makes retaliation inappropriate. Two mechanisms solve this problem: reaction sequencing and hijacking.

Here's how *reaction sequencing* works: The storytelling engine examines every Actor to determine what roles, if any, that Actor fits, but the engine can examine them in an order best suited to your dramatic purposes. My engine gives Fate first crack at every Event; if Fred shoots Joe and Fate requires that Joe can't die yet, then Joe falls to the ground, lies there a moment, and then opens his eyes and says, "Garsh, it was only a flesh wound." That's Fate's work.

After Fate has had a pass at the Event, the witnesses come next. They consist of anybody who's on Stage with the Subject and DirObject but is neither of these two. At this point, witnesses have a chance to intervene. Next comes DirObject's reaction, and last is the Subject's reaction.

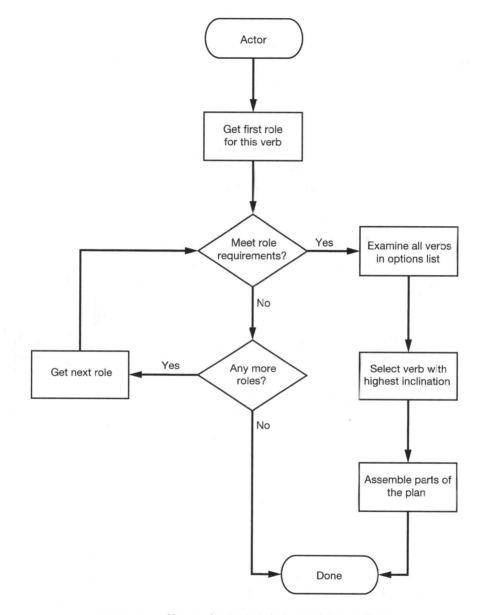

FIGURE 16.1: How an Actor goes about reacting to an Event.

The storybuilder, in creating a role, must specify whether any of its Verb options are *hijacking*. If so, then any Actor who chooses that Verb *hijacks the storyline*. Hijacking prevents any other Actors from subsequently reacting to the Event, as diagrammed in **Figure 16.2**.

Try walking through an example using Figure 16.2. Start with an Event: `Fred Punches Joe`. First, Fate reacts to the Event. Say that Fate finds no role to play, so it takes no action. Next, the witnesses react. One of the witnesses is Joe's big brother, who finds a role to play and ends up choosing the Verb `Intervene`. This Verb has its `hijacking` flag set to `True`, so Joe's big brother hijacks the storyline, taking you all the way down to the bottom of Figure 16.2, "Done."

From Plan to Execution

The simplest structure for a storytelling engine uses *immediate execution* of Verbs; as soon as an Actor decides on a Verb, he or she executes it. There's no delay between intention and execution. An engine like this is easy to build.

However, there are all manner of dramatic situations that immediate-execution systems can't handle. The first problem is *deferred execution*, in which an Actor chooses a reaction that shouldn't take place immediately. For example, big tough Fred punches wimpy Joe, and Joe, knowing he can't fight Fred, decides to wreak revenge by painting Fred's house pink while Fred's away. Joe doesn't want to execute his plan immediately; he wants to wait for the proper moment. Besides, he needs time to gather his paint and brushes.

Solving this problem vastly complicates the storytelling engine. It won't do to simply specify an execution time at some point in the future; what if Joe shows up, paint bucket in hand, while Fred's mowing his lawn?

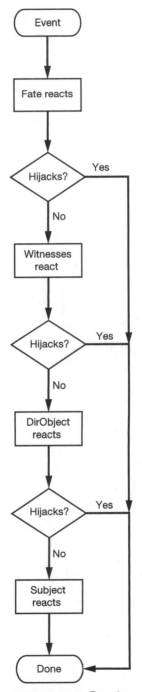

FIGURE 16.2: Reaction sequencing and hijacking.

No, deferred execution requires a more complex approach. First, every time an Actor decides on a reaction, that reaction is entered into the *plan list*, which is just a temporary holding pen for plans that are still cooking. When a plan enters the plan list, it's given a *preparation time*, the amount of time delay required before the plan can even be considered for execution. Most plans have preparation times equal to zero, ensuring that they're carried out immediately. The plan sits in the plan list until its preparation time has expired—but it's still not ready for execution! One more hurdle must be surmounted.

When the plan comes out of the plan list, the situation at that moment might not be conducive to carrying out the plan. (Fred might be mowing his lawn, for example.) So the plan moves from the plan list to the *opportunity list*, which is a holding pen for plans whose audience requirements haven't been met. Every Verb has certain requirements for the presence or absence of other Actors, called *audience requirements*. For example, romantic Verbs often require the privacy of Subject and DirObject and, therefore, the absence of other Actors.

Refer back to Chapter 13, "Verbs and Events," for more discussion on audience requirements and variables.

Every Actor has an opportunity list of plans waiting for execution; every time the Actor changes Stages, or another person enters or leaves the Actor's current stage, the Actor consults his opportunity list to determine whether the situation is ripe for carrying out one of the plans waiting in the opportunity list. If so, the Actor proceeds to execute that plan.

 Doesn't this mean that some plans sit rotting in the opportunity list for a long time? What if the right conditions are never satisfied?

This is certainly a possibility. If Dick wants to get Jane alone to romance her, he might never get his chance, but one small trick greatly improves Dick's chances. Dick doesn't wait passively for Jane to walk into his Stage when he's alone; he monitors Jane's location and, as soon as Jane is alone, he goes to her Stage so that he can carry out his plan.

 That's not realistic! How can Dick possibly know that Jane is alone?

Remember what I said about dramatic reality versus physical reality? This is storytelling—you don't allow yourself to be distracted by accounting details. You want Dick and Jane alone together, so you grab the first opportunity you can.

 But what if Jane is alone because she's taking a shower? Dick can't just barge in!

True. This problem is dealt with by a variable I call `Territoriality`, which is the degree to which an Actor feels comfortable on a given Stage. Each Actor has a `Territoriality` value assigned to every Stage. For example, Dick has a high `Territoriality` for the baseball field because he hangs out there a lot and a low `Territoriality` for, say, the shopping mall. Jane's `Territoriality` values for these two Stages might be the reverse of Dick's. In the same way, Dick's `Territoriality` for Jane's shower is zero: He will never go there. Problem solved.

If all the audience requirements are met, the plan pops out of the opportunity list and is executed, at which point it becomes an Event. **Figure 16.3** illustrates this arrangement.

At this point, other Actors consider their roles and react to the Event, as shown previously in Figures 16.1 and 16.2. And so the cycle of life continues…

None of these complexities arises in a storyworld with just one Stage. If all Actors share the same Stage, you don't need to worry about audience requirements or opportunity lists, and Figure 16.3 is unnecessary. Similarly, if you confine yourself to immediate execution, you don't need a plan list. If you're just getting started with interactive storytelling, you might want to defer working on these more complicated problems.

Deferred Reactions

Another dramatic situation that immediate-execution systems can't handle arises from the use of Gossip (discussed in Chapter 14, "HistoryBooks and Gossip"). If a person learns of an Event through Gossip, immediate reaction is impossible. If Mary tells Joe's buddy Clem that Fred punched Joe, Clem can't use the Verb `InterveneVerbally`—the Event is long past! However, Clem might still want to react to the event by, say, having a little talk with Fred. This is what I call a *deferred reaction*. In a deferred reaction, the choice is made long after the Event; in deferred execution, the choice is made immediately after the Event, but execution is deferred to a later time.

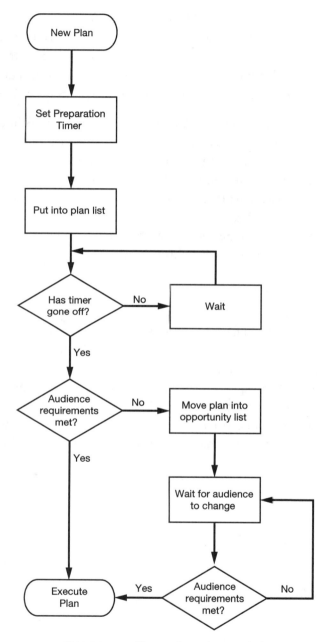

FIGURE16.3: How a plan gets executed.

If you build a storytelling engine with Gossip, you'll need a system for handling deferred reactions. Fortunately, deferred reactions are, at heart, no different from immediate reactions; they simply use different roles. Therefore, your roles for deferred reactions differ from your normal roles only by a specification that the Actor is not a witness to the Event (that is, not present at its execution).

For example, suppose that Fred Punches Joe and you have defined three roles: Victim, BuddyOfVictim, and GirlfriendOfVictim. They are all immediate reaction roles. Suppose you want to add a role for somebody who hears about the Event through Gossip and wants to admonish Fred to behave himself in the future. This new role, Gossipee, can't take any of the immediate reaction options. It's a different role that's considered when the Actor hears the gossip about Fred and Joe. The role includes in its specification a statement that the Actor is not a witness to the Event, but has heard of it through the Gossip process.

Wrapping Up

Every interactive storytelling engine needs some scheme for sequencing the story's events. The mechanics of sequencing can be complicated, depending on how much spatial and temporal complexity you permit in your storyworld. The central concept that makes sequencing possible is using roles, which are sets of commands that specify the conditions under which they can be played, the options the role-playing Actor can consider, the factors that influence the Actor's choice, and any emotional or physical changes that ensue as a direct result of the Event.

CHAPTER 17
Development Environments

THE FIRST TASK FOR ANY DESIGNER of an interactive storytelling technology is creating an engine capable of generating interesting, robust drama. This is only the first task, however; the designer must also make that engine accessible to the storybuilders who will use it. Accessibility is provided through a *development environment*, a suite of programs that storybuilders can use to create, edit, test, and tune a storyworld. This chapter explains the elements of a good development environment.

Historical Background

Once upon a time, long long ago, software was short and simple, mostly because computers were small and simple. Back in the 1940s, the earliest computers were programmed in binary machine language: lots of 1s and 0s entered with toggle switches. That method, still in use in the 1970s, was fine for tiny programs of a few dozen bytes. As programs became bigger, however, the tedium of entering binary code became overwhelming, so programmers switched to hexadecimal numbers instead of binary. Entering "A9 00" is a lot easier than "10101001 00000000."

Hexadecimal machine code is fine for slightly larger programs. When writing programs in machine code, however, programmers discovered that a few kilobytes of code was the upper limit. Modifying these programs created all sorts of new bugs. With larger programs, programmers were taking two steps forward and slipping 1.9 steps back.

Next came assembly language, which substituted alphanumeric contractions for hexadecimal. Instead of typing "A9 00," you entered "LDA #00," which, as any old-timer can tell you, means "load the accumulator with a value of zero." Here are two versions of the same code:

Machine Code	Assembly Code
A9 03	SQUARE LDA #03
85 35	SPACE STA NX
A5 43	LDA S
4A	LSR
C5 42	CMP L
BO 1F	BCS CYCLD

Although the two columns represent identical code, assembly code is easier to understand (after you've memorized the mnemonics) than machine code.

Assembly language was a big improvement over machine language, and programmers were able to write some fairly substantial programs with it. For example, I led one team that wrote about 50KB of code in assembly language.

Although we weren't at the upper limit, we could tell that if the program got much larger, our problems would multiply.

At this point, two factors combined to create a demand for something new. First, computers were spreading out into a broader range of uses; these new uses required programs so large that they would be impossible to manage in something as simple as assembly language. One response to this problem was the creation of the C language, a kind of "super assembly language" that enabled programmers to write much larger programs.

The second factor was the need to make computers accessible to people other than programmers. Scientists wanted to write scientific programs without having to hire programmers, businessmen needed a faster way to get the programs they needed, and teachers needed a simple language to introduce students to programming. Three languages were created to meet these needs: FORTRAN for scientists, COBOL for businessmen, and BASIC for students. (At the time, it didn't look this simple, but this is how things look with 20-20 hindsight.)

As programmers learned more about software and began attempting more ambitious projects, however, programs grew ever larger, and the methods that worked with small programs just didn't with bigger programs. The classic example is the GOTO statement, which tells computers to go to another place in the program and work from there. It's rather like those step-by-step software installation instructions that say "If your computer already has a floopgoggle, then go to step 5." This method works fine with short instructions and one or two GOTO statements, but with thousands of instructions and scores of GOTO commands, you can get totally lost trying to figure out what goes where. Programmers call this type of program "spaghetti code" because the intertwined instructions are just too messy to keep straight. So computer scientists invented languages such as Pascal that had no GOTO command and required programmers to use more structured systems. I, like many other programmers, grumbled at the constraints on my freedom (we called Pascal a fascist language), but after using the language we realized it really did make the trains run on time.

By this time, programmers had divided into two groups: systems programmers and applications programmers. Systems programmers worked in assembly language and C, writing the low-level programs that ran computers directly.

Applications programmers worked in high-level languages like Pascal, writing programs that did useful things for paying customers.

Meanwhile, the demands of various special-interest groups continued to grow, and computer scientists realized they needed to provide more than just special-purpose programming languages. They needed to offer something less abstract and generalized, something more narrowly targeted to the particular users' needs. The appearance of personal computers intensified this problem and created a huge new class of users who weren't programmers but were willing to pay for software that gave them new capabilities.

For example, VisiCalc, the first spreadsheet program for personal computers, was a simple number-crunching program specialized for dealing with the lists of numbers common in budgets. Although users didn't realize it, VisiCalc was a programming language; a computer scientist later proved that a sufficiently large spreadsheet program could, theoretically, solve any problem that a regular computing language could solve. But VisiCalc was a narrow-purpose computing language, devoted exclusively to the problems of crunching numbers. Its single-mindedness made it easier to learn, which in turn made it accessible to non-technical users. Thus, the third major group of computer people (after systems programmers and applications programmers) were created: users who wanted to use computers to organize their work. Applications programmers no longer wrote programs that directly solved problems; instead, they wrote applications (such as spreadsheets) that users could easily program to solve their problems.

The early *adventure game generators* are a more pertinent example of user-level programming. Back in 1976, Crowther and Woods created the classic game Adventure. Its internal structure was simple, requiring more in the way of data than code. By 1979, there were programs that provided an "adventure game engine" along with a "content editor" that enabled anybody to create an adventure game by entering the relevant content data. These adventure game generators required little technical expertise. Nowadays dozens of adventure game generation programs are freely available on the Internet.

Similarly, the early 1980s saw the development of programs that teachers could use for providing educational content to their students. Since then, the concept has been expanded and refined to include level editors for games, character editors for role-playing games, macro editors for photo-retouching programs, scripting capabilities for word processors, and so on. All such programs have two fundamental components: an engine that runs the system using user-supplied data and a content editor that permits users to enter and edit that data. More elaborate programs include testing facilities that enable users to experiment with variations and quickly see the results. Taken together, this entire system of programs (engine, editor, and tester) constitutes a development environment.

The Importance of Development Environments

It should be obvious that interactive storytelling software, by whatever means it is accomplished, will be big. A lot of data is required to specify the Actors, story components, Verbs available to Actors, Props, Stages, and so forth. Consequently, development environments for interactive storytelling have to be elaborate affairs, which forces the new requirement in Lesson #38.

Lesson #38
The development environment is just as important as the engine.

In other words, building a powerful engine for interactive storytelling isn't good enough; to be of any utility, that engine must be accompanied by a powerful development environment. My own experience is that the development environment requires at least twice as much effort as the engine. After all, with an engine, you're just crunching numbers, but with a development environment, you have to provide a good user interface, which is always a demanding task.

Elements of Development Environments

The specifics of a development environment will, of course, be tied to the specifics of the engine it feeds data to, but I can offer some general principles in the following sections.

Algorithmic Entry

The most profound decision you can make about your development environment is whether it will include algorithmic capabilities for storybuilders. The simple approach is to permit storybuilders to control only data: numbers, images, sounds, and so forth. This approach is easier for people to understand and quite simple to implement. You merely present check boxes, radio buttons, scrollbars, and other standard data entry components for your storybuilders. You'll have a lot of these components, to be sure, but they're conceptually easy to design and understand.

The next level up is including boolean algorithms, which are simple true-false calculations that most people can understand. They enable storybuilders to include simple if-then decisions in their storyworlds. For example, a storybuilder might want to declare that, if an Actor is a gal, the story goes one way, but if the Actor is a guy, it goes another way. If the Actor is old and frail, a certain Event happens, but if he's young and strong, another Event happens. And so on.

Be warned, however, that making boolean algorithms available to storybuilders makes your development environment much more complex because you now must include expression-editing capabilities. Storybuilders must be able to assemble any combination of boolean variables and boolean operators. Think of all the boolean variables a storyworld might include: variables that specify an Actor's gender, a Stage's accessibility to an Actor, a Prop's visibility, or whether an Actor has already completed an action. Your storybuilder could well want to put together an expression such as this one:

```
IF (Actor1 is female) AND (Actor2 is male) AND (Actor2 is not married)
➥AND (NOT(Actor2 has gone out on a date with (anybody other than
➥Actor1)) OR NOT(Actor1 has gone out on a date with (anybody other
➥than Actor2))) THEN...
```

Pretty messy, huh? If you're going to permit boolean algorithms, you've got to be able to handle the resulting expressions.

But wait—it gets worse! Why should your storybuilder be prevented from entering numerical relationships such as this one:

```
IF (Love[Actor1 for Actor2] > Love[Actor1 for Actor3]) THEN...
```

Of course, including this type of expression means you have five new operators to offer (=, >, <, ≥, ≤) as well as all the numeric variables. Lots more work for you. Ugh!

But wait—it gets even worse! The preceding expression asks whether Actor1 loves Actor2 more than Actor3. It's a fairly obvious basis for a choice such as

"Should I leave Actor3 for Actor2?" But what if you also want to include a little natural inertia in Actor1's decision? In other words, she's not going to leave Actor2 for Actor2 if she loves Actor2 just a smidgen more than Actor3. She needs to love Actor2 a *lot* more than Actor3 to justify the pain of breaking up with Actor3. So now the formula looks like this:

```
IF (Love[Actor1 for Actor2] > Love[Actor1 for Actor3] + 10) THEN...
```

Oops. Now you've gotten yourself into arithmetic. And the slippery slope has no natural stopping point; if you permit a simple arithmetic operation such as + 10, how can you deny one like this:

```
IF (Love[Actor1 for Actor2]²·⁵ > SQRT(SIN(Love[Actor1 for Actor3])))
➥THEN...
```

And there you are, deep in the fires of Math Hell.

I suppose you could make some sort of arbitrary constraint, such as limiting storybuilders to the four basic arithmetic operators (+, -,×, ÷), but you can be sure some storybuilders will chafe at the arbitrariness of your restriction. "Just give me square roots; that's all I need," they'll plead. "Just one more division of troops and we'll finish off those Viet Cong, Mr. President."

In for a penny, in for a pound. If you're going to include full arithmetic expressions, why not go whole hog and permit arithmetic modifications such as this one:

```
IF (Actor2 slaps Actor1) THEN Love[Actor1 for Actor2] = Love[Actor1 for
➥Actor2] - 27
```

This expression means that if Actor2 slaps Actor1, then Actor1's love for Actor2 will be diminished by 27.

Or how about this obviously useful bit of code:

```
IF (Actor2 murders brother of Actor1) THEN {

    i = 0;

    WeFoundAVictim = FALSE;

    WHILE ((i < ActorCount) AND (WeFoundAVictim))  {
```

```
    IF (Actor#i is kin of Actor2) THEN {

        WeFoundAVictim = TRUE;

        Victim = i;

    }

    increment i;

}

IF (WeFoundAVictim) THEN {

    Plot dark and bloody revenge

}

}
```

This little code snippet might be hard for nonprogrammers to read, but basically all it does is sweep through the list of Actors, looking for one who is kin to the murderer, and then selecting that kin Actor for dark and bloody revenge. Obviously this capability is useful, but it takes you beyond Math Hell and into the even lower levels of Programming Hell. How deep do you want to go, Dante?

Some Suggestions

I toiled with these problems for years, and did come up with a few ideas.

Eliminating Loops

First, it's possible to steer clear of Programming Hell with a scheme using *selection loops* that take algorithmic arguments. Here's how it works: First you create a standardized function called PickBestActor. It has the loop buried inside it, but the storybuilder never knows. From the storybuilder's point of view, it's just a function that picks the Actor who best fits some specification. That specification is an arithmetic expression that the storybuilder hands to the function as an argument, like so:

```
MyChampion = PickBestActor(Strength[])
```

It says "My champion will be the Actor with the highest value of Strength." You can extend the idea as follows to say "The gal picks the guy with the best overall combination of good looks and money":

```
ThePerfectHusband = PickBestActor(GoodLooks[] + Wealth[])
```

In practice, I have found it necessary to include both a boolean and a numeric argument to the function:

```
ThePerfectHusband = PickBestActor(GoodLooks[] + Wealth[], IsNotMarried)
```

The gal picks the guy with the best overall combination of good looks and money *and* who is not already married.

For this function to work, you'll need to supply versions of it for everything an Actor might want to choose, as in these examples:

```
"I reach for my (PickBestProp(Lethality[], IsAWeapon))."
```

```
"I take my date to (PickBestStage(RomanticAtmosphere,
➡NobodyElseThere)."
```

This scheme relieves the storybuilder of the cognitive load of writing selection loops; in practice, I have found little need for other kinds of loops.

Canned Formulae

Even with this scheme in place, however, I have found that math scares away most storybuilders. Most seem capable of handling boolean expressions, but balk at algebraic formulae. This fear is particularly crippling with respect to inclination formulae, which are important components of many interactive storytelling technologies. They specify the degree to which an Actor is inclined to take a particular course of action. Suppose, for example, that an Actor is faced with danger and must choose between fight or flight. The inclination formulae might read like so:

```
Inclination[Fight] = Courage[] - Prudence[]
```

```
Inclination[Flight] = Prudence[] - Courage[]
```

This kind of math is too difficult for most storybuilders to use on a regular basis. More than any other factor, math fear is what prevented people from using the

Erasmatron. There is, however, a way to ameliorate the problem: Constrain the form of the formula and allow users to specify just two factors to control it. **Figure 17.1** shows how I do it in the Erasmatron.

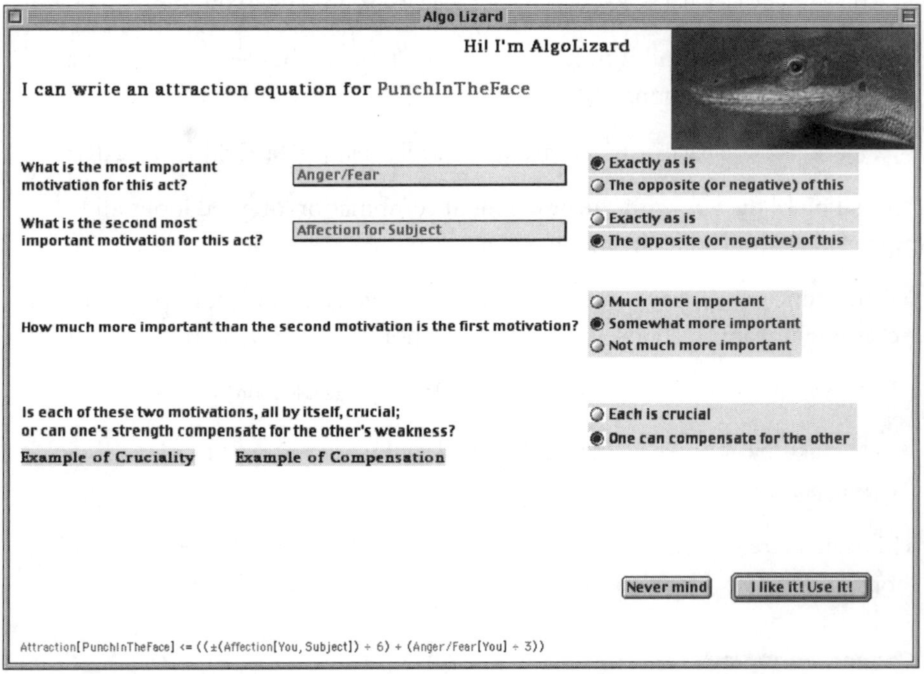

FIGURE 17.1: Algorithms without tears.

The two variables selected for this inclination formula are the Actor's Anger/Fear mood and the negative of the Actor's Affection for the Subject. The first motivation, Anger/Fear, is somewhat more important than the second motivation because it controls the weighting factors used. Finally, the concept of cruciality versus compensation is a little tricky, but it determines whether the formula's basic form is additive or multiplicative. Compensatory relationships are additive, and cruciality-based relationships are multiplicative.

Compensation is the easier concept to understand. In the earlier example of a gal choosing a husband, wealth could compensate for good looks, and vice versa. Therefore, she would be just as likely to pick a good-looking poor guy as a wealthy ugly guy—although she'd prefer a good-looking rich guy.

Cruciality is a little more difficult to understand. Suppose, for example, that Actor1 is contemplating an action that might have the side effect of antagonizing Actor2. Actor1 might have reason to fear Actor2's reaction. In this case, the inclination formula might look something like this:

```
Inclination[Antagonize] = Irritability[Actor2] × Power[Actor2]
```

Two factors are at work here, and both are crucial to the question of whether antagonizing Actor2 is an undesirable outcome. The first factor is the degree to which Actor2 might be antagonized by the action; the second is the power that Actor2 has to inflict harm upon Actor1. For example, if Actor2 is a mellow but powerful person, there's no cause to fear antagonizing him because you know he won't be antagonized. Conversely, if Actor2 is easily antagonized but impotent to do anything about it, Actor1 need not fear his reaction because he can't hurt Actor1 anyway. Thus, cruciality means that *both* factors are absolute requirements, but they can intensify each other. Compensation means that *either* factor can drive the decision.

Attraction Formulae

A further simplification is to replace inclination formulae with *attraction formulae.* The difference between these two is simple: An inclination formula is specific to a single situation, but an attraction formula is permanently attached to its Verb.

Consider, for example, the Verb Slap. Imagine that a gal might want to slap a guy in two completely different situations. In one situation, he has been overly forward in his affections and she wants to forcefully reject his advances. In the other situation, he has deliberately insulted her and she wants to retaliate. In a system using inclination formulae, each situation would have a different formula for the inclination to slap. The rejection-slap might take into account the gal's affection for the guy, but the retaliation-slap would not, like so:

```
Inclination[Slap] = Temper[Gal] - Affection[Gal for Guy]

Inclination[Slap] = Temper[Gal] + HowMuchTheInsultHurt
```

Thus, inclination formulae can be finely tuned to each specific situation.

An attraction formula, however, would assign an intrinsic basis for the slapping action, meaning there would be one formula for both slapping situations:

```
Inclination[Slap] = Temper[Gal]
```

The advantage of this approach is also its disadvantage: It's a simpler, one-formula-fits-all approach, requiring storybuilders to write one formula just once. But because that one formula must fit different contexts, it's less dramatically precise.

Tuning Formulae

Canned formulae offer storybuilders salvation from Math Hell, but they don't address the need for tuning those formulae. I doubt anyone is algebraically nimble enough to perceive all the consequences of a system of formulae as large as those encountered in sets of inclination formulae. In other words, the first draft of the inclination formulae is likely to yield undesirable results. The hero always fights and never flees, even when hopelessly outclassed. The heroine rejects every marriage proposal, no matter how attractive. To deal with these problems, the development environment must provide a tuning system in the form of various testing mechanisms. It's too much to ask storybuilders to write inclination formulae, play the storyworld, and then go back and adjust the inclination formulae. Storyworlds are too complicated for that kind of simple-minded approach.

I call the first testing mechanism the *quicktest*. It assembles a statistical representation of how formulae behave under a wide variety of situations. Inclination formulae always come in sets (one formula for each option available in that situation). Therefore, if each formula has two variables, a set of formulae with two choices has four variables, a set of formulae with three choices has six variables, and so forth. For example, in a three-choice set with six variables at play, select random numbers for each of the six variables and calculate which inclination formula has the highest result; that tells you which choice would be made under those circumstances. Then note which choice was made. You repeat this process many times, counting how many times each option is chosen. It's no problem doing it, say, a thousand times because this is precisely the kind of task that computers do well. Then you display the results in a pie chart (see **Figure 17.2**).

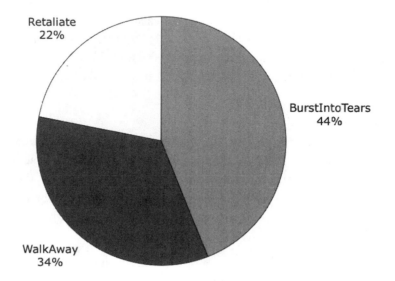

FIGURE 17.2: Pie chart for an imaginary quicktest.

Or you can extend the process by repeating the whole procedure, except this time, set the first variable to the maximum value you have defined for it, and use random values for the other five. That generates another pie chart. Then do the whole thing all over, this time using the middle value of the first variable and randomizing all the others. Do it one more time, using the minimum value of the first variable. Then do this entire three-step process all over again, once for each variable, with one pie chart for its maximum value, one for its middle value, and one for its minimum value. All in all, this procedure generates 18 more pie charts. By examining those pie charts, storybuilders can figure out how well the various inclination formulae work and what adjustments must be made to get results more closely approximating their expectations. Most people will find the quicktest too tedious, but if you're the statistical type, it might be worthwhile to try.

The Achilles' heel of statistical testing methods like these is the role that historical elements play. If your inclination or attraction formulae contain terms that refer to the HistoryBook, generating useful statistical calculations is impossible. For example, suppose that a gal's inclination to slap a fresh guy depends on whether she has already rebuffed him. The inclination formula would include that historical element, which of course can't exist in a one-shot test such as the quicktest. It's possible in some cases to force the value one way or the other in the statistical test, but doing this raises a variety of new problems. All in all, the problems of handling historical elements are so great as to make them impractical.

Setting the Context

Statistical tests yield results only for theoretical situations: using purely random values for variables or using maximum and minimum values. The actual situation in a real storyworld is never so cleanly theoretical. Moreover, the storybuilder might know that the particular corner of the storyworld being tested can be experienced only in certain contexts that presume a narrow range of values for some variables.

For example, suppose you're testing a storyworld in which a wedding can take place. In this storyworld, it's pointless to test for situations in which the bride hates the groom. Moreover, the context demands certain relationships, moods, and attitudes of other Actors in the scene. Accordingly, a fair test of the inclination formulae should have those presumptions built in.

Therefore, storybuilders must be able to assign certain contextual values before the test. Moreover, they might want to set values by a variety of logical conditions. For example, they might want a random selection from the entire cast, from only males, from males who are present, from males who are present and are kin of the protagonist, and so forth. This selection can become immensely complex, and it seems unlikely that, in the early stages, storybuilders will want that much control. However, when designing your development environment, keeping this capability in mind for future versions would be prudent.

Threadtests and Rehearsals

Storybuilders can also benefit from another kind of testing facility: the ability to start a story going at any point and see how it develops in a variety of situations.

A *thread* is a sequence of Events following a single point in the storyworld. A *threadtest* starts at that single point and generates a thread. It repeats the process many times, building up an ensemble of threads. It then assembles those threads into a single statistical structure showing how the story is likely to develop from the starting point.

 But doesn't that depend on the values of all variables at the starting point?

Indeed it does; therefore, the threadtester should be able to generate values for all those variables. It's the same problem discussed previously under "Setting the Context." Some simple capabilities for context-setting might be advisable.

Threadtesting is necessary to expose two nasty problems that can arise in a storyworld:

▶ **Threadkillers:** These situations terminate the action. An unanticipated situation prevents anything from happening, and so the story simply dies. A threadtester can recognize and record threadkillers and present the results to storybuilders.

▶ **Loopyboobies:** Fred punches Joe. This infuriates Joe, who punches Fred back. This makes Fred so angry that he punches Joe again. Joe punches Fred, Fred punches Joe, and it goes on forever because the storybuilder's inclination formulae don't take into account that people get tired. A threadtester can recognize and count loopyboobies and warn storybuilders about them.

Typically, the problem of loopyboobies has two solutions. First, use moods to shut down excessive behavior. The punching raises the Anger value quickly and raises the Fatigue value more slowly. If your engine is using end-weighted addition, Anger rises quickly but soon tops off, and Fatigue climbs more slowly. The storybuilder need only include a negative value for Fatigue in the inclination formula to ensure that the fighters eventually tire of their battle and give up.

Second, you can make an explicit reference to the HistoryBook. You simply check how many times the contemplated course of action has already been carried out, and then forbid the action if it has already been executed too many times.

Should the storybuilder have responsibility for checking for loopyboobies, or should the engine automatically check for them?

Good question. On the one hand, loobyboobies arise only in special situations, so dumping this responsibility onto storybuilders seems fair. However, it's possible to build a loopybooby detector into the engine and then assign "loopybooby maximum values" to each Verb. For each Verb, the storybuilder need only specify the maximum number of times the Verb can be executed by one Actor during a specified period. The engine can then enforce this restriction.

Loopyboobies come in many degrees, according to the number of steps they contain. The previous fighting example is a simple two-step loopybooby, but three-step, four-step, and even five-step loopyboobies can be just as embarrassing as two-step loopyboobies.

A *rehearsal* is simply a threadtest that starts at the beginning of the story. It's the final test of the storyworld; a series of rehearsals should visit every corner of the storyworld. Here's where the computer shines bright; it can carry out thousands of rehearsals while you're wasting time in meetings arguing about what color the box liner should be. With the proper design, you can put those rehearsals to good use. The trick is to organize the resulting mass of data into patterns that reveal any weaknesses in the storyworld.

The simplest analysis lists the frequencies of Verb executions. Some Verbs are used more often than others; this list reveals that pattern. In the mathematically ideal design, all Verbs are used equally often, but dramatic considerations have more weight than mathematical symmetry. Verbs with the highest Import value shouldn't occur often, but Verbs with low Import can. After all, you don't want mass murders, meteor impacts, and suicides to be as frequent as salutations, comments on the weather, and suggestions for dinner. This analysis is most useful at the bottom end: Verbs that are never executed are big red flags waving the message that the inclination formulae leading to them are unduly restrained.

ComeFrom Analysis

The perplexed storybuilder facing the situation of Verbs that are never executed will want to look at the *ComeFrom* data, which are tables of situations in which a Verb is an option. To assemble these tables, the engine must have the capability to store every decision made—not just which option was chosen, but what options were available. This data enables the engine to build a table for each Verb showing how many times it was an option versus how many times it was chosen. If a Verb is often an option but is never chosen, it's a simple matter to fix the problem by adjusting the inclination formula. But if it's *never* an option, the problem lies in a Verb upstream from the deficient Verb.

Here's an example. Suppose your romantic storyworld never culminates in weddings. For some reason, heroines are not accepting marriage proposals. If you run a ComeFrom analysis, you might discover that the Verb `AcceptMarriageProposal` was an option 27 times, but was never actually chosen. This problem is easy to fix; you merely examine the inclination formula for `AcceptMarriageProposal` and tweak the inclination formula upward a bit. If, on the other hand, the ComeFrom analysis demonstrates that `AcceptMarriageProposal` was an active option zero times, you know that the upstream Verb, `ProposeMarriage`, was never executed. So you turn your attention to `ProposeMarriage` to determine why it was never executed.

A ComeFrom analysis also enables storybuilders to see where a Verb execution comes from: the proportion of Verbs upstream from the Verb in question. Suppose, for example, that the Verb `BurstIntoTears` shows up with an appropriate frequency. Uncautious storybuilders might congratulate themselves on this happy result and leave it at that. However, more prudent storybuilders will examine the ComeFrom analysis and discover, say, that `BurstIntoTears` has two upstream Verbs—`Insult` and `Jilt`—and that every single execution of `BurstIntoTears` resulted from an execution of `Insult`. For some reason, the verb `Jilt` never led to the result `BurstIntoTears`. Clearly, this situation demands further investigation.

You can make the ComeFrom analysis even more useful by ranking Verb executions by relative infrequency of choice. In other words, it can offer the storybuilder a list of situations in which a particular choice was rarely or never made. That list might look like this:

```
BurstIntoTears:    8/38

Insult:            8/29

Jilt:              0/9
```

On 29 occasions, BurstIntoTears was an option of the Verb Insult; on 8 of those occasions, BurstIntoTears was chosen. On 9 occasions, BurstIntoTears was an option of Jilt; on none of those occasions was BurstIntoTears chosen.

You can extend this process even further. The development environment can be designed to allow storybuilders to tune inclination formulae without understanding any math at all—a development you can be sure most storybuilders will welcome. This magic is accomplished by using linear equations in all inclination formulae. (A linear equation, roughly speaking, is one that takes the form Constant1 × Variable1 + Constant2 × Variable2).

To take the math out of storybuilders' lives, use ComeFrom analyses that enable them to navigate through the webwork of cause and effect until they find a problem. At that point, you display the output frequency pie chart shown earlier in **Figure 17.2**. The storybuilder selects a slice of the pie and clicks on one of two buttons: Make It Bigger or Make It Smaller. The system then adjusts the coefficients in the inclination formula to implement the storybuilder's choice. A simple increment or decrement moves the pie chart in the desired direction, but the storybuilder will have to come back and check the results after a subsequent rehearsal.

 Why just "Bigger" and "Smaller"? Why can't the system permit the storybuilder to just set the pie chart to the desired proportions?

That, it turns out, is impossible to do without much more effort. The killer problem is the uncertainty of the values of variables used in the inclination formulae for all the options. Simply increasing a coefficient by, say, 10% will not increase the frequency of choice by 10 percent. The effect of that change depends on all the other coefficients (which you can figure out) and all the variables (which you can't).

It's possible to pull off this magic trick by storing all the values for all the variables that led to these results. For example, suppose a storybuilder is attempting to correct the problem with BurstIntoTears coming from Jilt. The output frequency pie chart looks like **Figure 17.3**.

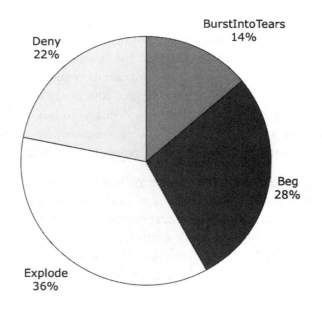

Consequences of Jilt

FIGURE 17.3: A pie chart for the consequences of the Verb Jilt.

The storybuilder graphically manipulates the pie chart to show the desired percentages. The software could then run a series of tests; each test would calculate the inclination formulae for each set of variable values and determine the statistical results. By altering the values of coefficients, the software could eventually identify a set of coefficients that would yield the storybuilder-specified percentages. This testing would entail an enormous amount of computing—but hey, that's what computers are for!

Debuggers

A *debugger* is a program that allows a programmer to step through code that's under development. It shows, step by step, exactly what's happening, how values are being changed, how the program jumps from one place to another. The best analogy to a debugger would be a DVD player that enables you to step through the movie, frame by frame, but can also fast forward under several conditions. This magical DVD player would be able to fast forward until it came to the next frame meeting any particular condition you care to define. And while it's at it, a debugger can show you the value of every variable at work at each point in the progress of the story. You can even set a debugger to run until something attempts to change the value of some variable. Programmers consider debuggers essential parts of any programming development environment.

So including a debugger in your own storytelling engine seems appropriate. However, I have doubts about the utility of a debugger for storybuilders. A debugger must show the engine running step by step; to use it, a storybuilder must be intimately familiar with the engine's operation. This knowledge might be too high a demand to place on storybuilders. On the other hand, a debugger can be an excellent tool for helping storybuilders understand the engine's operation. You can write all the documentation you want, but until storybuilders see the engine ticking over, its operation won't be clear.

A Programming Note

Threadtesters and debuggers are tricky to program. They require you to sprinkle intervention code all through the engine. Thus, whenever the engine does something that the threadtester might want to know about, you must insert an If statement that checks whether the threadtester is running, and if so, control must be diverted to some monitor routine that accumulates testing data.

Debuggers are even more demanding. You must devise a model of your engine that you can present to your storybuilders, and then insert an observer at that point to halt the engine's operation and give storybuilders access to the engine variables. The calculations your engine carries out must be presented to storybuilders, which requires displaying the calculations that are underway.

Finally, you will likely need to give storybuilders ways to run quickly through uninteresting portions of the engine's operation. If your engine operates in a purely procedural fashion, you can probably use something like *breakpoints*, which are stopping points that programmers use to check the program's state at those specified instants. More likely, you'll need to provide storybuilders with special constructs that permit stopping the engine operation based on declared story conditions. In any event, you'll probably find this the most difficult programming problem of the project.

Script Editing

A *script* is a short user-written program operating inside a larger program, used to customize applications or to handle repetitive chores. Many big applications have some sort of scripting system. All scripting languages are fairly simple, but considerable variation remains. Some scripting languages, such as Lingo for Macromedia Director, require extensive study to master, but a few can be picked up with a little experimentation.

It's difficult to conceive of an effective interactive storytelling system that doesn't use some sort of scripting language. Storybuilders must not only specify what Actors look like or what their personalities are; the most important task is to specify what they DO—and that takes you into territory that isn't far from darkest Programming Hell, if not actually inside it.

Creating a scripting language is a major task in building technologies for interactive storytelling, and it's made doubly difficult by most storybuilders being mathphobic. The designer must therefore go to great lengths to shield storybuilders from the fiercest denizens of Programming Hell.

Kill the Keyboard

The simplest way to shield storybuilders from Programming Hell lies in dumping the keyboard. Most script-editing systems use keyboard input, an appalling violation of the most elementary concepts of user interface design. With keyboard input, storybuilders can access a conceptual space of 26^N possible options (N is the number of keystrokes). Most scripting systems, by contrast, use only a few dozen variables and a few dozen operators in tightly constrained combinations. In more prosaic terms, with keyboard input you can say a gazillion wrong things to a scripting system and only a handful of correct things. Keyboard input is fine for professional programmers or others who are willing to learn all the abstruse textual details of a scripting system, but storybuilders can't afford to spend years mastering arcane technicalities. Besides, the purpose of a computer is to *help* people, not judge their syntax errors. Accordingly, keyboard input is inappropriate for interactive storytelling scripting systems. Pop-up menu-driven systems work better.

 Come on! Menu-driven systems are slow and clumsy; everybody knows that. Keyboard input is much faster.

That depends. If you're a programmer, typing `sudo killall -9 BOMArchiveHelper` might be lightning fast, but storybuilders aren't programmers and could take 10 minutes to get the right syntax for this command. For these people, a properly designed menu-driven system really is faster than keyboard input.

 But the number of menus you'd need to handle all the variables in an interactive storytelling engine would be prohibitive.

On the contrary, I found that I could lay out the script component menu headings along the left edge of the window; clicking on a menu heading displays all the menu options. This system works perfectly well inside an 800 × 600 window, using a scripting system with more than 400 defined terms, as you can see in **Figure 17.4.**

Lesson #39
Use menu-driven systems for script editors.

Inverse Parsing
A major benefit of menu-driven systems is that they permit *inverse parsing,* which is parsing that takes place before rather than after data entry.

 How can I parse storybuilders' input before they even enter it?

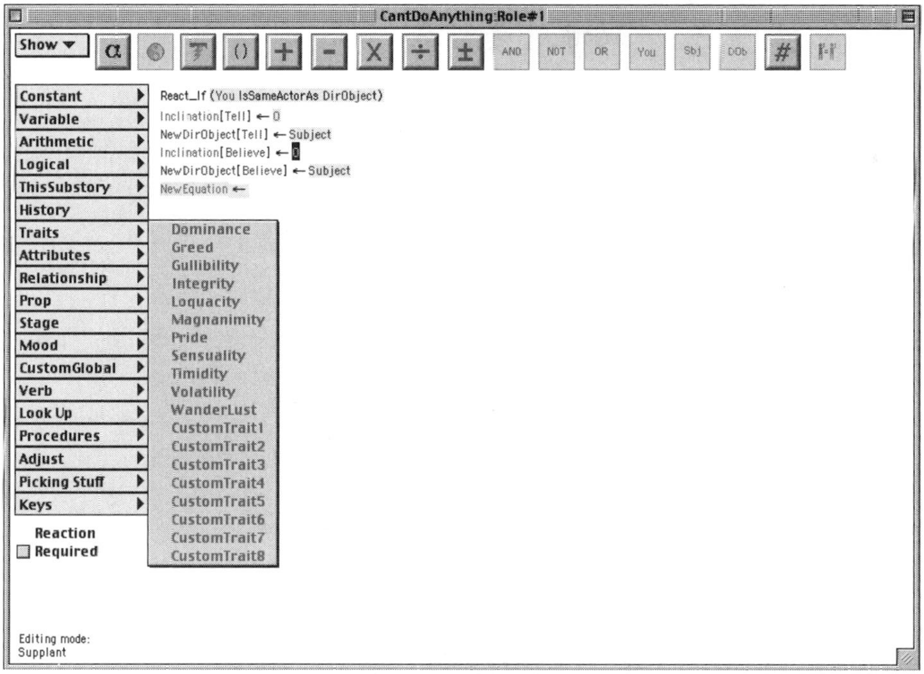

FIGURE 17.4: A menu layout for the Erasmatron scripting system.

You parse the possibilities, not the input. Say that a storybuilder has selected something to edit. Certain options are inappropriate for that selection, and an inverse parser determines what options are inappropriate and disables their menu items. The result is that the storybuilder can select only good, wholesome items for input.

And while you're at it, you might want to "semi-disable" menu items rather than fully disable them. A semi-disabled menu item is still displayed in a color to indicate that it's not fully accessible, but if the storybuilder goes ahead and selects it, an alert pops up to explain why that item is disabled and what must be done to enable it. This approach goes a long way toward reducing storybuilder frustration.

Preset Arguments with Full Prompts

However, a well-designed menu structure is only part of the overall user interface for a scripting system. For example, storybuilders should never have to guess what goes where. Whenever a storybuilder selects a script component that requires arguments to be supplied, those arguments should be set as default values or clearly marked as undefined.

For example, suppose a storybuilder wants to use the `Affection` variable in a script formula. This variable takes two arguments: the person holding the affection and the person for whom the affection is held. Therefore, when the storybuilder selects the `Affection` variable, it should be presented as

```
Affection[OfWhom, ForWhom]
```

I underline the two undefined terms to clearly indicate to the storybuilder that something is wrong with them, that more needs to be done. The labels for the terms indicate exactly what they mean.

Lesson #40
Clearly indicate and define required but undefined arguments.

The basic concept is simple: Storybuilders should never be required to remember to include something. This rule extends down to whatever lines of script you require. If every script must have a statement that assigns a value to, say, a variable called `Result`, the bare-bones version of the script should say

```
Result = WhatNumber?
```

If your scripting system requires storybuilders to enter expressions for multiple values, every script should be initialized to include statements for every value. To put it another way, if your scripting system ever needs a message statement along the lines of `Undefined value for X`, you have screwed up (unless you have provided an underlined cue value but the storybuilder failed to use it.)

Lesson #41
Provide all required lines of script on script initialization.

Another rule is ridiculously simple but often overlooked:

Lesson #42
Lose the acronyms. Spell it out.

If you're using keyboard input, contracting "line printer" to "lp" can be worth a programmer's time, but if you're not using keyboard input, this problem vanishes. You can spell out words such as "Affection" without burdening storybuilders, and it makes the script more readable.

But doesn't that eat up too much screen space?

Not in my experience. Remember, storybuilders are not given to writing out long formulae with dozens of terms. Most of the script lines they write will be short and simple.

Here's another simple rule that dramatically improves script readability:

Lesson #43
Use strongly typed, color-coded variables and functions.

In any interactive storytelling system, you're likely to have five basic types of values: Actors, Stages, Props, numbers, and booleans. Your scripting system should be strongly typed; that is, only Actor-type variables should be allowed in Actor-type script slots, only Prop-type variables in Prop-type slots, and so forth. Moreover, these types should be color-coded onscreen. I use red for numbers, black for booleans, blue for Actors, green for Verbs, orange for Events, pink for Props, and brown for Stages. At the very least, color-coding makes the scripting window fun to read!

How is this menu-driven system used for different modalities of text entry, such as insertion and replacement?

I use prefix keys, such as Ctrl and Alt. The default text-entry mode is replacement. The storybuilder clicks once on any term, and that term is highlighted. Then the storybuilder selects a menu item, and the chosen menu item replaces the selected term. In this system, you don't use insertion; instead, you use something I call *outsertion*. Outsertion adds a new operator and retains the original selected term inside that operator. For example, if I want to add 10 to the value of Affection, I don't insert an addition sign after the word "Affection"; instead, I select the word "Affection" and then hold down the Ctrl prefix key while selecting the menu item for addition. The result looks like this:

```
(Affection[Subject, DirObject] + WhatNumber?)
```

One warning: Editing systems require heavy use of parentheses to clearly indicate exactly what belongs where. Even when you're simply adding a group of numbers, parentheses are necessary to keep the editing system workable. The editor inserts the parentheses in direct response to storybuilder actions, so you can get odd-looking expressions such as this:

```
(((Affection[Subject, DirObject] + 27) + Temper[Subject]) +
➥Anger[Subject])
```

A nice feature to include is pop-up replacement menus; if a storybuilder clicks and holds on any term, a pop-up menu lists every variable that could replace the selected term. However, these pop-up menus can become cumbersomely long, so I cannot wholeheartedly recommend the idea.

A Few Nice Touches

Now it's common for editors in programming environments to show the range of any enclosing punctuation (parentheses, braces, or brackets). It's a good idea, and you should probably implement something like it in your editor. I tried a variation on the standard system. Any time a term has been selected, a storybuilder can click a button that highlights the contents of any operator, function, or array variable. In other words, if you want to know what something acts on, select it by clicking once, and then click and hold on the Contents button and the contents of that item will be highlighted. It's easier to pull off than clicking on a skinny parenthesis, and it works quite well.

Another odd possibility is to dispense with horizontal scrolling by allowing *substitution characters*, such as Greek letters. Whenever a line grows too long, a storybuilder can select the contents of any portion of the line (using the Contents button described previously) and click the Substitute button, which creates a new line of script containing the selected material and replace that selected material with the Greek letter.

Here's a before-and-after example:

Before:

```
Inclination[Punch] = Anger[Subject] - SQRT(Affection[Subject,
➥DirObject] + Gullibility[You]
```

After:

```
β = SQRT(Affection[Subject, DirObject] + Gullibility[You]
```

```
Inclination[Punch] = Anger[Subject] - β
```

Why go to all this trouble to replace horizontal scrolling?

Because sometimes lines get so long that it's difficult to figure out what they mean. Worse, the stuff hanging off the right edge of the window is often ignored and becomes the source of nasty bugs.

Why not simply allow storybuilders to have a wide window?

Because somebody will always build an expression wider than the window.

Seems like a lot of trouble for a tiny problem.

Yes, it probably is; that's why I list it as "a nice touch" rather than an important feature.

Wrapping Up

The hand of man is only as powerful as the tool it grasps. Storyworlds are big, complicated structures; attempting to build one with an inadequate development environment is as futile as attempting to bring down a wooly mammoth with a rock. Indeed, the size and richness of the storyworld that can be created is commensurate with the size and richness of the development environment used to create it. Simple tools yield simple products; if you hope to attain true interactive storytelling, you will surely need to build powerful development environments.

PART V

Applications

CHAPTER 18
The Erasmatron

I FIRST BEGAN GROPING IN the direction of interactive storytelling in the early 1980s, while running the games research group at Atari. Of course, at that time, the 8-bit, 1MHz computers we were using were completely inadequate to the task of interactive storytelling, so I wasn't even thinking in terms of such a grandiose objective. Instead, I wondered if I could design a game about interpersonal interactions. The videogames of the time were all quite simple-minded and impersonal— couldn't something be done to get some social interaction in games?

Early Efforts

My first crack at the problem was a little game I called Gossip, with eight actors: the human player and seven computer actors. Each had a telephone. The player would point to one of the actors (who then became the "interlocutor") and click to make his or her telephone ring. In a stunning display of technical virtuosity (for the time), the interlocutor would pick up the telephone and say "Air-Ro?" (This was Randy Smith's clever technology.) Then the player would point to a second actor and click. At this point, the player's face would alter to show a neutral emotional expression. Pushing the joystick up would change the expression to an friendly smile; pushing it up a second time would elicit a big, friendly smile and vigorous up-and-down nodding. On the other hand, pushing the joystick down would trigger a slight frown; pushing it down a second time would produce an angry glare and emphatic sideways head-shaking. In this manner, the player could express his feelings of affection or disdain for the designated actor.

Having declared his feelings, the player could then watch as the interlocutor declared his own feelings toward that person. They could continue their conversation by sharing opinions of other actors, or they could hang up. Other actors might call the player to express their feelings.

The gameplay was simple: People like people who like people they like. In other words, you could endear yourself to somebody by feigning affection for those he likes. You could also endear yourself by declaring contempt for those he hates. The strategy in Gossip, then, was to tell everybody what they wanted to hear. Of course, if your inconsistencies became widely known, nobody would like you, and you'd lose the game.

Gossip was certainly primitive. I never thought of it as a full game design; instead, it was a design study for a much larger game, Excalibur. The player, as King Arthur, had to retain his knights' loyalty, but their own interpersonal rivalries drove them apart and could indirectly affect Arthur. If Percival, for example, feuded with Arthur's brother Kay, Percival's hatred for Kay would translate into disaffection for Arthur. The player had to monitor these rivalries and occasionally intervene with special goodies for Percival to retain his loyalty.

In 1987 I took another stab at the problem with my game Siboot. By this time, I had realized that language was a major problem because the range of behaviors required of drama demanded a larger vocabulary than could be had with the simple nonlinguistic input systems used in games. Therefore, with the help of Dr. Christa Hansen, a psycholinguist from Stanford, I developed the concepts of an inverse parser and a graphical sublanguage, discussed in more detail in Chapter 10, "Language-Based Strategies." These components provided the foundation of the game. The game that resulted was unconventional; players used the language to converse with actors and exchange information. The primitive language used in the game was presented to the player as a telepathic language enabling actors from different species to communicate. It wasn't a commercial success, but is certainly my most creative effort. You can find Macintosh and PC downloads of the game at a number of sites on the web; searching for "Siboot" should get you there.

The Erasmatron Engine

In 1991, I decided the time had come to commit myself to solving the problem of interactive storytelling. In the dozen years since then, I have developed and refined a technology for just this purpose. Much of that technology is described in previous chapters. The personality model I developed, for example, is presented in detail in Chapter 11, "Personality Models."

My version of a drama manager I called *Fate*. I have previously mentioned Fate in Chapter 16, "Sequencing." Fate is always given the first opportunity to react to any Event that takes place; this gives Fate the ability to intervene in every situation and bend it in another direction. Fate is my proxy (as storybuilder) in the storyworld, my personal representative. I strive to endow Fate with my dramatic intentions. I also endow Fate with the ability to act independently; once each day Fate is activated and examines the developing story from a global perspective; should Fate identify a need for action, it uses this opportunity to set up that action. I call this mechanism a *plotpoint*.

The engine's basic structure is described in Chapter 16, "Roles and Sequencing." It's a reactive engine; every Event occurs as a reaction to some previous Event. Only Fate can initiate Events, using plotpoint powers. It uses Verbs and Events as described in Chapter 13, maintains a HistoryBook as explained in Chapter 14, and implements anticipatory behavior in conformance with the ideas presented in Chapter 15.

Data Types

In Chapter 17, "Development Environments," I referred briefly to *data types*, a standard concept in computer science, when dicussing the types of variables and functions, such as Actors, Stages, booleans, and so forth. Deep inside the computer, there are only numbers, but to make programming less error prone, computer languages such as C++ implement data typing. At the beginning of each program, the programmer must list each variable used in the program and declare its data type. For example, a simple integer is declared to be of type short, which is a number stored in only two bytes of memory. Another data type called long is a number stored in four bytes of memory. Text is declared to be of data type char, short for "character." (That's why I insist on the cognomen "Actor" for virtual characters in the storyworld; it's too easy to confuse the character "%" with the character "Harry.") The big idea of data typing is simple: You can't mix apples and oranges. You can't use a short where you require a char, and vice versa. Data typing automatically catches lots of pesky little mistakes that would otherwise cost many hours of debugging time.

The Erasmatron uses exactly eight data types—no more, no less. They are Actors, Verbs, Stages, Props, Events, Groups, Numbers, and Flags. Storybuilders cannot mix these data types together. A command requiring an Actor can be filled in only with an Actor. To make matters even easier, the data types in the Erasmatron are color-coded, as shown in this table:

Data Type	Color
Actor	Blue
Verb	Green
Stage	Brown
Prop	Pink
Event	Orange
Group	Purple
Number	Red
Flag (boolean)	Black

Color-coding makes it easy to see exactly what's going on in the Erasmatron.

Roles

Roles are defined in Chapter 16, "Sequencing." In the Erasmatron, roles are defined by what I call *reaction formulae*, which are boolean expressions defining the specifications for the role. Here is a simple reaction formula for the role of the victim of a punch:

```
ReactIf (You IsSamePersonAs DirObject)
```

This formula reads like a command: "You will react to the Event if you are the same person as the DirObject." Note that the long phrase "are the same person as" has been compressed into a single word; functionally, it operates as a single relationship.

The concept of a reaction formula becomes useful when you consider complicated contexts, such as the role of the male friend of the punchee who might want to intervene:

```
ReactIf (NOT(You IsSamePersonAs DirObject) AND (Male[You]) AND
➥(Affection[You, DirObject] > 5))
```

This formula reads like so: "You will react to the Event if you are not the DirObject, and you are a guy, and you have plenty of Affection for the DirObject." As you can see, this form of expression permits storybuilders to specify almost any context.

Scripts

I described scripting systems in Chapter 17, "Development Environments." In the Erasmatron, every role has its own script that specifies:

▶ The reaction formula, specifying whether an Actor should execute the rest of the script.

▶ Changes in the Actor's relationship with the Subject of the Event: in other words, that Actor's emotional reaction to the Event.

▶ Changes in the physical environment arising from the Event, such as the transfer of ownership of a Prop. These changes are normally handled in a role executed by Fate.

▶ The Verb options available to the Actor for reacting to the Event.

▶ The secondary objects (SecObjects) associated with each Verb option. (SecObjects are explained in Chapter 13, "Verbs and Events.")

▶ The inclination formula for each Verb option.

The scripting editor in the Erasmatron uses all the ideas presented in Chapter 17, such as color-coded entry, replacement editing, full wording, underlining used as cues, and mouse-driven editing.

Inclination Formulae

Most of the effort in building a storyworld in the Erasmatron goes into creating and tuning inclination formulae. I offer here an example of a set of inclination formulae and how they are handled. The Verb to which the Actor is reacting is Punch; the Actor is the DirObject. The Actor has four options: WithdrawGrumbling, RunAway, Punch, or DrawAGunOn. The inclination formulae for these options are as follows:

```
Inclination[WithdrawGrumbling] = 2

Inclination[RunAway] = 1 - AngerFear[You]

Inclination[Punch] = Strength[You] - Strength[Subject]

Inclination[DrawAGunOn] = 5 × LogicalToNumber(Prop[Gun].Owner
➥IsSameActorAs You)
```

Now let's go through this mess line by line. The first line is the easiest: You simply say that the inclination to WithdrawGrumbling is 2. That fixes the base level; the Actor will take that option unless some other option gets a higher Inclination value.

The second line is a bit more complex; it says that the Inclination to RunAway is based on the Actor's AngerFear mood. An Actor with an AngerFear mood of 10 will be raging with fury, and Actor with an AngerFear mood of –10 will be quaking in fear. An Actor with an AngerFear mood of 0 will not be feeling Anger or Fear. Note that you subtract the mood from 1; this means a positive value of the mood (meaning that the Actor is angry) disinclines him to RunAway, and a negative value for the mood yields a positive result, inclining the Actor to RunAway.

The next line says that the inclination to return the punch is equal to the difference in Strength between You (the Actor considering the options) and the Subject (the Actor who just punched You). In other words, if You is stronger than the Subject, You will be inclined to punch him back, but if You is weaker than the Subject, You will be disinclined to punch him back.

The last line is complex. It's easiest to understand if you work backward, from right to left. "You" has already been explained. IsSameActorAs is a boolean test; it asks whether the Actor in front of this term is the same Actor as the one in back of this term. In a more brutal mathematical language, you would simply use an equals sign (Actor1 = Actor2), but I designed the Erasmatron scripting language to be understandable without a lot of mathematics.

Prop[Gun].Owner is a mess. It refers to the Actor who is the owner of the Prop known as Gun. It's a number equal to the index of the Actor who owns the Gun. In plain English, it answers the question "Who owns the gun?"

Therefore, the entire expression inside the parentheses (Prop[Gun].Owner IsSameActorAs You) asks whether the owner of the gun is the same person as the Actor executing the script. It's a long-winded way of asking "Does You have the Gun?"

LogicalToNumber is a function that takes a logical value ("true" or "false") and turns it into a number ("1" or "0"). This value, when multiplied by 5, yields 5 or 0, depending on whether You has the Gun. In other words, if You has the Gun, the inclination to DrawAGunOn will be 5; if You does not have the Gun, the inclination will be 0.

So suppose that the Actor in this case is moderately afraid (AngerFear[You] is -3), weaker than the Subject (Strength[You] - Strength[Subject] = -3), and has no Gun. Then the results will be as follows:

```
Inclination[WithdrawGrumbling] = 2

Inclination[RunAway] = 4

Inclination[Punch] = -3

Inclination[DrawAGunOn] = 0
```

In this case, the Actor will choose to RunAway. Hence, the engine will build a plan with the Actor as the Subject, RunAway as the Verb, and the previous Subject as the new DirObject.

Time in the Erasmatron

The Erasmatronic conception of time is, well, mechanical. There's a central clock, which ticks off one minute with each tick. With each new tick, the engine repeats a lengthy procedure, as explained in Chapter 16. The first step in this procedure is searching through the plan list looking for plans that are ready to execute. When such a plan is found, the engine doesn't immediately execute it; first it checks to make certain the appropriate audience conditions exist for its execution. If so, then the engine executes the plan; otherwise the plan goes to the opportunity list for deferred execution.

Plan Execution

Executing a plan is a ridiculously simple matter: the engine moves the plan from the plan list into the HistoryBook, where it becomes an Event. At the same time, it takes the current clock time and stores it in the TimeOfOccurrence slot of the Event record. The engine also figures the CausalEvent and stores it in the appropriate slot.

Movement and Space

The Erasmatron deviates most from common practice in the area of movement. There's no map in a storyworld; there are no spatial relationships among locations. There are only Stages, which impose simple spatial relationships on Actors. All Actors sharing a Stage are able to interact with each other freely, but only Actors sharing a Stage can interact with each other. Actors can move from one Stage to any other instantly; there are no travel times. One special Stage, called Limbo, holds Actors who are out of action. No activity takes place in Limbo; putting Actors in Limbo is like banishing them to Siberia.

The engine controls most movement. So long as there's activity on a Stage, no one is allowed to enter or leave. After the activity dies out, the engine starts to move Actors to other Stages, and new Actors can enter the Stage. For each Actor, the storybuilder specifies his or her Territoriality for each Stage. As I explained in Chapter 16, Territoriality isn't a desire to control a Stage, but a proclivity to return to that Stage. For example, a 16-year-old Valley Girl would have a high Territoriality value for the shopping mall Stage and a low Territoriality value for the pool hall Stage. Males would have low Territoriality for the women's bathroom, and horse lovers might have high Territoriality for the stables.

The storybuilder can intrude on this process by entering an *Appointment* in the script for a Verb. An Appointment specifies the time for an Actor to go to a Stage; in moving Actors, the engine gives priority to Appointments.

Gossip in the Erasmatron storytelling engine follows the principles laid down in Chapter 14, "HistoryBooks and Gossip."

Additional Odds and Ends in the Engine

There remain a number of minor features in the system. One is *Spying*, which reflects a major difference between drama and real life. In real life, people can, if they wish, speak together, confident that they're not being overheard. Such is not the case in drama. The two actors lean over the table to each other, whispering their plan to foil the antagonist, and then depart; the curtains behind their table part to reveal—the antagonist! Drama oozes with unlikely circumstances because they allow interesting dramatic convolutions. Sure, it isn't realistic; this is drama, not simulation.

The Erasmatron storytelling engine permits this kind of behavior. One Actor can be set to spy upon another, and for the next 24 hours, the Spy shadows the Spied-Upon, witnessing everything the Spied-Upon says and does, all without being detected.

Another minor detail is a special data type called Group, which is a set of Actors defined to act as a social unit. For example, a storybuilder might build a Group representing a gang, and then treat the gang as a single object. The leader could exhort the group as a whole, accept the group's cheers and huzzahs, lead the group into a fight with another gang, and so forth. Group interactions are uncommon in drama; most interactions involve only two people. But a few interactions demand group treatment, so the engine provides for these situations.

Future Directions

The Erasmatron is now at Version 3.2. I am preparing for a major revision of the technology with Erasmatron 4.0. This new version will contain a streamlined personality model, improved facilities for storybuilders to create and tune inclination formulae without requiring expertise in mathematics, and improvements in computations for anticipation.

Complete information on the Erasmatron technology can be found at www.erasmatazz.com.

CHAPTER 19
Research

RESEARCH ON INTERACTIVE STORYTELLING goes back to 1985, when Brenda Laurel addressed the notion in her doctoral thesis. A group of graduate students at MIT began exploring the relationship between narrative and computers in the early 1990s. Agent-based technology drifted toward storytelling issues in the mid-1990s, and Stanford hosted the Interactive Story Systems conference in 1995. That early work was tentative, but people were definitely starting to show interest. Janet Murray published her popular book *Hamlet on the Holodeck* in 1997, describing some of the efforts and possibilities.

Conferences addressing topics related to interactive storytelling were held in Avignon, France, in 2001 and Darmstadt, Germany, in 2003. "Narrative Intelligence," a collection of academic papers, appeared in 2002. Several dozen research papers on aspects of interactive storytelling have appeared in the past few years. This chapter presents a digest of some of that work.

Interactive storytelling lies on the frontiers of research; accordingly, no common vocabulary or even any consistent frame of reference exists. Every researcher, including me, approaches the problem fresh and concocts whatever schemes and terminology seem right. Bombarding you with this diverse terminology will surely befuddle you; I therefore take the liberty of rephrasing many of these ideas in the terminology I've established in this book. In most cases, my rephrasing robs the original work of some of its robustness, so I urge readers to consult the original research work when possible. I have supplied references to many of these works in the endnotes.

Generic Issues

First, I want to present a number of major points that touch on many of these research efforts. Most of these research efforts have been prepared for academic consumption, and as such, they cannot be applied immediately to the task of building interactive storytelling systems. Research projects aren't intended to yield software that can be sold in stores; what matters is to create and develop ideas for what commercial operations call the "feasibility stage." The goal is not to actually finish the software, but to demonstrate that it could be finished with an adequate expenditure of money and resources. Realistically, one graduate student working for two years can't be expected to build a working system for interactive storytelling. The previous chapters of this book should have demonstrated the massive and complex nature of any technology for interactive storytelling.

Accordingly, these efforts must be appraised not as working technologies but as speculative exploration of interesting concepts. If you require them to prove their merit with working demonstrations, you'll inevitably be forced to conclude they just don't work. A more constructive approach is to merely extract the best ideas and leave it at that.

Hammers and Nails

An apropos aphorism here is "When you've got a big enough hammer, everything starts to look like a nail." A number of these research efforts are attempts to treat interactive storytelling as the perfect nail for the hammer of some well-developed technology from computer science. These efforts pose particular problems for this book because few of you are likely to be familiar with current technologies in computer science. I shall attempt to at least characterize those technologies as the need arises, but sometimes rendering a complete explanation of the idea for nontechnical readers is impossible.

Boolean Thinking

Computer scientists have built a large and powerful set of concepts for solving a wide range of problems. This set of concepts is not just a random pile; they are all interrelated in a complex intellectual structure. Fundamental concepts underlie a structure of ideas that researchers continue to expand and build ever higher. In this way, computer scientists have been able to coordinate the efforts of many brilliant people over the course of decades, establishing an impressive intellectual edifice.

This edifice was built to solve engineering problems. Computer scientists have tackled a wide range of problems, but they have veered toward more mechanical problems because these problems are the ones they can solve. When they have attempted to tackle softer problems, such as natural language, they have encountered frustrating obstacles and made less progress.

The perfect example of computer science at its best is the programming of the Mars robots Spirit and Opportunity. These two robots operate millions of miles away from their human controllers, in a harsh and alien environment, with absolutely no opportunity for assistance should they err. They use their cameras to view their surroundings, and their software analyzes the images in 3D to figure out locations and sizes of rocks, the slope and texture of the ground, and so forth. They plan safe routes over rocky and uneven ground. They have to be able to carry out minor repairs on their own software and evaluate their own mechanical problems. This is complicated stuff, yet they have performed magnificently. These machines are a triumph of computer science.

But all these tasks are engineering problems, expressible in precise mathematical form. There are no uncertainties, no probabilities, no soft factors. Everything the robot needs to know it can calculate, and the results of its computations are black and white. These robots aren't programmed to make judgment calls based on hunches or soft factors. That's not their department—computer science doesn't do that kind of thing well.

 What about fuzzy logic and other methodologies for handling uncertainty?

True, computer scientists have made many stabs at handling uncertainty, but these efforts have not enjoyed the triumphs that hard-core approaches can claim. Many interesting and impressive results have been obtained using fuzzy logic, but so far this area of effort is more a field of opportunity than a spire of triumph.

The problem with the most common computer science technologies is their emphasis on boolean data structures. Fundamentally, a boolean value is a stupid number. The numerical value of pi is 3.14159265358979, but the boolean value of pi is 1, as distinct from 0. Seeing the world through boolean eyes eliminates all color and all shades, leaving just two values: black and white (see **Figure 19.1**).

FIGURE 19.1: On the left, arithmetic imagery; on the right, boolean imagery.

This black-and-white vision is what computer scientists tend to do with dramatic reality. They build large datasets containing statements like this:

An apple is a fruit.

An orange is a fruit.

A banana is a fruit.

All fruit is edible.

Only edible things can be eaten.

All Actors have the boolean attribute Hungry.

If the Hungry flag is true, then the Actor sets a goal "to eat."

The Hungry flag is set to true eight hours after an Actor last ate.

After a thing is eaten, it no longer exists.

This kind of dataset makes it possible for actors to determine that they are hungry, decide that they need to eat, search for something that's edible, and then eat it. By expanding this pile of statements, computer scientists believe that they can attain any level of dramatic fidelity they want. **Figure 19.2** illustrates the way they see it in their mind's eye.

First try   More work   Someday

FIGURE 19.2: Every day, in every way, better and better!

The problem with this thinking is that it underestimates the number of logical statements needed to make "someday" happen. The most ambitious effort in this direction is the CYC project (www.cyc.com), which attempts to capture all the basic information necessary for what we call "common sense." The CYC team has already compiled millions—I do not exaggerate—of such statements and it hasn't reached completion. Common sense is a subset of what's needed to express all the laws of drama. Obviously, the task of applying this boolean methodology to interactive storytelling is far beyond our reach.

 Does that not suggest the task is impossible? How do you know that a numerical approach will be any less humongous?

Consider a drawing, shown in **Figure 19.3**, based on the previous images.

At heart, Figure 19.3 is a collection of curving lines, not a collection of pixels. The images in Figure 19.2 are composed of pixels, all black and white. The more pixels, the better the image. Figure 19.3's drawing is not composed of pixels, however; its core data structure is a curve, which is a numeric data structure, not a boolean data structure. Note how the drawing is able to capture the human essence of the images in Figure 19.2 without having to store thousands of pixels. It consists of only a few dozen curves. The drawing is a more artistic construction because it emphasizes the parts of the image you're interested in (eyes, mouth, and hand) and suppresses those parts you're not interested in (clothing, details of the hat, wrinkles). Sure, the best bitmaps look more realistic, but they have a high cost. The drawing in Figure 19.3 requires less information than the first-try bitmap, which it's clearly superior to. In other words, for a certain amount of work on your part, the numeric approach gives you more fidelity than the boolean approach.

FIGURE 19.3: A drawing, not a bitmap.

Scott McCloud makes this point powerfully in his book *Understanding Comics*. He discusses it in terms of the abstraction with which an image is presented and the effect that more abstraction leads to wider applicability of the image. He offers a visual representation of the concept at `www.scottmccloud.com/inventions/triangle/triangle.html`.

This is what the current emphasis on boolean thinking misses. At the lowest levels of effort, the boolean approach is more readily controllable and easier to work with, but in tackling big complex problems such as interactive storytelling, the boolean approach requires more true/false combinations than can be realistically assembled.

The following sections are a synopsis of the various research reports I have been able to discover.

The Oz Project

The late 1980s saw lots of excitement in the computer science community over an idea referred to as "intelligent agents." The concept is to create a body of software that addresses a particular task and give that software some kind of human face. Instead of designing everything in machine-like terms, agent technology approached the problem as a matter of teaching a computer agent to behave properly. This approach was largely a matter of changing the software designer's point of view, but much of this thinking bled over into other areas. The most prominent example is the "help wizard" who appeared onscreen to give advice, answer questions, and offer help. These wizards didn't work out because they were much dumber than any wizard, so user-wizard interaction was largely frustrating for users. Eventually designers of these systems laid off most of their user interface wizards and shipped the survivors to a back room.

A number of researchers, however, saw merit in the idea of applying agent technology to entertainment software. Dr. Joseph Bates led the first effort in this direction, the Oz Project, at Carnegie Mellon University in the early 1990s[1]. The agents, called "woggles," were balls with eyes that could move around their environment by bouncing. Most of the research effort went into designing good personality models for the woggles, which could in turn be translated into interesting behavior.

The crucial flaw in this effort, in my opinion, lay in the emphasis on the character model at the expense of the verb set. The woggles are interesting creatures, but they can't *do* very much because verbs were built into the system only to demonstrate woggle personality. My definition of interactivity places all the emphasis on the verbs in the design. By giving short shrift to verbs, the designers created a completely computable but ultimately moribund virtual universe.

 But this work was done more than a decade ago! It's primitive because it broke new ground.

You're absolutely right. The Oz Project is important for the pioneering nature of the work. The project trained a group of researchers who are now at the cutting edge of entertainment software design: Joe Bates himself, Peter Weyhrauch, Phoebe Sengers, and Michael Mateas. The spin-offs from this project testify to its importance: Zoesis, a company attempting to commercialize the Oz technology (www.zoesis.com); the Façade project (described later in this chapter); and additional research efforts.

Barbara Hayes-Roth at Stanford also pounced on agent technology at an early stage and took it in new and different directions. Her company, Extempo Systems (www.extempo.com), uses agent technology for training and entertainment software.

Experience Management

The solution you come up with is dictated by the problem you perceive. In designing Experience Management[2], the authors, Andrew S. Gordon and Nicholas V. Iuppa, start off with the perception that narrative and interactivity are not absolutely incompatible, but tend to work against each other. They see the central problem as establishing a balance between player control (interactivity) and dramatic control (narrative). One other perception dominates their thinking: that a narrative has only one or a few correct endings. For this reason, they see their challenge as confining the player to the preferred storyline.

Adventure game designers have faced this problem for more than 20 years; the standard solution in adventure games is a foldback scheme, as I described in Chapter 7, "Simple Strategies That Don't Work." If the player insists on going off on a tangent, the designer must somehow return that player to the expected path. Brian Moriarty used and satirized the standard solution in 1986 with Trinity. In this game, the player is at a park and is expected to move in a certain direction. Should the player attempt to move in the wrong direction, blades of grass rise up together and push the player back. It was an absurd solution, but it accomplished its intended effect of keeping the player moving along the correct path.

Gordon and Iuppa rely on foldback, dressed up in high-falutin' academic language. The example they offer posits that the player is expected to follow his friend Richard into a cafe. Should the player refuse to conform to their expectations, they offer a series of increasingly insistent options to make it clear to the player that he damn well better do what's expected of him and get his stupid butt into that cafe. As examples, the authors offer:

> "As I walk back home, I notice the cafe at the edge of the park and see that Richard is heading in this direction."

"As much as I try to ignore Richard and head back home, he seems to always be ahead of me, making his way toward the cafe at the edge of the park."

"As I come around the corner and pass a magazine stand, I see that there is a cover-story article praising the wonderful food at the cafe at the other edge of this very park—just as my stomach begins to rumble with hunger."

Get the hint, you stupid player?

What's the difference between this approach and some of the intrusive techniques offered in Chapter 12?

This approach is more heavy-handed than the techniques described in Chapter 12, "Drama Managers." See especially the section "Correcting the Player."

This technology, which the authors christen "Experience Management," provides a clever model for implementing this foldback scheme. They apply concepts from computer science to formally represent the knowledge implicit in the developing story and to indicate the storybuilder's expectations for players. Each event in the storyworld must include formal statements defining the key tidbit of knowledge that event represents and specifying the storybuilder's expectations as to how players should change their knowledge in response to that tidbit. All this knowledge representation then feeds the *predicate logic* (a technical term for logical calculations) that determines how to respond to players' actions.

All this high-powered computer science technology seems to do nothing more than select which foldback option will be inflicted on stubborn players to enforce proper behavior. The technology doesn't actually create or compose those foldback options; it doesn't recognize that the player has deviated from the required path.

You're being unfair. This technology wasn't developed to implement a general-purpose interactive storytelling system; it was developed for educational applications. The goal of the system is to get the player to the correct solution for a tricky problem.

True, but even as an educational application, this strategy fails. If the player wants to drive his car off the cliff, designers shouldn't create guard rails that magically appear and bounce his car back onto the road or magic guardian angels who catch the plummeting car and waft it back onto the road. No, they should let the car fall to its destruction and tell the player, "See what your stupid decision led to? Wanna try again?" That's the whole point and purpose of using computers: They let players fail without real-world consequences. Students using an educational application don't truly understand the material until they see it in both the light and the darkness, the right and the wrong, the success and the failure. So let them fail!

Story Traces

Interactive storytelling is so difficult that any foothold you can get is worth trying. There are so few technologies on which to base your work that it's worthwhile to examine any relevant technology for its applicability. Elizabeth Figa and Paul Tarau have done just this with WordNet[3] (described in some detail in Chapter 10, "Language-Based Strategies"). They have attempted to harness the power of WordNet to build technologies useful to interactive storytelling. Their goal is to build a library of story traces and story projections.

A *story trace* is an abstract reduction of a story, the skeleton of the story, as Figa and Tarau put it. They propose to extract story traces from a variety of stories, using WordNet to deduce the story trace by examining the relationships among the words in the story. This process will yield a library of story traces that can be used as templates against which a developing story could be matched. Thus, as the player plays with the storyworld, a story trace is extracted from the story created so far, and that trace is matched against the templates in the library. The best-fitting template is then used to take the story to its next step.

That next step is what Figa and Tarau call a *story projection:* a fragment of a story that can be treated as a single dramatic atom. Story projections are actual selections of story fragments that fit a given ontology, described as a set of matching rules. They allow a reader to focus on a single aspect of the story seen as a unit—for instance, what happens to a certain character, what takes place at a given location, and so forth. As yet, their work hasn't reached the stage at which it can generate stories.

Façade

As of early 2004, Façade, developed by Michael Mateas and Andrew Stern, is without doubt the best actual working interactive storyworld yet created[4]. It combines a number of off-the-shelf software technologies with some brilliant innovations.

Façade is impressive in a number of areas. It offers a 3D first-person view of the stage and actors (see **Figure 19.4**).

FIGURE 19.4: A screenshot from Façade.

The player is a dinner guest at the home of Trip and Grace, whose marriage is falling apart. It's a one-act play on a single stage with just two nonplayer characters. This narrow focus is one factor in the success of Façade; by tightly confining the dramatic situation, Mateas and Stern have brought the problem within reach. Trip and Grace are fully realized 3D objects; they can walk around, gesticulate, and display facial expressions. This 3D action by itself is not revolutionary, but its integration with the overall storytelling system is a great accomplishment. To pull it off, Mateas and Stern created A Behavioral Language (ABL), a custom language for controlling bodily movements. This language allowed them to specify stage directions for actors in response to the developing dramatic situation. They also created a natural language processing system for interpreting the player's typed-in speech and a "reaction decider" language for choosing context-specific reactions to the player's speech and physical actions.

Moreover, Façade runs in real time. Rejecting the turn-sequenced systems that I and others prefer, Mateas and Stern have tackled the problem of maintaining real-time drama. The construct at the core of their system is called a *beat*. A beat is what I call an Event; it's a single dramatic atom, although it's expressed as a sequence of audiovisual steps. For example, the beat that launches the storyworld has Trip open the door and welcome the player. Trip opens the door, steps back, greets the player, and invites entry. All these actions constitute a single beat.

Where turn-sequenced Events simply happen in one fell swoop, a beat takes place over an extended period and can be interrupted. This is closely analogous to my system for hijacking the storyline, although Mateas and Stern have gone further by creating a clever system that keeps interrupted beats on hold while the interruptions are dealt with, and then returns to the interrupted beats or abandons them if they are no longer dramatically appropriate.

The core of the dramatic expression comes in the system for sequencing beats; their system uses something very similar to my own system for roles and inclination formulae. What I call a reaction formula, they call a precondition; what I call an inclination, they call a weight.

Mateas and Stern implement a simple drama manager in their system by adding another factor to their inclination formulae based on the dramatic tension. The storybuilder assigns to each beat an individual tension value that is applied to the selection of the succeeding beat. The basic idea is that each succeeding beat should have more tension than the previous one, until the story reaches its climax, at which point the drama manager switches to beats with diminishing tension.

The Façade technology doesn't address issues such as gossip, secrets, lies, multiple dimensions of relationships, or variable audience requirements for executing a verb. By focusing their attention on a precisely confined dramatic context, Mateas and Stern have obviated the need for these technologies, permitting them to attack and solve all the problems of that confined context. The result is without question the best overall interactive storyworld produced as of early 2004.

 Mateas and Stern also participate in an excellent blog, Grand Text Auto, at `http://grandtextauto.org/`.

The Dr. K- Project

One of the more charming aspects of the universe of interactive storytelling is the collection of wild and crazy ideas that have been tried. The Dr. K- Project, by Brandon Rickman, definitely falls into this category[5]. It was carried out as part of a master's thesis, and so doesn't reflect the kind of concerted effort seen in many other projects. Instead, it offers a pleasantly bizarre approach to the whole problem of interactive storytelling.

Rickman has dispensed entirely with the notion of a story as a temporal sequence of events. Instead, he takes advantage of the computer's special capabilities to offer something that—well, it's difficult to describe. Perhaps the sample interaction he offers best characterizes the concept:

> A place. A tea chest. A body bag. A scrap of paper. An assassin. A character. Something happens.

> [User selects "A character".]

> A place. A tea chest. A body bag. Some scenery. An assassin. A rascal. Something happens.

The result of the user's input is to replace "a character" with "a rascal." If you're wondering where the story is, well, there isn't any story. Rather, as best as I can tell, the software presents an unfolding vignette. The user selects phrases from the phrase list, which causes the selected phrase to expand into something more detailed. Simultaneously, ignored phrases fade into generalities.

Weird as this might seem, it demonstrates an interesting technology. Mr. Rickman has taken the concept of an object hierarchy as used in object-oriented programming and applied it to drama. He has created a hierarchy of classes based on four basic classes (props, scenes, actors, and actions) with a variety of other sub- and superclasses to build a system that can readily move in either direction in the hierarchy. The result is this "unfolding vignette."

HEFTI

The DNA in cell nuclei is a biological computer. It not only stores the information that constitutes genetic heritage, but it expresses that heritage by processing the proteins that create the cells forming human bodies. Even more impressive is DNA's ability to recombine and alter in ways that permit living creatures to adapt to changes in the environment. This biological computing system is immensely powerful; a researcher has already used DNA to solve a mathematical problem that would have taken years to solve with conventional computers. The preparation and chemical analysis of the sample took many months; the actual computation took a fraction of a second.

So it shouldn't be surprising that computer scientists have looked to DNA for inspiration in radically new approaches to computing. A major subfield of computer science research, called *genetic algorithms*, is dedicated to this idea. Much has been learned about how to build virtual genes, how to combine them, and how to set up populations of virtual systems that learn from their environment.

It occurred to Teong Joo Ong and John Leggett of Texas A&M University that genetic algorithms might prove a useful approach to the problem of interactive storytelling, so they built a software system to do just that[6]. They called it HEFTI: the Hybrid Evolutionary-Fuzzy Time-based Interactive storytelling system.

At this point, I must excuse myself with the observation that the HEFTI documents are written with more than the usual academic abuse of the English language. Multiple rereadings of these documents leave many unanswered questions. My explanation of this technology will be inadequate. I must accept some responsibility, for I do not have a computer scientist's intimate familiarity with the latest jargon, but the obtuseness of the documentation's writing is the primary obstacle.

The HEFTI system is complex, comprising five major components. The Evolutionary Programming Subsystem (EPS) component is the most critical. It uses genetic algorithms to assemble virtual chromosomes representing story threads. These chromosomes are compared to story threads the storybuilder provides; the best-fitting chromosome becomes the story thread used in interaction with the player.

The Fuzzy Decision Based System (FDBS) "imposes constraints, modifications, and evaluations on the solution instances with rules and variables in the knowledge base." Translated into plain English, this means nothing more than "the FDBS crunches some numbers." Presumably it does so using the techniques of fuzzy logic.

The Knowledge Base is a pile of storybuilder-specified data. Its fundamental component is the *story component*, the author's term for what I call a Verb. A story component is defined as "the representation of a particular time step in the story," but the authors don't define "time step." The storybuilder strings these story components together into story threads, which appear to be representative sequences of story components. The Knowledge Base also contains Contextual

Sets, used to "categorize various plot units, events, scripts, actions, and characters within the story components." Aside from "story components," none of these terms is explained further.

The Graphical Object Library (GOL) is a collection of graphics data and methods that provide imagery and animation for the system's output. When the HEFTI engine has decided what it wants to do, it directs the GOL to display the appropriate imagery onscreen.

The last component of the HEFTI system is the Integrated Authoring Environment (IAE), based on XML. This development environment provided with the engine feeds data into the Knowledge Base. Here's an example of the code used in the IAE:

```xml
<storyline>

  <timestep order="1" name="introduction" sequence="and">

    <set type="introduction" pickatmost="1">

      <element name="act_10" addfitness="1"/>

    </set>

  </timestep>

  <timestep order="2" name="wolf threat" sequence="and">

    <set type="wolf threat" pickatmost="1"/>

  </timestep>

  <timestep order="3" name="wolf attack" sequence="and">

    <set type="wolf attack" pickatmost="2" placement="remove"/>

  </timestep>

  <timestep order="4" name="wolf's plan" sequence="and" loop="true"
➥condition="{isPigStillAvailable}==true OR {isWolfDead}==true">

    <set type="wolf's plan" pickatmost="1" placement="noremove">

      <element name="act_13" addfitness="2"/>
```

```
        </set>

    </timestep>

</storyline>
```

This sample exemplifies the wrong approach to development systems. It's program code for programmers, incomprehensible to the kind of creative talent needed for storytelling. So long as development environments look like this code example, only programmers will write storyworlds, and we'll continue to get the same old clichéd stories.

The only storyworld the authors built with their technology appears to be an abbreviated version of "The Three Little Pigs." They were able to get the wolf to attempt to eat the pigs, and they managed to get the pigs to run away. One small step for a man…

IDTension

Nicholas Szilas, the developer of IDTension[7], uses a model for narrative that's based on five fundamental concepts:

▶ **Goals:** States desired by various actors in the story.

▶ **Tasks:** Procedures that must be performed to achieve goals.

▶ **Segments:** Subtasks.

▶ **Obstacles:** Factors that prevent a segment from being performed.

▶ **Values:** Moral dimensions applying to segments; for example, if the segment requires an actor to tell a lie, and the actor has a high Value for honesty, a conflict is created within the actor.

Volition is expressed through nine high-level verbs: decide, inform, incite, dissuade, accept, refuse, perform, condemn, and congratulate. These nine verbs revolve around the concept of making difficult decisions. The first verb, decide, lies at the center of this constellation of verbs; the verb perform represents the actual implementation of the decision. Incite and dissuade are meant to allow another actor to influence another actor's decision, either positively or negatively. Accept and refuse are reactions to incite and dissuade. Finally, after a decision is performed, another actor can react to that event with the verbs condemn or congratulate.

Note that this decision structure is boolean at heart, meaning an actor doesn't choose among various options. Instead, the actor decides whether to take a single course of action. Although this decision is theoretically indistinguishable from the more normal choice among several options, in practice, it just doesn't match the way characters in drama behave. They often have multiple choices, and they don't run down the laundry list of choices, considering and rejecting each in turn until they come to the one option they like.

The sample storyworld that Szilas offers has five actors, two goals, three tasks, two obstacles, and two values. The underlying story concerns a murder. A witness, Mr. D, claims that he saw Anna fleeing the murder scene. Joe, the protagonist, is Anna's husband, and their two friends are Bill and Sylvie. The various components of the storyworld are thus:

▶ Actors: Mr. D, Anna, Joe, Bill, and Sylvie.

▶ Goals: Make witness retract testimony, get rich.

▶ Tasks: Kill the witness, bribe the witness, rob the bank.

▶ Obstacles: Not enough money to bribe witness, police don't believe retraction.

▶ Values: Nonviolence, respect for the law.

Here is a fragment of a story generated by IDTension and this storyworld. I have translated the broken English of the original into more fluent English:

Anna tells Joe he could try to bribe Mr D, the witness.

Joe accepts Anna's advice.

Bill advises Joe to kill Mr D.

Joe refuses to do that.

Joe tells Anna he might kill Mr D.

Anna advises him not to do so.

Joe tells Anna he wants to bribe Mr D.

Anna advises him to do so.

Bill advises Joe to kill Mr D.

Joe meets Mr D.

He offers Mr.D some money for changing his testimony, but Mr D. wants a lot of money, and Joe is not rich enough.

He then decides to get money.

He tells Anna about it.

Joe tells Sylvie he might kill Mr D.

Sylvie advises him not to do so.

Joe tells her he is trying to get money.

He tells Bill about it.

Bill advises him that he could rob the bank.

Joe accepts.

He tells Anna he wants to rob the bank.

Anna advises him to do it.

He tells Bill about his intention.

Bill advises him to do it.

He tells Sylvie about his intention.

Sylvie advises him not to do so.

Joe robs the bank, and he is successful.

He pays Mr D.

He obtains Mr D's withdrawal of testimony.

This story demonstrates some of the features of the IDTension technology. Joe is able to draw inferences about the need to gain money to pay off Mr. D and to weigh his friends' advice against his own values. All in all, IDTension works as a logical exercise. Its dramatic content, of course, is low, but we can't expect much of a first attempt. Interestingly, Szilas reports the same difficulties building an actual storyworld that other authors report (and that I experienced). Apparently, building storyworlds isn't as easy as building interactive storytelling engines.

The Virtual Storyteller

Virtual Storyteller[8], a project carried out at the University of Twente in the Netherlands, is part of a much larger project, AVEIRO, which aims to present a complete virtual theater, including storytelling, music, and dancing. The authors built the system as a set of autonomous agents organized by a *director agent* (a drama manager). In other words, each storyworld is populated with a complement of actors who operate with their own goals, but before they can act, they must obtain the approval of the director agent, whose task is to maintain plot integrity. The actors are responsible for the consistency of their own behavior.

The director agent has three means of affecting actors' behaviors. First is disapproval of their proposed actions; if the director agent disapproves of an actor's proposal, the actor won't carry out his or her plan. Approval is based on whether the actor's proposal is consistent with the plot's overall direction.

The second means of control is motivational; the director agent can give an actor a goal to pursue. The director agent can't command an actor to perform a specific action, as that action might not be consistent with the actor's personality. Therefore, the director agent provides only the goals the actors are meant to attain.

The third means of control is environmental: The director-agent can introduce new actors or objects into the storyworld. These new factors would presumably influence the original actors' decisions in a direction favorable to the plot.

The authors don't describe how all this is done. They state: "The director is able to judge whether a character's intended action fits into the plot structure, using both storyworld knowledge and general knowledge about what makes a 'good' plot." They use a standard rule-based reasoning system, which uses an inference engine that references a set of facts and rules the authors specify. These facts and rules aren't described, however.

Their system is not designed for interactivity; the director's role is too intrusive to accommodate the needs of an independent player. Obviously, the director can't order players to accept a new goal. It might be possible to achieve interactivity by shielding the player from the director agent's interference. As far as I can tell, no presentable storyworld has been built using this system.

InterTale

Karin Berndtsson and Lena Kindmark, the authors of InterTale[9], came up with an interesting idea: Sift through a large body of similar stories and find a group of stories with similar architecture. They used Grimm's fairy tales as their database of stories and isolated about 40 stories they thought had similar structures. They called them "stories with a turning point." In each story, three people attempted to solve some problem. The first two tried obvious approaches and failed, but the third tried something different and succeeded. Berndtsson and Kindmark built a narrative grammar based on this pattern.

This technology was integrated with another technology, Toilet Entertainment Systems, and the result was presented in May 2002 at an exhibition in Gotheburg, Sweden. Users of the public toilets interacted with the technology by choosing among six tiles next to the toilet paper dispenser. The results of their actions were printed onto the toilet paper. No mention was made as to whether the printing technology was inkjet or laser.

Story Grammars

Dr. R. Raymond Lang resurrects a line of research that was active in the 1970s: story grammars. This research, carried out in the younger days of computer science, had failed to produce acceptable results and was abandoned in the 1980s. Dr. Lang revived the line of research because subsequent developments in computer science have opened new possibilities.

This research diverges from research on interactive storytelling, as its goal is an engine that can generate stories without player intervention. There's a long line of such efforts, dating back to TaleSpin, a program James Meehan created for his doctoral thesis in 1976.

Here's a sample of the kind of output the TaleSpin system could generate:

> Betty was famished. Betty wanted to get some berries. Betty wanted to get near the cranberries. Betty walked from her cave down a pass through the valley across a meadow to the bush. Betty took the cranberries. Betty ate the cranberries. The cranberries were gone. Betty was not hungry. The end.

The thrust of this line of research concerned knowledge representation, not storytelling. Computer scientists had realized that what's called "intelligence" relies heavily on the manner in which knowledge of the world is organized in the mind. They therefore experimented with many ways of organizing information, one of which evolved into the broad field now called *narrative intelligence*.

Lang's story grammar system, called JOSEPH[10], furthers this line of research. Here's some sample output from JOSEPH:

> once upon a time there lived a peasant. peasant was married to wife. one day it happened that peasant quarreled with the wife. when this happened, peasant felt distress. in response, peasant took a walk in the woods. peasant found a pit when he looked under the bush. when this happened, peasant desired to punish wife. in response, made it his goal that wife would be in the pit. peasant tricked wife. wife was in the pit. peasant lived alone.

In storytelling terms, this sample isn't anything to write home about, but in computer science terms, it's a step forward. The program is able to calculate emotional reactions to events, calculate actions generated by emotions, and form plans.

The killer problem with all these story generation technologies is that they aren't designed to be interactive and could not readily be modified for interactivity. The methods used treat the story as a single block of output, not a collection of reconfigurable pieces. The player could perhaps provide initial conditions and watch as the computer generates a story built around those initial conditions, but I don't see this as a marketable solution.

Perhaps some bright researcher will figure out a way to modify the basic methodology to permit on-the-fly revision of the storyline, thereby making genuine interactivity possible. My guess is that these story generation technologies will not lead directly to interactive storytelling, but that portions of them will be integrated into drama managers for interactive storytelling.

Interactive Drama Architecture

Dat ol' debbil "plot versus interaction" so haunts the minds of some researchers that their entire approach to interactive storytelling is formulated around the apparent dilemma. Such is the case with the Interactive Drama Architecture that Brian Magerko and John Laird created[11]. Their fundamental idea is to monitor players closely and make corrections when they deviate from the intended plot; their goal is to achieve "balance" between plot and interactivity.

They seem to have ordered their thoughts well; they define a goodly set of terms for their system. They have a Director, who functions as a drama manager; their smallest combinable unit is the beat, which assembles into scenes, which assemble into acts, which assemble into stories. Sad to say, they don't provide any details of how their system might function. It appears to be a work in progress.

DraMachina

The impressive idea in Stephane Donikian's DraMachina[12] is the notion that the tool defines capabilities. Donikian therefore set out to build a powerful tool for creating interactive storyworlds. This tool doesn't appear to be built with any particular storytelling engine in mind. Instead, it offers a general way of organizing the many components of a storyworld: the actors, props, stages, scenes, dialogue, and so forth. These components are then organized and output as an XML file that any storytelling engine can read.

Personal Narrative Agents

"If you can't beat 'em, join 'em" might be the slogan best describing the efforts of Jeff Rawlings and Joe Andrieu[13] to build interactive storytelling technology. Instead of attempting to impose a dramatic arc onto the player, their idea is to find a dramatic arc that fits the player's actions. This is accomplished by means of a *Personal Narrative Agent* (a "drama manager," in my terminology) who monitors the player's actions and searches through a set of *Narrative Forms* that serve as templates for mini-stories. The Personal Narrative Agent identifies the Narrative Form that best fits the player's situations and actions and plugs it into the ongoing narrative. This approach is similar to Figa and Tarau's, with "Narrative Forms" replacing "story projections" (which I call "Events").

The Personal Narrative Agent forms hypotheses about the player's motivations, tests those hypotheses by running test situations past the player, and then acts on the hypothesis best supported by the player's choices.

The concepts Rawlings and Andrieu describe are impressive, but for the moment they are just that: concepts. As far as I know, they haven't yet built working software that implements these concepts.

HTN- and HSP-Based Technologies

Marc Cavazza and Fred Charles, researchers at the University of Teesside in Britain, have published a number of works presenting important components of interactive storytelling technology[14]; they appear to be assembling a full suite of technologies for integration into a complete system at some point in the future.

One of their technologies is based on Hierarchical Task Network (HTN) technology. This technology, developed over several decades by computer science researchers, sets up a hierarchy of goals and tasks. At the top of the hierarchy are goals; each one is broken down into subgoals, which are subdivided further and further until they have been broken all the way down to tasks that can be executed. **Figure 19.5** depicts a simple version of this scheme. In this diagram, goals are represented by ovals; tasks that can actually be carried out are in rectangles.

This simple scheme exemplifies the problems I cited earlier in the sections "Hammers and Nails" and "Boolean Thinking." Decades of research have honed the technology of HTNs to a fine edge; applying this advanced technology to the still-childish technology of interactive storytelling seems a fine opportunity to pursue. The tool, however, shapes the hand of the user, so the boolean thinking implicit in HTNs carries over into interactive storytelling. Although this technology performs magnificently when, say, guiding robots over the surface of Mars, its handling of romantic situations is a little off, as shown in **Figure 19.6**.

Not quite Romeo and Juliet, is it?

HTNs have another flaw: their inability to prepare plans that extend over a long period and interleave with other plans. Realizing this, Cavazza and Charles added another technology to their system: Heuristic Search Planning (HSP). This technology is more powerful, so it shouldn't surprise you that it makes more demands on the storybuilder. Specifying relationships among the various story components is a more complicated task with HSP than with HTN; the authors concede that this complexity might be a source of difficulty in recruiting talented storybuilders to use their system.

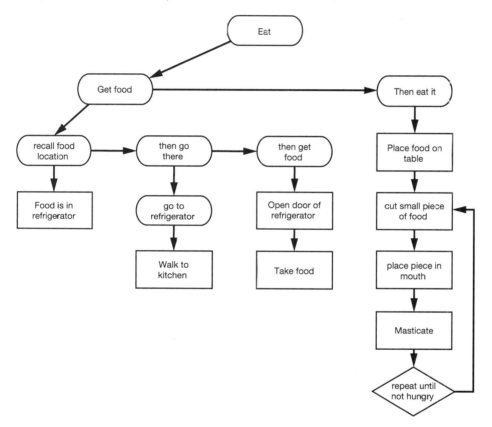

FIGURE 19.5: A simple Hierarchical Task Network.

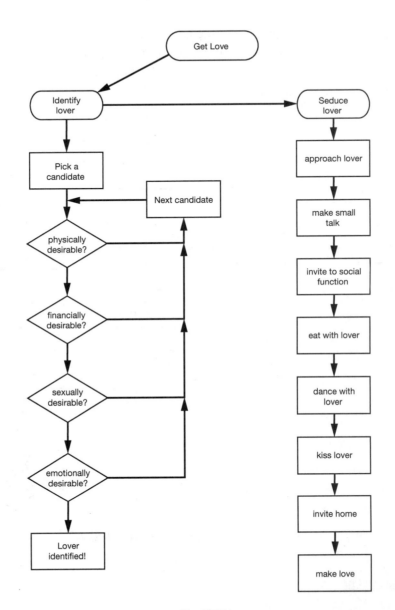

FIGURE 19.6: The HTN for romance.

The authors have also experimented with using speech recognition for user input; their results indicate that players directly commanding actors does not work well. Instead, they recommend that players use speech input to give warnings, information, or advice to their actors. These inputs can then be integrated with the planning mechanism (the HTN and HSP) to guide the actors' decisions. Last, the authors have integrated their software with a 3D engine that shows actors moving about on the stages.

Wrapping Up

The research efforts discussed in this chapter go off in all directions; there are few common elements, although drama managers show up frequently. Several researchers prefer to use the term "beat" where I use the term "Event." Aside from these components, there isn't much commonality in the research underway. Chalk it up to the youth of the field. Give it 10 or 20 years and they should have, at the very least, a common vocabulary.

The pace of research into interactive storytelling is so rapid that this chapter will likely be obsolete by the time the book is published. You can keep up with the stampede by consulting Andrew Stern's excellent index of all things related to interactive storytelling[15].

1. Dr. Joseph Bates, Oz Project: http//:www-2.cs.cmu.edu/afs/cs.cmu.edu/project/oz/web/oz.html.

2. Andrew S. Gordon and Nicholas V. Iuppa, Experience Management: www.ict.usc.edu/~gordon/TIDSE03.PDF.

3. Elizabeth Figa and Paul Tarau, WordNet: http://logic.csci.unt.edu/tarau/research/, http://logic.csci.unt.edu/vista/index. htm, and www.cogsci.princeton.edu/~wn.

4. Michael Mateas and Andrew Stern, Façade: www.quvu.net/interactivestory.net/.

5. Brandon Rickman, Dr. K- Project: www-2.cs.cmu.edu/afs/cs/user/michaelm/www/nidocs/Rickman.html.

6. Teong Joo Ong and John Leggett, HEFTI: http://dl.aace.org/12719.

7. Nicholas Szilas, IDTension: www.idtension.com.

8. Virtual Storyteller: http://wwwhome.cs.utwente.nl/~anijholt/artikelen/cve_2002.

9. Karin Berndtsson and Lena Kindmark, InterTale: www.playresearch.com/publications/2003/intertale.pdf.

10. Dr. R. Raymond Lang, JOSEPH: http://www-2.cs.cmu.edu/afs/cs/user/michaelm/www/nidocs/Lang.pdf.

11. Brian Magerko and John Laird, Interactive Drama Architecture: www.eecs.umich.edu/~magerko/research/ magerko.AAAI.2002.pdf.

12. Stephane Donikian, DraMachina: www.dramachina.com/.

13. Jeff Rawlings and Joe Andrieu, "Player-Protagonist Motivation in First-Person Interactive Drama," Proceedings of TIDSE Conference 2003, pp. 31–44.

14. Marc Cavazza and Fred Charles, HTN and HSP: http://www-scm.tees.ac.uk/users/f.charles/publications/ publications.htm.

15. Andrew Stern, InteractiveStory.net: www.quvu.net/interactivestory.net/links.html.

CHAPTER 20
Distant Relatives

A VARIETY OF EFFORTS ATTEMPT to use the computer in some fashion that seems kinda-sorta narrative. In this chapter, I discuss some of these efforts and their relationship to interactive storytelling.

Interactive Fiction

In 1976 Don Woods released his greatly expanded version of Will Crowther's Colossal Cave Adventure, and a genre was born, originally called *adventure games*. Scott Adams created the first version of the game on a personal computer in 1979. He built a general-purpose editing program that made it possible to create completely new games using the same architecture. (Few people know that Rob Zdybel at Atari created a similar tool at about the same time.) Originally known as "adventure games," this genre has a simple structure. Several dozen rooms are populated by a variety of objects, obstacles, and antagonists. Players see only a textual description of the room they occupy; their goal is to wander through the maze of rooms to reach some desired goal. Player commands are entered with a tiny subset of English. Initially, the parsers in adventure games handled just two-word sentences specifying a verb and an object: "Go north," "Take book," "Eat cookie," and so forth. Later, parsers grew more complex, permitting the use of synonyms (such as "Go north," "Move north," "Walk north") and recognizing extended sentences (for example, "Open door with crowbar").

Despite their name, adventure games were really intricate puzzles, not games. Players mapped huge labyrinths of rooms, taking props from one room to overcome an obstacle in a distant room. Much of the gameplay consisted of encountering an obstacle, trudging through long sequences of rooms to obtain a prop, trudging back to the obstacle, attempting to use the prop to overcome the obstacle, failing, and then wandering off in search of some other solution.

The genre was pushed forward by Infocom, a company formed by MIT computer scientists who had built a much better parser. Their adventure games expanded the genre's expressive reach because they showed much creativity in combining rooms, props, and obstacles with interesting puzzles.

The next step in the evolution of adventure games was Sierra Online's creation of *graphic adventures*; these games were structurally identical to the original form, which were consequently renamed *text adventures*, but they included pictures of rooms rather than textual descriptions. Graphic adventures supplanted text adventures, and the form culminated in the visually spectacular game Myst and its sequels. Adventure games, however, were still nothing more than puzzles in terms of their gameplay, and the genre faded away.

An avid subculture devoted to the genre remains, however. They have given it the more dignified name *interactive fiction,* but it's basically just the same old text adventure architecture with additional bells and whistles. There are now a number of editing systems that make it possible to create interactive fictions (for example, TADS and Inform) as well as websites devoted to the genre, competitions for the best work, and so forth. A particularly active group is the Society for the Promotion of Adventure Games (SPAG)[1].

Interactive fiction is certainly interactive, and it's fictional in the sense of being made up, but it's certainly not storytelling. Some practitioners of the field write eloquently of the glorious narrative possibilities, but the actual creations remain elaborate puzzles.

 One of the better sources on interactive fiction is `www.xyzzynews.com/index.html`.

An old example illustrates the way that adventure games are dressed up with emotions. In Infocom's classic game Planetfall, Floyd the robot befriended players early in the game. Floyd helped out in all manner of ways and provided lots of humorous diversions. But then, in a moment of danger to the player, Floyd charged forward and sacrificed himself to save the player. Players were overwhelmed with the moment's emotional power. This great moment, I must point out, was absolutely noninteractive. There was nothing players could do to avert it. Players could insult Floyd, abuse Floyd, ignore Floyd, and he'd still nobly sacrifice himself. This behavior was programmed into the game.

Lesson #44
Interactive fiction will not lead to interactive storytelling.

Hypertext Fiction

Another field of effort is the serious exploration of *hypertext fiction* as a medium of artistic expression. It's an old field: Mark Bernstein started Eastgate Systems to develop the medium in 1982, and two decades later, he's still plugging along[2]. Because of Bernstein's efforts, there's now a substantial body of work.

Hypertext fiction is most easily imagined in terms of the Web. Imagine a story presented on perhaps a hundred different web pages, with links embedded in the text that take you to other pages in the story. Instead of reading the story linearly, the player can traverse it by a large number of paths.

 It sounds terribly confusing. Couldn't I read about the death of a character I haven't yet been introduced to?

Good hypertext fiction authors can prevent obvious bloopers like this, but the experience certainly befuddles some readers. That's part of the appeal of the medium: You have to read not just between the lines, but behind them. You have to proceed with some questions unanswered, some details left out, until you discover the answers. This effort instills a deeper understanding of the story. More advanced hypertext fiction engines, such as Thespis and CardShark, offer logical constraints on the links between story segments.

Although this medium hasn't enjoyed commercial success, it has attracted the attention of a number of academics interested in developing its theoretical possibilities.

Lesson #45
So far, hypertext fiction offers little more than interesting academic possibilities.

Note: Other interesting sites on hypertext fiction are `www.storysprawl.com.` *and* `www.markbernstein.org/talks/HT01.html.`

Digital Storytelling

Another distantly related field goes by the name *digital storytelling*[3]. Practitioners have no interest in interactivity; their motivation is the moviemaking power that computers confer upon unfunded artists. One flavor of this school sees digital storytelling primarily as a means for everyday people to record the stories of their lives. Families can assemble family histories, children can create and record their own little stories, and so storytelling comes to Everyman. All this work can be published on the Web, without the intermediating role publishers play, releasing a tidal wave of narrative material that until now had faded into history with the passing of each generation. Although the concept is interesting and worthy, it has no bearing on interactive storytelling and little to teach prospective story-builders.

Another variation on this field is referred to as *machinima*: the use of 3D graphics engines to create movies. Artists must often rely on graphic elements the engine provides; if the engine is designed for first-person shooter games, the results are sometimes skewed. I recall with pleasure a machinima production in which two soldiers from the game Halo discuss the philosophical underpinnings of their nature as killers and wonder aloud as to why they must behave as they do. Meanwhile, two of their enemies watch from afar, trying to comprehend their new unwarlike behavior.

The main point about digital storytelling is that, although it's carried out on computers, it makes no attempt whatever to provide interactivity. The computer is used as a tool for creating video in the conventional sense. The player doesn't alter the story in any fashion.

Lesson #46
"Digital" does not mean "interactive."

Scriptwriting Software

Hollywood has such a voracious appetite for stories that a little industry has sprung up offering writers advice on how to create stories for Hollywood. Some of these efforts are more academic in tone; some have all the charm of a get-rich quick scheme ("100 proven tips and tricks from the experts!"). Some, however, represent serious attempts to understand the dynamics of storytelling as practiced by Hollywood, and none is more ambitious than Dramatica, a software product designed to help screenwriters prepare better screenplays[4].

Dramatica boasts a huge theoretical foundation; the documentation alone runs to hundreds of pages, and the dictionary of terms is 57 pages long. Although I normally disparage software that requires humongous manuals, my criticisms don't apply to Dramatica because its documentation explains the theory behind the software, not just the buttons to click. I confess that I don't understand the theory; it's simply too big to digest without a major commitment of effort.

Nevertheless, I'm mightily impressed by the abstraction the authors have developed in their theory.

The theory suffers a bit from an overwrought attempt at elegance, however. There are four classes: physics, universe, psychology, and mind. Each class is separated into four types; for mind, the types are memory, conscious, preconscious, and subconscious. Each type is further divided into four variations; for memory, they are truth, evidence, suspicion, and falsehood. Each variation is subdivided into four elements; for suspicion, these elements are order, change, inertia, and chaos. All told, then, there are 256 elements. Each grouping of four is set out in a square (see **Figure 20.1**). This geometry often produces useful insights, but it breaks down in just enough cases to undermine my confidence in the system.

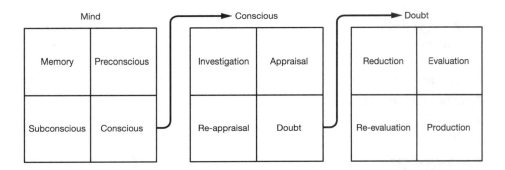

FIGURE 20.1: Each up/down, left/right, and diagonal pairing has some special significance in Dramatica's theory.

More important to interactive storytelling, the theory is not computerized in any applicable form. The software acts as a multifaceted prism offering many revealing points of view of a screenplay; it's meant to be used to refine existing screenplays rather than create original ones. I believe the Dramatica theory could form the basis of an interactive storytelling engine if considerable effort were made to nail down all its concepts in fully computable form.

Role-Playing Games

I have previously dismissed computer games as unsuited for developing interactive storytelling for a variety of reasons; however, role-playing games (RPGs) deserve special consideration. Although they often hew closely to the standard hack-and-slash style, a few efforts show more interest in genuine character development. Some have tried to flesh out their characters; a few offer dialogue a bit more interesting than the standard fishing-for-information fare. One RPG, Deus Ex, shows some promise in its plot development. Another product vaguely related to RPGs, Grand Theft Auto, similarly offers a few sparkles of potential. The possibilities of this form arise not so much from what has been accomplished as from the frequently declared and fervently held intention of RPG designers to pursue deeper character development in their games. They are certainly giving it the old college try, and the market's generally favorable reactions suggest some potential here.

Sadly, however, personality models in RPGs seldom include relationship information, and emotional relationships among characters can't be developed because the verbs in these games seldom address relationship issues. Without human relationships, how can you build a storyworld of any merit?

Simulations

Computer simulation is an old field that has enjoyed something of a renaissance in recent years. A new generation of designers has sought to apply simulation to a much wider range of problems than was previously addressed. The old emphasis on a simulation's utility for predictive purposes has been shoved aside for a new emphasis on its educational value. This emphasis has instilled a more relaxed approach toward mathematical exactness and system verifiability, freeing up the field to address all manner of new subjects: renaissance politics, the dynamics of business meetings, and urban crime, for example. This more liberal attitude has encouraged some designers to add storytelling elements to their work. These efforts are in their early stages and so aren't well developed. In their excitement over the potential of storytelling to enhance simulations, some designers have shown more enthusiasm than productivity, making some rather excessive claims. The potential is real even if the product isn't here yet, and I think we can expect to see some interesting experiments in this field. These people aren't working on interactive storytelling, but they might be able to put narrative concepts to work in educational applications.

Narrative Intelligence

Computer scientists have long struggled with the problem of creating artificial intelligence that can be applied to human problems as opposed to mechanical ones. A central realization in this effort is that the intelligence relies on knowledge, so *knowledge representation* has arisen as a major field in computer science. Figuring out how to organize data in bank accounts or flight schedules is easy, but how are ideas such as marital fidelity, integrity, or love represented? How can the meaning of these ideas be specified to a computer? Early researchers, such as Roger Schank, zeroed in on narrative as one mean by which people encode social knowledge. Much subsequent research has attempted to define the structures of narrative in terms that can be used in a computer. Although no breakthroughs have been achieved, some interesting ideas are being developed in this field. Designers of interactive storytelling systems would do well to keep abreast of developments in narrative intelligence. However, it doesn't directly address the problems of interactive storytelling.

Wrapping Up

The intersection of storytelling and computers has become a hot topic in many areas of human endeavor. Scriptwriters, pure artists, business consultants, the military, game designers, educators, and computer scientists have attacked the problems of that intersection with great energy and ambition. Although each of these related fields of endeavor has some interesting angle on the problem, most share a common weakness: a failure to address the element of interactivity.

---

1. TADS: www.tads.org; Inform: www.inform-fiction.org; SPAG: www.sparkynet.com/spag.

2. Mark Bernstein: www.eastgate.com.

3. For more information on digital storytelling: http://tech-head.com/dstory.htm.

4. Dramatica: www.dramatica.com/.

CHAPTER 21

Prognostications

WHAT FUTURE AWAITS INTERACTIVE STORYTELLING?

Two schools of thought compete: evolutionary and revolutionary.

The Evolutionary School

This school believes that interactive storytelling will evolve out of the games industry. Unsurprisingly, it consists mostly of people currently working in the games biz. Optimists all, they are confident that with continuing effort they can improve the medium to the point that it rivals Hollywood in narrative depth.

Unquestionably, games have made progress in integrating a story into the game. In Chapter 7, "Simple Strategies That Don't Work," I related the history of that effort. I also explained why these efforts will never achieve true interactive storytelling. I did not, however, unload the full blast of logical devastation onto this pathetic line of reasoning; it's time to unleash my inner tyrannosaurus onto this sniveling weakling of an argument.

The Wrong Verbs

Recall the most important lesson of this book, which I presented in Chapter 2, "Interactivity": "Interactivity depends on the choices available to the user." Recall the emphasis I placed on that lesson. Now it's time to place the evolutionary argument into the jaws of this lesson.

What choices does the storified game make available to players? The answer is clear: Although the stories jammed into games are ever more elaborate, the choices available to players haven't changed. Players must make the same choices they have always faced: shooting, moving, sneaking, hiding, acquiring, and so forth. The artwork has changed, the video is better, but there has been zero evolution in terms of choices available to players. And because those choices define the interactivity, you can conclude that, in terms of interactivity, there has been zero evolution in these games.

If the games industry were to demonstrate some sort of evolutionary progress in integrating stories into games, you could see it in the verbs. At first you'd see a few simple verbs with dramatic significance, and with each passing year, you would see a few more such verbs, some dramatically richer verbs, and so forth. So far, the progress seen in this direction has been at best debatable. A few embellishments in game backstories and context have opened a tiny crack of possibility that hasn't been much exploited. Game designers can point to a few extra neurons in the brains of their dinosaurs, but at this rate of evolution, we'll be colonizing stars before we get interactive storytelling in games.

The Wrong Themes

This horse may be dead, but I'm not done kicking it. There's still the matter of thematic content. Games have well-defined themes: action, spatial reasoning, and puzzle-solving. Those themes just don't lend themselves to high drama. Yes, there have been plenty of Hollywood action movies, but these movies don't succeed on the merits of their stories. It's the violence, action, and spectacle of action movies that underlie their popularity. I suppose you could argue that action movies give games a worthy target to aim for, but it's a small target. In the broad continuum of cinema, pure action doesn't cover a lot of territory. Most successful Hollywood movies have a modicum of story that lies far beyond what games now attain. Moreover, action movies remain a target far above the reach of current games—even *Godzilla* had more character development than most of today's games.

Market Factors

Okay, the horse is long dead, half-rotten, and riddled with maggots. I'm still not done kicking. I've saved my best kick for last: the inertia of the market.

Markets are nowhere near as perfect as your freshman economics course led you to believe. Markets are burdened with lots of friction and anti-competitive factors. The person who builds a better mousetrap will likely be buried by the slick marketing campaigns of big companies with inferior mousetraps.

The core concept here is that a superior product cannot make itself known without marketing—and marketing is expensive. We have built a huge and impressive economy capable of developing and delivering a myriad of products to customers. That economy is composed of all manner of elements connected in a bewilderingly complex structure. There are producers, distributors, and retailers who must get to know each other. There are customers who learn which retailers offer what kinds of products. It's all a huge and expensive infrastructure, and altering that infrastructure is inordinately expensive.

A Marketing Fairy Tale

For example, suppose you produce the hottest, coolest, wildest game ever built. This baby is the perfect extrapolation of everything that sells well in today's market. It's got great graphics, great animation, great video, great sound, great music, great action, and so forth. It's what every marketing executive dreams of: It's just like yesterday's smash hit, only better! You'll have no problem selling this baby to a publisher. They can instantly see why it's going to be a smash hit, so they'll produce a million copies and devote millions of dollars to the marketing campaign.

It won't be hard for them to sell the game because the distributors will love it, too. Distributors aren't games fanatics, but they certainly know what sells, and they can readily see that your game is just like what sold so well last year, so it's a no-brainer from their point of view. Salivating, they whip out their checkbooks at the sight of your game.

The retailers will be no different. They know a hit when they see it, and they'll give this baby generous shelf space. So customers will be sure to notice your game and will certainly buy lots and lots of games. Hooray for you!

A Marketing Nightmare

But now look at it from the other side. Suppose you were to create the perfect interactive storytelling product. It offers genuine, true-blue, red-blooded interactive storytelling with real drama. You take your work of genius to a games publisher. What happens?

The games publisher will look at you long and hard and say something like this: "I really hope you find a publisher for this product, because I love it and would very much like to play it. But I can't recommend that we publish it because it's not like last year's hit game. As great as it is, we just can't sell it."

These words are pretty much the ones I heard when I first tried to interest publishers in interactive storytelling in the early 1990s, but suppose you get lucky or that publishers have changed. Suppose you find a publisher with the vision to recognize that interactive storytelling will take off soon. Suppose this publisher agrees to take your storyworld.

You're still dead because he'll never find a distributor willing to take the product. Distributors are even less visionary than publishers; they make all their decisions by the numbers. They compare every candidate product with the most similar product they can find, and then project its sales based on that similarity. When they consider your storyworld, they'll be hard put to find something comparable. They'll eventually come up with some obscure failure of a game —which will tell them that your product can't sell. Down go the thumbs.

But say that somehow, you get lucky again. You have a rich uncle who owns a distribution company, or the owner of a distribution company was just visited by the Ghost of Christmas Future, or some such. Somebody agrees to take your product. Huzzah!

Don't rejoice yet. You still have to get retailers to carry your product. And why should they? They know what sells and what doesn't sell, and your product most definitely does *not* smell like last year's smash hit. Your product will languish on their shelves, taking up precious shelf space and not moving. They'll lose their shirts if they stock your storyworld. You lose.

But wait! In for a penny, in for a pound. You're already three steps down a ridiculous fantasy, so you might as well suppose that you succeed in finding a major retail chain that agrees to stock your product. There's a computer error at Wal-Mart and they order a million copies. What luck!

Forget it. They'll put it on the shelves next to all the other games. What kinds of customers visit those shelves? Gamers! They're looking for the latest, hottest, coolest action game. They'll take one look at the box and complain "No shooting; no explosions; no monsters; no strategy—Bo-ring!" and they'll pass your product by.

Who would buy your storyworld? Lots of people! The problem is, they don't peruse the games shelves because they already know what they'll find there, and they don't want what they'll find there.

The conclusion to draw is simple: The games industry has spent more than two decades building a huge and efficient infrastructure for getting games into the hands of their customers. Along the way, they have precisely defined their target market; that precise definition allows them to spend their marketing money more effectively. Everybody involved in the business—publishers, distributors, retailers, customers, and noncustomers—knows what to expect from it. It took billions of dollars to get the system tuned so accurately, but now it works to the profit of all. If your product is out of tune with that system, you lose, which is precisely the case with interactive storytelling. It's not a matter of design genius or technological constraints. The greatest game designer in the universe, equipped with magnificent hardware and an army of programmers and artists, couldn't crack this nut. The cement has hardened, and there's no room left in this infrastructure for change.

But doesn't this argument apply with even greater force to the revolutionary school?

Indeed it does, but the revolutionary school acknowledges this problem as the primary one it must overcome. The thrust of the argument is that no evolutionary path exists from the "here" of games to the "there" of interactive storytelling—at least, not in marketing terms. Any deviation from the well-defined market for games will encounter resistive forces that prevent expansion of that deviation. Therefore, there's no advantage in using games as the starting point for reaching interactive storytelling, and indeed that marketplace will hold us back. Better to start from scratch than try to crawl out of the hole that games have dug themselves into.

The Revolutionary School

These marketing considerations lead me to conclude that a new infrastructure must be built up if we are to find customers for interactive storytelling. We need to build a completely new marketplace with different developers, different publishers, different distributors, different retailers, and, above all, different customers. Indeed, the most important factor in developing this new industry will be the clear differentiation of interactive storytelling from games. People confusing interactive storytelling products with games will be the kiss of death; they'll dismiss them as quickly as they dismiss games. Perhaps some sort of high-falutin' terminology to emphasize this distinction will be necessary at first: "interactive literature" or "interactive cinema" or some such. I suspect that bookstores will be the preferred retail outlet for these products; they have a tone and atmosphere that will help differentiate interactive storytelling from the games industry.

What about the Internet? Isn't it better for guerilla marketing?

Yes, but retail outlets remain absolutely necessary to the development of a mass market. Given the high costs of developing the retail channel, the first companies in the industry will probably establish a market identity via the Internet, develop a revenue stream from that source, and use that revenue stream to obtain venture capital for the jump to retail. The danger with this strategy lies in the Internet's tendency to attract specialized audiences who demand product changes that would move the product away from the mainstream. If an interactive storytelling company acquiesces to this market pressure, it forecloses its option to move into retail channels; if it stands firm, it will eventually lose those aficionado customers. Therefore, the jump to retail must be carefully timed.

Nevertheless, I think this Internet-first approach is the most likely means of getting the interactive storytelling industry off the ground. It doesn't cost much to develop small concentrations of customers on the Internet, and high marketing costs are often fatal to startups.

 Isn't it a little rich for the infamous prophet in the desert to be advocating a market-driven argument for the development of the industry?

Not in the least. I consider my arguments to constitute a quite reasonable, middle-of-the-road analysis. It is the games industry that has moved to the extremes of crassness, short-termism, and narrow marketing. I seek a mass market for interactive entertainment, not the hobby market for games we now have. I have incessantly nagged for greater breadth of appeal. Many years ago, in what was perhaps the finest speech I have ever given, I said at the Computer Game Developers Conference:

> *I dreamed of the day when computer games would be a viable medium of artistic expression—an art form. I dreamed of computer games expressing the full breadth of human experience and emotion. I dreamed of computer games that were tragedies, games about duty and honor, self-sacrifice and patriotism. I dreamed of satirical games and political games; games about the passionate love between a boy and girl, and the serene and mature love of a husband and wife of decades; games about a boy becoming a man, and a man realizing that he is no longer young. I dreamed of games about a man facing truth on a dusty main street at high noon, and a boy and his dog, and a prostitute with a heart of gold.*

It is the mass-market approach that I have always advocated and that the computer games industry has rejected. I am surely the prophet in the desert, but the games industry lives in an oasis isolated from the rest of the world, and I am pointing the way to the wider world. Hence, there's nothing contradictory about my emphasis on a marketing-based approach—I've been pushing that line from the very beginning.

Implications of the Market-Driven Approach

Given that our strategy must be to build a new marketplace, how are we to proceed? As I have suggested, the first companies will likely make their appearance on the Internet. How long will this take? That depends primarily on what I'll call *technological shakeout*. At the moment, there are too many competing technological strategies for interactive storytelling and too few actual technologies. This book has presented many of those strategies, and it should be obvious that many of them are as yet only partially explored. It will take time for people to examine and develop their strategies. As they do, some strategies will be revealed to be dead ends and will be abandoned. This will permit greater concentration of effort on the remaining strategies, thus accelerating their development.

Increasing Awareness

Another important factor driving the development of an interactive storytelling industry is the increasing awareness of the topic's importance. When I first began working on the problem in the early 1990s, most people reacted to my explanations of interactive storytelling with incomprehension and incredulity. What was the point of interactive storytelling? Why would anybody ever want to buy such a product? They simply could not see any future in my efforts.

However, a number of strands were already in place, as I explained at the beginning of Chapter 19, "Research." Andrew Glassner's book, *Interactive Storytelling*, appeared in 2004 and as I write this, Lee Sheldon's book, *Character Development and Storytelling for Games*, is in preparation. **Figure 21.1** is a timeline showing the acceleration.

The pattern is clear: The pace of work on interactive storytelling is heating up. More and more people are becoming aware of this topic, and its importance is becoming increasingly obvious. That can only help the process.

				Character Development and Storytelling for Games	
				Interactive Storytelling (Glassner)	
			Narrative Intelligence		
Computers as Theater	Stanford Conference	Hamlet on the Holodeck	Avignon Conference	TIDSE conference	this book
1990		1995		2000	2005

FIGURE 21.1: Timeline of events in the interactive storytelling industry.

Predictions

What judgments can be made about the future of interactive storytelling? My guess is that the first genuine interactive storytelling product will make an appearance sometime between 2006 and 2008. There will, of course, be plenty of fraudulent claims, products with overblown claims to interactive storytelling; such fakes have been appearing for years. We probably won't recognize the real thing when it finally appears because it will be lost in the marketing noise. But 50 years from now, historians of interactive entertainment will have no problem putting their finger on the true pioneer.

As more true-blue interactive storytelling products appear, the snake-oil products will be pushed out of the marketplace. I believe that by 2010 we'll definitely have a nascent industry, with several small companies jockeying for position and developing the market. The decade until 2020 will be devoted to market consolidation as big companies buy out little companies, the market matures and expands enormously, and interactive storytelling becomes a mass medium. If I make it that long, I'll be 70 years old, and I'll be able to look back 40 years to the beginning of my dream of computer entertainment becoming a mature medium of expression.

Index